XIIIth
CENTURY CHRONICLES

XIIIth
CENTURY

Jordan of Giano

Thomas of Eccleston

Salimbene degli Adami

CHRONICLES

Translated from the Latin by

PLACID HERMANN O.F.M.

With Introduction and Notes by

MARIE-THERESE LAUREILHE

FRANCISCAN HERALD PRESS

Publishers of Franciscan Literature

Chicago 9, Illinois

NIHIL OBSTAT
Mark Hegener O.F.M.
Marion A. Habig O.F.M.
Censores Librorum

IMPRIMI POTEST
Dominic Limacher O.F.M.
Minister Provincial

IMPRIMATUR
†Albert Gregory Meyer D.D.
Archbishop of Chicago

March 6, 1961

To

the Friars

of the days of St. Francis

who laid so well

the foundations of the Franciscan Order

FOREWORD

Marie-Thérèse Laureilhe published a French version of the three Franciscan chronicles of the thirteenth century in 1959 under the title *Sur Les Routes D'Europe au XIIIe Siècle*. She had done an earlier work on St. Dominic and the Dominicans in 1956, and had been encouraged to do the present work by the late Alexandre Masseron, a noted French scholar and friend of the Franciscan Order. His work, incidentally, that appeared some years ago under the French title *Les Franciscaines,* was re-translated, revised, enlarged, and republished in 1959 by Father Marion Habig O.F.M. and the Franciscan Herald Press under the title *The Franciscans.*

Miss Laureilhe's work contains, in addition to the complete chronicles of Brother Jordan of Giano and Brother Thomas of Eccleston and some selections from the chronicle of Brother Salimbene degli Adami, excellent introductions to each of these chronicles. These introductions I have translated directly from the French in this English volume. As far as the chronicles themselves are concerned, however, I have gone back to the Latin texts of these chronicles as contained in the latest versions available and worked directly from these, with the French constantly at hand. A list of the books that were especially helpful in this present translation will be found in the bibliography at the end of this volume.

I have also taken certain liberties with regard to the footnotes in the French volume. Most of them, of course, I have retained. Some, however, I have condensed, and some I have omitted. Occasionally I have added some of my own. The most important of these latter are indicated by the parenthetical T. N., signifying translator's note.

With regard to the frequent quotations from Holy Scripture, particularly in the chronicle of Brother Salimbene, the newest translation of the Confraternity of Christian Doctrine was used, except, however, when the newest translation did not convey the meaning Brother Salimbene had in mind in using the Vulgate version. In these instances the English translation from the Latin Vulgate was used.

But with it all, I feel very much in the position of Brother Jordan. While it is true I have not as yet attained the fulness of age of Brother Jordan, I have, however, long since reached the stage of his weakness. And, what is more to the point, I have often felt, in the course of this translation, that I should acknowledge and confess with Brother Jordan: "I who have so little ability for the task." Wherefore, like Brother Jordan, I beg in advance the indulgence of the reader and urge him to correct whatever needs correction and, if he so desires, to improve for himself the reading of the English translation.

Placid Hermann O.F.M.

CONTENTS

Maps

PREFACE

by Marie-Thérèse Laureilhe

St. Francis of Assisi was truly a man who lived according to the Gospel, a thorough disciple of Christ. He and his companions chose to imitate as perfectly as possible the life of the Divine Master: "The Rule and Life of the Friars Minor is this, namely, to observe the Holy Gospel of our Lord Jesus Christ by living in obedience, without property, and in chastity."[1] They observed the rule of evangelical poverty, humility, and charity; and they went the limit in this observance, even to the Cross itself, because they knew that the teachings of the Gospel cannot be followed only half-way and that the tepid are rejected.

At the moment of His ascension to the Father, our Blessed Savior gave this supreme command to His disciples: "Go into

---

1. The Second Rule of St. Francis, chapter 1 (Meyer, *The Words of St. Francis*, p. 285).

the whole world and preach the Gospel to every creature."[2]
St. Francis, who had the signal honor of seeing the marks of the
Passion of his Master imprinted upon his own flesh, was not
able to follow this command of our Lord himself; but, as soon
as his companions had increased sufficiently in number, he
sent them traveling through the world preaching the Gospel
by word and by example.

In 1226, at the death of St. Francis, the Order of Friars
Minor counted twelve organized provinces: Tuscany, the
Marches of Ancona, Lombardy, the Terra di Lavoro,[3] Apulia,
Calabria, France, Provence, Spain, Germany, Syria, and England. These provinces gave birth to others and, in the
fourteenth century, there were thirty-four provinces. In the
second half of the thirteenth century, according to estimates,
there were between 30,000 and 35,000 friars divided amongst
some 1,130 convents.[4]

We possess some vivid and interesting sources that describe
the spread of the Franciscan Order across the world and the
founding of the first provinces. Several Friars Minor kept
journals of their march forward. They belonged almost to the

---

2. Mark 16, 15.
3. A region just below central Italy, on the western coast. It might be
   noted here that provinces quite generally were broad in extent and
   were ruled by ministers provincial, subject of course to the minister
   general of the whole Order. Because of the difficulties of communi-
   cation within each province, the single provinces were generally
   divided into two or more custodies, as they were called, and each
   custody was ruled by a custos in the name of the minister provincial
   and with a certain dependence upon him. Thus Germany, for example, already in 1223 was divided into four custodies. (T.N.)
4. Le P. Gratien, *Histoire de la fondation et de l' évolution de l'Ordre
   des freres Mineurs au XIII siecle*, Paris-Gembloux, 1928, pp. 514 et
   seq.

first generation of Franciscans or to the friars who entered the Order shortly after the death of Francis. This direct testimony is of great value. These chroniclers describe for us the provinces which they helped to found, but, like all chroniclers of this period, they delight in turning aside from their main subject to recall one memory or another that does not seem to us to have much connection with the main story; yet, because of these digressions we are given information about many details of Franciscan history that, in the mind of the author at least, are connected with the main subject.

In 1221, Brother Jordan of Giano was sent to Germany; the memoirs he dictated in 1262 have an important value for us. His chronicle is a direct and vital testimony concerning the expansion of the Order into Germany and toward the East of Europe. Besides, entering the Order as he did while St. Francis was still alive, he knew both him and his first companions. He is the only chronicler who describes in detail certain events of the life of St. Francis between 1217 and 1221; and he played an active role at the time of the violent crisis that shook the Order between 1230 and 1239 and brought about the deposition of the minister general, Brother Elias.

Brother Thomas of Eccleston, around 1260, wrote the history of the founding of the province of England. He describes in detail the arrival of the first brothers from France, and we are made to witness the birth and development of the English province. But the author informs us also about other topics. He tells us also about the deposition of Brother Elias and about his successors, in particular about his English confrere, Brother Haymo of Faversham.

We have the good fortune to have these first-hand, vital documents about the growth of the Order in Germany and

England. For France, which was already a prosperous and well-organized province when the province of England was founded, the texts that describe the beginnings of the province are limited to a few pages, even to a few lines. Happily, Brother Jordan of Giano and Thomas of Eccleston tell us briefly about these beginnings. These two report some anecdotes that are fairly significant, and thanks to these and to a few other brief texts we are able to catch a glimpse at least of the grand beginnings of the province of France.

But neither Brother Jordan nor Brother Thomas tells us about the life of the average Franciscan in France and the rather rare texts that tell us about the beginnings of the Order in France do not tell us much more. If we wish to know, as far as France is concerned, the life of the simple friar in his convent in the way that we know this in Germany from what Brother Jordan tells us and in England from what Brother Thomas tells us, we must have recourse to a chronicler who lived in France from 1247 to 1249, the Parmesan friar Salimbene degli Adami. He wrote his chronicle between 1282 and 1287, but his trip to France was the great event of his life and he describes the provinces of France and Provence with many picturesque details. He takes us into the interior of the convents in a more intimate way than does Brother Jordan or Brother Thomas. He describes events that took place about the time at which these other chronicles come to an end and he documents the developments of the Order.

The style of these several chronicles poses a difficult problem for the translator. He must try to keep the flavor of the medieval style, but he must also not weary the reader. The medieval sentences are often long in the Latin, and they do not have the clarity of the Ciceronian periods. It is necessary therefore to lighten these sentences. It does not destroy the exactness of the translation to do so by breaking up the sentences into smaller units and by changing the punctuation marks. The golden rule for translating was given by St. Thomas Aquinas: "It is the business of a good translator to guard the sense of the truths he translates, while he adapts the style to the nature of the language in which he expresses them."[5]

The chronicles of Brother Jordan and of Brother Thomas are presented in their entirety. But only a portion of the chronicle of Brother Salimbene is given; for, it was found necessary to omit many of his interminable digressions and wearisome sections and to eliminate many of the too numerous biblical quotations that often hold up the narrative unduly.

---

5. T h o m a s   A q u i n a s, prologue to the *Opusculum contra errores Graecorum.*

THE CHRONICLE

OF

BROTHER JORDAN

OF GIANO

INTRODUCTION

1. THE AUTHOR

The chronicle written by Brother Jordan of Giano is almost the only text that gives us information concerning the life of its author; outside of this source, there is no mention made of this friar except the few lines in the chronicle of Matthew of Paris and the few lines of Nicholas Glassberger, a compiler of the sixteenth century, who set down a physical and moral portrait of this chronicler in these words: "This same Brother Jordan was one of the first brothers sent by Blessed Francis to Germany. He was a man of swarthy appearance, small in stature, cheerful in spirit, kind, and ready for every good work. He was remarkable for his spirit of obedience. He did not give any recognition to signs of sanctity in a

Friar Minor nor did he consider them of any importance if they were not accompanied by obedience."[1]

The chronicle of Brother Jordan permits us to reconstruct his life. He is, however, much less prolix and much less vain than his confrere Salimbene; he does not spread himself in useless details, and he is much more interesting.

Brother Jordan presents himself to us with this formula: "Brother Jordan of Giano, of the valley of Spoleto"; this is all we know of his origins, and his family remains unknown. Giano is a little mountain village in Umbria, about fourteen miles northwest of Spoleto. We know of the existence of a convent of Friars Minor there through a list of the year 1343, but we know nothing more about it. Since Brother Jordan informs us that he was a deacon in 1221, we can estimate that he was born about 1195 or a little before this. He was probably a deacon at his entrance into the Order for he does not tell us when the subdiaconate and the diaconate were conferred upon him though he tells us that he was ordained priest when he was already a Friar Minor. Glassberger informs us that Jordan was received into the Order by St. Francis; if this information is exact, this would place the entry of Brother Jordan into the Order before the voyage of St. Francis to the Orient in 1219; and this is probable, for it is from the year 1219 on that our chronicler gives in detail the history of the Franciscan Order.

After his entry into the Order, Brother Jordan lived in Umbria. In 1221 he was included, in spite of himself, in the

---

1. Nicholas Glassberger, *Chronica fratris Nicolai Glassberger, Ordinis Minorum observantium*, ed. by the Fathers of the College of Saint Bonaventure, Quaracchi, 1887 *(Analecta Franciscana*, Vol. II), p. 54.

mission sent to Germany and from that time on his life was intertwined with the history of the Friars Minor in that country.

In September, 1221, he left Italy; he stayed first at Salzburg, then at Speyer; in June 1222, he was assigned to the apostolate in the villages of Speyer, Worms, and Mainz. In 1223, he was ordained priest and lived at Speyer. In 1224, he was at Mainz as guardian, that is, as superior of the convent; on September 8, 1224, he traveled to Thuringia where he was well received by the people; he contributed toward the planting of the Franciscan Order in Erfurt, Eisenach, Gotha, Nordhausen, and Mühlhausen. He remained in Thuringia until about 1239. Still, he went back to Italy twice in between, once in 1230 and again in 1238.

Brother Jordan is then silent about his life during the three following years, but the chronicler Matthew of Paris publishes in his *Chronica Majora*[2] several letters concerning the invasion of the Mongols, two of which, dated 1241, are signed: "Brother Jordan, of the Order of Friars Minor, vicar of Bohemia and Poland," and "Brother Jordan, vice-minister of Bohemia and Poland." Now we have three serious reasons for attributing these letters to our Brother Jordan: the style is the same; he makes comparisons with Tuscany and Lombardy; he employs Italian turns of style. This therefore accounts for one blank period of his life.

In 1242, we find him in Saxony at the provincial chapter at Altenburg. He was elected vicar of Saxony at this chapter.

---

2. Matthew of Paris, *Ex Mathei Parisiensis Cronicis majoribus* (edited by F. Liebermann), *Monumenta Germaniae Historica*, Scriptores XXVIII, pp. 107-389.

From then on there is a new blank period and we do not meet him again until 1262 at the chapter at Halberstadt, "old and weak"; he died, no doubt, not long thereafter, and according to one tradition, he was buried at Magdeburg, but this cannot be established with certainty, since the Franciscan documents of that village have been destroyed. Brother Jordan is mentioned in the Franciscan Martyrology as blessed under the date of November 7.[3]

In reading the chronicle of Brother Jordan, our impression is that its author is an agreeable person and one easy to live with. Glassberger tells us that he was "cheerful of spirit." His chronicle confirms this for us; the humorous stories are numerous. Brother Jordan has a sense of humor and he knows how to get himself out of difficult situations with a witticism, a joke.[4] In critical moments, when the brothers were on their travels, in a country unknown to them, where they risked death by starvation, our brother does not complain but preserves his good humor.[5] Is not this the mark of a true Franciscan? Brother Jordan of Giano, under difficult circumstances, knows how to conduct himself as a true son of St. Francis and to find "perfect joy" where most people think they are victims of the worst calamities.[6]

---

3. Cf. *Acta sanctorum*, November, Vol. III, p. 322 and *Martyrologium Franciscanum*, a P. Arturo a Monasterio, latest edition, Rome, 1938, p. 430. The Bollandists mention Brother Jordan, but they admit that there is no trace of a cult rendered to Brother Jordan who according to them was inscribed on a list of Franciscan saints about 1335.
4. See numbers 27 and 63 of the chronicle.
5. See number 21.
6. See Chapter 8 of *The Little Flowers of St. Francis,* translation by Raphael Brown, pp. 58-60 (Hanover House, Garden City, New York, 1958). (T.N.)

A man of a cheerful nature and one who does not complain is the friend of all and when Brother Jordan met again the brothers over whom he was superior, on returning from a long trip, they showed their affection for him in a moving way.[7] The people too, distrustful at first, were quickly won over.

Glassberger tells us that "he was a man remarkable for his spirit of obedience." He was sent to Germany where, as he expected, the "cruelty of the Germans" would bring him martyrdom; he went, against his own wishes, but he obeyed without a murmur.[8]

Finally, Brother Jordan was a pious man, understanding thoroughly the meaning of striving for perfection. His entire chronicle proves this to us. There are indeed valid reasons for calling him blessed.

These qualities gained for him offices within the Order: these were the office of guardian, that is, superior, of the convent of Mainz, and the office of custos, or head of a group of convents, in Thuringia; he was also vicar of the minister provincial of Saxony and of the minister provincial of Poland. These qualities merited for him also two missions of trust. He was sent to Italy in 1231 to present to the minister general John Parenti the wishes of the brothers of the provincial chapter of Worms. In 1238, he was charged with another very delicate mission: Brother Elias, the minister general, had angered the Franciscans by his arbitrary acts and by sending meddlesome and therefore unpopular visitators to the provinces. This stirred up an appeal to the Pope. It was Brother Jordan who was chosen for this difficult mission and he took

---

7. See number 59 of the chronicle.
8. See number 18 of the chronicle.

part in the meeting at Rome of the brothers delegated by the other provinces for the same purpose.

Brother Jordan, therefore, led an interesting life. Toward the end of his life, he enjoyed recounting his memories to the brothers and they enjoyed hearing what he had to say so much that they insisted that he set them down in writing. Brother Jordan consented. He excused himself in advance, however, in the prologue of his chronicle, for any failings of his memory because of his age and for the rudeness of his style. The simple narrative, without pretensions, is a document of primary importance.

2. THE MANUSCRIPTS AND EDITIONS

Between 1861 and 1871, the scholar George Voigt, professor of history at Leipzig, discovered a manuscript among the papers of his father John Voigt, the archivist at Koenigsburg. It was a copy, made by John Voigt, of the chronicle of the thirteenth century by Brother Jordan of Giano. George Voigt, after searching in vain for the original, published this copy in 1871,[9] though he was not able to correct the inaccuracies of the text.

But, after certain archives of Koenigsberg had been transferred to Berlin, another scholar, Dr. Perlbach, discovered the original manuscript. This made possible the publication of a better edition. The Franciscan Fathers of the College of St. Bonaventure at Quaracchi published the Berlin manuscript.[10] They corrected certain inaccuracies, but they did not make all

---

9. Jordan de Giano, *Die Denkwuerdigkeiten*, 1217-1238, *des Minoriten Jordans von Giano*, edited by George Voigt, Leipzig, S. Hindel, 1870.
10. *Analecta Franciscana*, Vol. I, 1885.

the verifications they could have made, and so some rather dubious phrases have remained in this edition. The manuscript of Berlin is the work of a copyist of the second half of the fourteenth century who worked without too much care; he has often placed one word for another and skipped whole lines. The editors of Quaracchi are continuing to correct the manuscript and to attempt a reconstruction of what is missing. On the other hand, the manuscript stops with the events of 1238. Since Brother Jordan wrote his chronicle in 1262, it is proper to ask if the manuscript is complete. The abruptness with which the text breaks off leads to the conclusion that it is not complete.

George Voigt searched in vain for the rest of the text in the complete catalogues of manuscripts. But Dr. Henry Boehmer had the good fortune to discover in the *Landesbibliotek* of Karlsruhe a manuscript of the fifteenth century, a fragment; in it he found numbers 57 to 62 of our chronicle, the final number that recounts the events of 1238, and a resume of the history of the province of Saxony up to 1262. The manuscript then changes its character and we have nothing more than a simple catalogue of the ministers provincial of Saxony. The chapter held at Halberstadt in 1262 marks the turning point between these latter parts. Up to this date, the evident unity of the narrative suggests that we attribute the entire text to Brother Jordan. What follows this date is a continuation written by a different author. Boehmer calls it "Continuatio Saxonica."[11]

---

11. Father Leonard Lemmens O.F.M. edited these latter parts (from 1238 through the continuations) in the *Archivum Franciscanum Historicum*, Vol. III, 1910, p. 47-54. In the accompanying article,

Continued on page 10

Doctor Boehmer undertook to investigate the problem. Conceding that the manuscript dictated by Brother Jordan was copied at least twice, he searched to see if he could not perhaps find fragments elsewhere, in particular if he could not perhaps uncover traces of it in Poland, since the Berlin manuscript had come originally from a convent in the ancient kingdom of Poland, that of the Friars Minor in Thorn.

In studying the Polish chronicles, Boehmer noticed that the Polish chronicler John of Komerow or Komerowski had inserted in certain of his works whole passages from the chronicle of Brother Jordan. John Komerowski was a Friar Minor of the Observance of the last part of the fifteenth and the first half of the sixteenth centuries; he held various offices, among which was that of minister provincial of Poland, and he wrote several works. In 1512, he wrote the *Tractatus cronice fratrum Minorum Observancie a tempore Constanciensis Consilii et specialiter de provincia Poloniae.*[12] In 1534 to 1535 he revised

---

Continued from page 9

he points out that the similarity of style between the parts up to 1238 and the next part up to 1262 and also the fact that Glassberger and Komorowski (mentioned here later) refer to this latter part as written by Jordan suggest that the whole up to the chapter at Halberstadt was written by Brother Jordan. After the chapter at Halberstadt there follow two distinct continuations: the first, 1262 to 1295 is quite similar in general make-up and style to Brother Jordans writing; the second, from 1295 to 1359, is a very brief list of the ministers provincial of the Saxony province. Lemmens suggests that the first of these two latter parts may have been written by Brother Jordan's scribe, Brother Baldwin of Brandenburg. The rest seems to have been added merely to fill out the chronicle to the date 1359. (T.N.)

12. John Komerowski, *Tractatus cronice fratrum Minorum Observancie a tempore Constanciensis Concilii et specialiter de provincia Poloniae,* ed. by Heinrich Zeissberg, Archiv fuer oesterreichische Geschichte, Vol. 49, 1872, pp. 297-425.

this work and published it under the title *Breve memoriale Ordinis Fratrum Minorum.*[13] In the first of these works he copied whole phrases from Brother Jordan and almost word for word numbers 64 to 67 and number 70. In the second work we find either entirely or in part numbers 3 to 6, 9 to 17, 19, 20, 22, 23, 25, 29, 54, 55, 61 to 67 and some phrases from other numbers. In examining the texts at hand Boehmer concluded that John Komerowski did not have a copy of the Berlin manu- script but that the latter manuscript and the manuscript of this compiler were both based on a common and more complete source.

But John Komerowski was not the only one who had knowledge of the text of Brother Jordan. This chronicle is inserted almost in its entirety in the chronicle of Nicholas Glassberger.[14] This brother, born in Olmuetz in Moravia, entered the Order of Friars Minor of the Observance in 1472 in the convent of Amberg in Bavaria. He lived in Munich, then from 1483 on in Nuremberg where he wrote his chronicle between the years 1506 and 1509. Nicholas Glassberger under- took to write the history of the Franciscan province of Strass- burg at the command of the guardian of Nuremberg. But it is not merely a chronicle of this province; it includes also a history of the various ministers general and likewise a history of the province of Saxony and of that of Bohemia.[15] This chronicle is, therefore, almost a general history of the Order.

---

13. John Komerowski, *Memoriale Ordinis fratrum Minorum,* Wydali Xawery Liske and Antoni Lorkiewicz, Monumenta Poloniae historica, Vol. 5, 1888, pp. 1-406.

14. Nicholas Glassberger, *op. cit.*

15. Glassberger also copied out the *Chronica XXIV Generalium,* which he said he transcribed "suffering from the cold and under great inconvenience."

For it Glassberger copied from documents in archives and extracts from books already published and from manuscripts. The work is a collection of diverse materials, but then neglecting to recast them the compiler has preserved for us a series of sources the originals of which we do not possess. Among these sources is the chronicle of Brother Jordan almost in its entirety, though Glassberger occasionally changes words in some of the texts. He must have used a manuscript that was a little more complete on certain points than those which we have. It is difficult to say if some of these supplementary phrases are additions or not. The portrait of Brother Jordan is probably a note by the latter's secretary, Brother Baldwin, but there is no proof of this. This can be said about the whole, though that it is the chronicle of Brother Jordan enriched with later additions.

Glassberger copied not only the text of Brother Jordan but also the rest called "Continuatio Saxonica," which is a list of the ministers provincial of Saxony and of the chapters that were held. The manuscript copied by Glassberger was even more complete than the maunscript of Karlsruhe, for the list in the manuscript of Karlsruhe ends with 1359 while that of Glassberger goes on to 1488.

One finds extracts from Brother Jordan in other narratives also, but Boehmer has proved that most of the other authors simply copied from Nicholas Glassberger. Yet, a Friar Minor of the convent at Basel who wrote a short chronicle a little after the general chapter of Lyons on May 26, 1325, transcribed an extract from the narrative of Brother Jordan.[16]

---

16. *Chronik der Strassburger Franziskaner-Provinz*, ed. by Fr. Leonard Lemmens O.F.M., Roemische Quartalschrift fuer christliche Alterthumskunde und fuer Kirchengeschichte, Vol 14, 1900, pp. 233-255.

It appears that he did not copy this latter directly, but that we have here a copy of a copy; the text seems touched up, for here and there it is found with marginal notes of some other origin and sometimes it is reduced to a simple summary.

After his careful work of textual criticism, Dr. Boehmer published his edition, taking for the basis of numbers 1 to 62 the Berlin manuscript and for numbers 63 to 78 the Karlsruhe manuscript. He corrected his text by comparing it with that of John Komerowski and that of Nicholas Glassberger. He concludes: "Since the libraries of Germany, Austria, Poland, and Russia are still far from having published the complete catalogues and exact descriptions of the other manuscripts, I do not despair of finding some day still other manuscripts of our text." Boehmer wrote that remark in 1908. Since that date, foreign and civil wars, aerial bombardments, invasions, military occupations have laid waste the countries toward the East, making uncertain any improvement on the edition of this German scholar.

3. The Style and Historical Value of the Chronicle of Brother Jordan

Although he was occupied with rather important offices in his Order, Brother Jordan was not really a learned man. He says of himself that he was "very ignorant" and he asks that the reader excuse the rudeness of his style. His Latin is not elegant and as soon as he attempts long rounded sentences, as in the prologue of his chronicle, his style becomes labored and the phrases show faults of construction. He uses Italian turns of style and his vocabulary is not without Italian influence.

Even though he is not a learned man, he nevertheless

shows great respect for learning in others; he never fails to praise the greater learning of certain of his confreres and he is completely in favor of the development of studies within the Order. He did not associate himself with the party of the "Zelanti," which was a group of extremists in the matter of strict observance, especially of poverty. This fact is a guarantee of his intellectual honesty and impartiality, for the writings of the "Zelanti" are often replete with manifestly exaggerated assertions.

What is the historical value of his narrative? Brother Jordan forestalls us when he writes that he is "old and weak," and he asks the reader to excuse the errors due to the failings of his memory. He writes with a certain garrulity and with the repititiousness of an old man. Paul Sabatier notes very justly: "In reading the chronicle, one thinks he is hearing the memories of an old soldier since certain details without value are laid hold of with a force of extraordinary embellishment."[17] He gives us a multitude of names of friars and the dates of events with great precision. Yet, like aged people, he gives more details about past events than about more recent ones.

Brother Jordan asks the indulgence of the reader, yet one rarely finds him at fault. He excuses himself once in that he does not recall whether the brothers who were martyred in Spain went on their journey there in 1219 or in 1218.[18] In another instance he gives the date 1219 for a general chapter that was probably held in 1217.[19] These are single items which we may easily excuse. Elsewhere, where we can compare his

17. Paul Sabatier, *Vie de St. Francois d'Assise,* definitive edition, Paris, Fischbacher, 1931.
18. See number 7 of the chronicle.
19. See number 3.

statements with other information, he seems always to be very exact. His penchant for humorous anecdotes, however, leads him perhaps to embellish a little the facts in the narrative of his interview with Pope Gregory IX,[20] but this is rather an isolated instance. We might add, for the sake of completeness, that he cites erroneously the name of a bishop.[21]

There are also some omissions, but these are rare. When he was custos of Thuringia, it is probable that he knew St. Elizabeth of Hungary, the wife of Louis IV, landgrave of Thuringia, but he merely mentions her once. This silence about a great saint of the Order is surprising.[22] Again, he knew well Brother Caesar of Speyer, minister provincial of Germany, who died a victim of the harsh treatment[23] inflicted upon the Order by Brother Elias, the minister general. Brother Jordan does not treat this last point which helped to bring about the deposition of Brother Elias, and he says no more of Brother Caesar. But we cannot complain very much about the omissions in Brother Jordan's work; these we have mentioned are indeed very few in number for a man who dictated his memoirs so many years after the events.

Brother Jordan is therefore a very important source for the history of the Friars Minor in Germany from 1221 to 1242. But it is proper to consider him also a valuable source for the history of St. Francis. He is the only one who gives any detailed information about the crisis that disturbed the Order

---

20. See number 63.
21. See number 22.
22. See number 25.
23. Brother Caesear was imprisoned by order of Brother Elias and met a violent death at the hands of a lay brother who had been appointed to guard him. This was in 1239(1240). It is not likely, however, that Brother Elias ordered his death. (T.N.)

of Friars Minor at the time of Francis' trip to the Orient in 1219 and about the events that followed in 1220 and 1221. He allows us to complete for these years the knowledge we have of the life of the saintly founder.

He gives us equally direct evidence on the circumstances that led to the deposition of Brother Elias, the minister general, in 1239, a deposition in which Brother Jordan had a part, since he was sent on the mission to Pope Gregory in 1238 to present to him the appeal of the brothers of Saxony against the demands of the visitators sent by Brother Elias.

It is therefore necessary to recognize this as a document of great importance. The sense of humor of its author makes the chronicle agreeable and easy reading matter. The narrative, vigorous as it is in its historical exactitude, is presented in a pleasing way. But Brother Jordan knows how to be moving too, and, when he tells us about St. Francis and about the memory of him among the brethen, he creates terms that are discreetly moving and we can understand the place the saintly founder of the Order held in the hearts of the brothers who knew him personally.

THE CHRONICLE
OF
BROTHER JORDAN OF GIANO

Prologue

Brother Jordan of Giano, of the valley of Spoleto, to the brothers of the Order of Minors established throughout Germany, for the present perseverance in good and for the future eternal glory with Christ.

Since many of the brothers have been edified by the things I have told them for time to time concerning the conversation and the life of the first brothers sent to Germany, I have often been asked by many of the brothers to set down in writing the things I have told them and other things too that I can recall, and to make note of the years of our Lord in which the brothers were sent to Germany and in which this thing or the other thing took place. But since, as an authority says, *it is like the sin of witchcraft to rebel, and like the crime of idolatry to*

17

refuse to obey,[1] I have decided to consent to the fervent wish of the brothers; this I do above all at the urging of Brother Baldwin of Brandenburg, who both of his own accord and at the command of Brother Bartholomew, then minister of Saxony, offered himself to do the actual writing.

Therefore, in the year of our Lord 1262, after the chapter celebrated at Halberstadt on *Jubilate* Sunday,[2] remaining in the place of the chapter, we set about to satisfy as well as we could the desire of the brothers, I doing the narrating and Brother Baldwin the writing.[3] And even though I myself wish to do this, nevertheless it must be conceded that you, as you well know, compelled me to do it, I who have so little ability for the task. If, however, human as I am, I should err through forgetfulness concerning the dates of the years, for I am already old and weak, I beg the reader's pardon, and I admonish him to charitably correct and amend wherever he finds I have erred. In the same way, if any one should wish to adorn the style of the writer with more polished words or correct the crudity of his language, we wish him well. For it suffices us to have given the material to those who are masters of language and skilled in the art of writing.

When I consider, on the one hand, my own littleness and that of the others who were sent with me into Germany, and, on the other hand, the condition and glory our Order has now attained, I am confused within myself and I praise in my heart the goodness of Almighty God and I am forced to extol before

---

1. I Kings 15, 23.
2. That is, the third Sunday after Easter. Jubilate is the first word of the Introit for that Sunday. In 1263 it was April 30.
3. In the first two sentences of this paragraph the text, as it has come down to us, is corrupt. The reading here is at least a close approximation to the author's meaning. (T.N.)

you this saying of the apostle: *For consider your own call, brethren, that there were not many wise according to the flesh,* who by their wisdom built up our Order; *not many mighty,* who proclaimed that it is to be preserved even with most strenuous efforts; *not many noble,* who by their favor undertook to support it; *but the foolish things of the world has God chosen to put to shame the wise, and the weak things of the world God has chosen to put to shame the strong, and the base things of the world and the despised has God chosen, and the things that are not, to bring to naught the things that are; lest any flesh should pride itself before him.*[4] That, therefore, we may glory in God, who in His wisdom founded the Order and through His servant Francis set it up as an example to the world, and not glory in man, it will be made clear in what follows when and how and through whom the Order has come down to us.

---

4. I Cor. 1, 26-28.

The Chronicle

1. In the year of our Lord 1207 Francis,[5] a merchant by trade, contrite of heart and inspired by the Holy Spirit, took up the way of penance clothed in a hermit's garb. But because enough has been said in the *Legenda*[6] about how his conversion took place, we will pass over it here.

---

5. The date given by Brother Jordan agrees with that given by Thomas of Celano (*Vita I*, 119), by Brother Leo, by the *Vita Aegidii*, by Alberic of Tres Fontaines, *l'Anonymus Perusinus*, and the *Chronica minor* ad 1216. But Thomas of Celano also gives the date as 1206 (*Vita I*, 109).
6. By 1262 there were many *Legendae* or lives of St. Francis in existence, notably the two by Thomas of Celano. It may well be, though, that here Brother Jordan is referring specifically to the *Legenda* of St. Bonaventure. In 1260, when he was minister general of the Order, St. Bonaventure was commissioned by the General Chapter of Narbonne to write a new life of St. Francis to take the place of the many in existence. This he did during the years 1260-1262. In 1266, at the General Chapter of Paris, this *Legenda* was declared the standard biography of St. Francis and all others were ordered destroyed. It is not known definitely just what was behind this order. Some have seen in it a simple attempt to ensure unity in the excerpts that were used in the Divine Office. Others have seen it as being inspired by the growing dispute between the Spirituals and the Community. Something of this may have been in it. Still, if we remember that

2. In the year of our Lord 1209, the third year of his conversion, upon hearing in the Gospel what Christ said to his disciples when he sent them out to preach, Francis immediately put aside his staff and purse and shoes and changed his garment, putting on the kind the brothers now wear, becoming an imitator of evangelical poverty and a zealous preacher of the Gospel.

3. In the year of Our Lord 1219 and the tenth year of his conversion,[7] in the chapter held at St. Mary of the Portiuncula, Brother Francis sent brothers to France, Germany, Hungary, Spain, and the other provinces of Italy to which the brothers had not yet gone.

4. But when the brothers who went to France were asked if they were Albigenses, they answered that they did not know who the Albigenses were; and so, being ignorant of the fact that the Albigenses were heretics, they themselves were put down for heretics. But when the bishop[8] and the masters

---

there were quite a few lives, both short and long, in existence, we might see it merely as an attempt to eliminate confusion and have one unified biography as the standard biography for the Order. In any case, the unfortunate result of the the decree was that most of the copies of the early biographies were destroyed and the few that remained were not uncovered until well into the eighteenth century. (T.N.)

7. This date is probably incorrect. It is more likely that Francis sent the brothers to these places in the Chapter of 1217. Cf. *Analecta Franciscana*, introduction to Vol. II, pp. XXV-XXIX.

8. Bishop Peter of Nemours, 1208-1219. The masters were the university teachers, theologians.

read their Rule and saw that it was truly in accordance with
the Gospel and Catholic, they took counsel about the matter
with the lord Pope Honorius.[9] The Pope, however, declared
in a letter[10] that the Rule was authentic, since it had been
confirmed by the Holy See, and that the brothers were in a
very special way sons of the Roman Church and true Catholics.
He thus freed them from the suspicion of heresy.

5.   Sent to Germany, however, was Brother John of Penna
with some sixty or more other brothers.[11] These, when they
came to Germany and, being ignorant of the language, were
asked if they wished to be sheltered or to eat, or the like, answered *ja;* they were accordingly treated kindly by some of the
people. And seeing that because of this word *ja* they were
treated kindly, they resolved to answer *ja* to whatever ques-
tions they would be asked. Whence it happened that when they
were asked if they were heretics and if they had come to
corrupt Germany as they had corrupted Lombardy and they
replied *ja,* some of them were cast into prison, others were
stripped and led naked to a dance[12] and made a ludicrous

---

9. Honorius III, 1216-1227.
10. The Bull *Pro dilectis filiis,* May 29, 1220.
11. Since the plural "missi sunt fratres" is used in the original text
    here, some think that at least one other name of a brother is miss-
    ing here. On the other hand, Brother Jordan would be the last to
    complain if it were suggested that he might have slipped up, using
    the plural construction with the "other sixty or more brothers" in
    mind. (T.N.)
12. Brother Jordan used the word *chorea* here, which means a dance.
    Some have thought that he might have meant *chora,* meaning rather
    a *local court.* Perhaps he had in mind the public place where the
    dance was held customarily. (T.N.)

spectacle before their fellowmen. The brothers, therefore, seeing that they would not be able to gather a harvest in Germany, returned to Italy. As a result of these things, Germany had a reputation among the brothers of being so cruel that they would not dare to return there except they were filled with a desire for martyrdom.

6. The brothers, however, who were sent to Hungary were conducted there by sea by a certain bishop from Hungary. And as they walked through the fields, they were derided, and the shepherds set their dogs upon them and kept striking them with their staves, the point, however, being turned away.[13] And when the brothers debated among themselves why they were being treated like this, one said: "Perhaps because they wish to have our outer tunics." But when they had given them these, they did not cease their blows. He added: "Perhaps they wish to have our under tunics also." But when they had given them these, they did not leave off their blows. He then said: "Perhaps they want our breeches too." When they gave them these, they stopped their blows and let them go away naked. One of these brothers told me that he had lost his breeches fifteen[14] times in this way. And since, overcome by shame and modesty, he regretted losing his breeches more than his other clothing, he soiled the breeches with the dung of oxen and other filth, and thus the shepherds themselves were filled with nausea and allowed him to keep his breeches. These brothers, afflicted with other insults too, returned to Italy.

---

13. A shepherd's staff had a crook at one end or a hook-like appendage; at the other end was a point. (T.N.)
14. Later, when this story is repeated in number 18, the number of times is given as six. Even this, which is probably closer to the truth, would be quite often. (T.N.)

7.   Of the brothers, though, who went to Spain, five attained the crown of martyrdom.[15] But whether or not these five brothers were sent out from this same chapter, or whether from the preceding chapter, when Brother Elias was sent beyond the sea with his companions, we are not sure.

8.   When the life and history of these aforementioned martyrs were brought to Blessed Francis, hearing that he himself was praised in them and seeing that the other brothers were taking pride in the sufferings of these brothers, in as much as he held himself in the greatest contempt and despised praise and glory, he spurned the accounts and forbade them to be read, and said: "Everyone should glory in his own suffering and not in that of another." And thus this whole first mission was brought to naught, probably because the time had not yet come for sending brothers out, since the time for everything is under the providence of heaven.[16]

9.   But Brother Elias[17] was appointed minister provincial by Blessed Francis for the territory beyond the sea. At his

---

15. The five were: Brothers Berard, Peter, Accursius, Adjutus, and Otho. Their feast day is celebrated on January 16. The place was Morocco, though, rather than Spain. (T.N.)

16. Eccles. 8,6.

17. Little is known of the early life of Brother Elias of Cortona. But he must have been a man of exceptional abilities since he merited so highly the esteem of St. Francis. His later life, however, was anything but exemplary. In 1239 he was deposed from the office of minister general. He left the Order and was excommunicated, but died reconciled to God. See: *Early Franciscan Government, Elias to Bonaventure*, Rosalind B. Brooke, Cambridge University Press, 1959. (T.N.)

preaching there, a certain cleric by the name of Caesar was received into the Order. This Ceasar,[18] a German born in Speyer and a subdeacon, was a student of theology under the master Conrad of Speyer,[19] a preacher of the crusade and afterwards bishop of Hildesheim. While Caesar was still in the world, he was a great preacher and a follower of evangelical perfection. At his preaching, while he was still in his native city, certain married women, putting off their ornaments, began to live humbly; their husbands, however, became angry and wanted to hand him over to be burned as a heretic. But he was snatched away by his master Conrad, and returned to Paris; afterwards, crossing the sea after the usual journey, he was converted to the Order at the preaching of Elias, as was already mentioned, and he became a man of great learning and good example.

10. After these things had been so disposed, the Blessed Father reflected that he had sent his sons to sufferings and labors; and therefore, lest, while others were working for Christ, he himself should seem to be seeking his own ease, for he was proud of spirit and did not wish anyone to excel him in the way of Christ but wished rather that he should excel all others, since he had sent his sons to uncertain dangers and amongst the faithful, burning with love for the passion of Christ, he himself the same year that he sent his brothers out, namely in the thirteenth year of his conversion, faced the certain dangers of the sea and, crossing over to the infidels, betook

---

18. See the notes about him in the introduction to this chronicle.
19. A renowned teacher at Paris and Mainz and a preacher of the crusade against Albigenses.

himself to the sultan.[20] But before he came before him, he was beset with many outrages and insults and, being ignorant of the language of his tormentors, he cried out amidst the blows: "Sultan! Sultan!" And thus he was led before the sultan, was honorably received by him, and was treated kindly in his infirmity. But since he could not harvest any fruit among them and was disposed to return home, he was led at the order of the sultan by an armed guard to the Christian army that was at the time besieging Damietta.

11.   Blessed Francis, when he had set out to cross the sea with Blessed Peter of Catania,[21] a doctor of laws, left behind two vicars, Brother Matthew of Narni and Brother Gregory of Naples. Matthew he put at St. Mary of the Portiuncula, so that remaining there he could receive those who were to be received into the Order; but Gregory he appointed to travel about Italy to strengthen the brothers. And because according to the first Rule[22] the brothers fasted on Wednesdays and Fridays and,

---

20. Melek el-Khamil, sultan of Egypt, 1217-1238. Francis arrived in the camp at Damietta on August 29, 1219.
21. Peter of Catania was one of the first to join St. Francis in his way of life.
22. The so-called *First Rule* of 1221 says only that the Friars were to fast from the feast of All Saints to the Nativity of the Lord, from Epiphany to Easter, and on Fridays. This *First Rule* was a revision of what is called the *Protoregula,* a very brief statement of the Friars' way of life which Pope Innocent III approved for St. Francis by word of mouth in 1209. The text of this latter is no longer extant, but it is hardly likely that it contained at that early moment of Francis' Order any particular legislation regarding fasting and abstinence. During the years between 1209 and 1221 this primitive Rule grew by additions at various general chapters, and, no doubt, the legislation mentioned by Brother Jordan was enacted during these years. After Francis' vicars had set about on their

with the permission of Blessed Francis, also on Mondays and Saturdays, and ate meat on other days when eating meat was lawful, these vicars celebrated a chapter along with certain older brothers of Italy, in which they ordained that the brothers were not to eat meat that had been procured for them on days on which meat was permitted, but only such meat as might be offered them by the faithful of their own accord. And in addition, they ordained that they were to fast on Mondays and on two other days, and that on Mondays and Saturdays they were not to procure for themselves milk products, but were to abstain from these, unless perhaps they were offered to them by the devoted faithful.

12. A certain lay brother became very angry over these constitutions, in as much as these vicars had presumed to add something to the Rule of the holy Father, and, taking with him these constitutions, he set out to cross the sea without the permission of the vicars. And coming to Blessed Francis, he first confessed his fault and asked forgiveness in that he had come to him without permission, impelled by this necessity that the vicars whom Francis had left in his place had presumed to add new laws to the Rule; and he added that the Order throughout Italy was disturbed over these vicars and

---

own to enact additional legislation, Francis revised the whole into the so-called *First Rule*, which, however, was not submitted to the Holy Father for approbation. Instead, it was revised again, put into more legal terminology, and submitted for the final approbation of Pope Honorius III in 1223. It received this approbation on November 29 in the Bull *Solet Annuere*. This latter Rule is called the *Second Rule* or the *Regula Bullata*. It is this Rule that is still in force for the Friars today. (T.N.)

over the other brothers who had presumed to legislate new things. After Blessed Francis had read the constitutions and while he was at table where meat had been placed before him for him to eat, he said to Brother Peter: "My lord Peter, what shall we do?" And Peter answered: "Ah, my lord Francis, whatever pleases you, for you have the authority." It was because Peter was educated and of noble birth that Blessed Francis, in his courtesy, honoring him, addressed him as lord. And this mutual reverence existed between them beyond the sea and in Italy. Finally Blessed Francis said: "Let us then eat, according to the Gospel, what has been placed before us."

13.   At this same time there was beyond the sea a certain prophetess who predicted many things that came true, wherefore she was called the tongue that speaks the truth. She said:[23] "Return, return, because on account of the absence of Brother Francis the Order is disturbed, torn asunder, and scattered." And this was true. For Brother Philip, who was over-zealous for the Poor Ladies,[24] contrary to the will of Blessed Francis who wanted to conquer all things through humility rather than by the force of legal judgments, sought letters from the Apostolic See. By these letters he wished to defend the Ladies and excommunicate their disturbers. Similarly, Brother John Conpella, after he had gathered together a large crowd of lepers, both men and women, withdrew from the Order and wanted to be the founder of a new Order. He wrote a Rule and presented himself with his followers before the Holy See to

---

23. Some such phrase as "she said" should be inserted here; it is missing in the manuscripts.
24. That is, the Poor Clares.

have it confirmed. And in addition to these things there were rumblings of other disturbances too that had arisen during the absence of Blessed Francis, just as that prophetess had said.

14. Brother Francis, taking with him Brother Elias, Brother Peter of Catania, and Brother Caesar, whom, as was said above, Brother Elias while minister of Syria had received into the Order, and some other brothers, returned to Italy. And there, after he had learned more fully the causes of the disturbances, he betook himself, not to the disturbers, but to the Lord Pope Honorius.[25] Father Francis cast himself down before the door of the lord Pope and did not dare to make a noise and knock at the room of so great a prince; but he waited expectantly until the Pope should come out of his own accord. When he did, Blessed Francis made the proper reverences and said to him: "Holy Father, may God give thee peace." And the Pope replied: "May God bless you, son." And Blessed Francis said: "My lord, since you are great and always oppressed with such great burdens, the poor cannot often gain access to you nor speak with you, when they have need to. You have given me many popes,[26] but give me one to whom I may speak when I have need; one who will hear and decide my problems and those of my Order in your place." The Pope answered: "Whom do you wish me to give you, son?" And Francis said: "The Lord of Ostia."[27] And he granted this. Therefore, when Blessed Francis explained to the lord

25. The pope was staying at Orvieto.
26. It may be that he is referring to the papal representatives who attended the general chapters of the Order.
27. Cardinal Hugolino who was elected pope in 1227 and took the name Gregory IX. He died in 1241.

of Ostia, his pope, the causes of his distress, the latter immediately revoked the letters of Brother Philip, and Brother John
was sent away from the Curia with his followers in shame.

15.   And thus, by the favor of the Lord, the disturbances
were quickly put down, and Francis reformed the Order according to his own statutes. And Blessed Francis, seeing that
Brother Caesar was a man learned in the Sacred Scriptures,
charged him to adorn with words from the Gospel the Rule
which he wrote in simple words.[28] And this he did. Many of
the brothers, however, because they had heard diverse rumors
concerning Blessed Francis, some saying that he was dead,
others that he had been killed, and still others that he had
been drowned, were much disturbed. But when they learned
that he was alive and had returned, it seemed to them in their
joy that a new light had risen for them. Blessed Francis, however, immediately went to St. Mary of the Portiuncula and
called a general chapter.

16.   Therefore in the year of our Lord 1221, on the tenth
day before the calends of June,[29] in the fourteenth year of the
indiction,[30] on Pentecost day, Blessed Francis held a general

---

28. This was the so-called "First Rule" of 1221.
29. May 23. To find the corresponding day on our calendar, remember
the Calends of the month are the first day of the month (here
June 1). Add 2 to the number of the days of the preceding month
and subtract from this the number of the day before the Calends:
3 plus 2 minus 10 - 23. (T.N.)
30. The indiction, according to Webster's New International Dictionary,
was a recurring cycle of 15 years, called in full the cycle of indiction. The number attached to it indicates the specific year within

chapter at St. Mary of the Portiuncula, and, as was the custom of the Order at that time, both professed and novices came to this chapter. It was estimated that there were three thousand brothers who came together at this time. The Lord Raynerius,[31] cardinal deacon, was present at this chapter, together with many bishops and other religious. At his command one of the bishops celebrated Holy Mass, and Blessed Francis is believed to have read the Gospel and another brother the Epistle. Since there were no dwelling places for so many brothers, the brothers lived, ate, and slept in tents of branches on a spacious and enclosed field; twenty-three tables[32] were

---

the cycle, as here, the 14th year of the indiction. There were several systems used: the Constantian in the East (which began with September 1, 312); the Imperial or Western used in Germany, France, and England (which began on September 24, 312); the Roman or Papal (which after the 12th century began with the birth of Christ). With the first two systems, to find the indiction, subtract 312 from the given year. With the last, add three years to the given year. And in each case, then divide by 15. The quotient is the number of the current indiction; the remainder is the year of the indiction. (T.N.)

There seems to be a double error in the date as given here. Pentecost that year was on May 30 and the year of the indiction was the ninth.

31. Raynerius Capocci, bishop of Viterbo, who died in 1252.

32. The details of two separate chapters, those of 1219 and 1221, are often confused by these early writers. Thus, for instance, they differ as to the number of those who attended, some giving 5000, some 3000. Likewise, some call the chapter of 1219 the chapter of mats; others, that of 1221 (capitulum storearum; capitulum de cortinis vel de tentoriis; or, as Brother Jordan puts it, sub umbraculis). Cardinal Hugolino was present in 1219. Brother Jordan here, surprisingly, says Francis "is believed" to have read the Gospel. Jordan was present, but by 1262 his memory of the occasion may have become dimmed and he too had difficulty in keeping the two

Continued on page 32

arranged in an orderly manner, well separated, and amply spaced. The people of the neighborhood served very willingly at this chapter, ministering bread and wine in abundance and rejoicing over the gathering of so many brothers and over the return of Blessed Francis.

In this chapter Blessed Francis preached to his brothers upon the theme: *Blessed be the Lord my God, who trains my hands for battle,*[33] and he taught them virtues and exhorted them to patience and to give a good example to the world. Likewise he preached a sermon to the people, and the people and clergy were edified.

Who can explain how great was the charity among the brothers at this time, and the patience, humility, obedience, and brotherly cheerfulness? I have never seen a chapter in the Order like that one, both as to the number of brothers present and the distinction of those who ministered to them. And, though there was such a great number of brothers there, the people supplied all things so cheerfully that after seven days of the chapter the brothers had to close the door and receive nothing further, and on top of it they had to remain there two days longer so that they might use up what had been offered and accepted.

Continued from page 31

chapters apart. The general picture this writer gets of the field, the tents, and the twenty-three tables set up about the field is this: for their meals, tables were set up at widely separated places around the large field (there were at least 3000 friars present); on these tables their food was placed and the friars would come to these tables, take what food they wished, and retire again to their tents where they "lived, ate, and slept." (T.N.)

33. Psalm 143, I (Confraternity edition).

17. At the conclusion of the chapter, that is, when the chapter was about to be terminated, it came to the mind of Blessed Francis that the establishment of the Order had not yet come to Germany. And because Blessed Francis was quite weak,[34] whatever was to said to the chapter on his behalf was spoken by Brother Elias. Blessed Francis, seated at the feet of Brother Elias, tugged at his tunic to attract his attention. Elias bent down to him to inquire what he wished, and then straightened himself and said: "Brothers, thus says *The Brother* (meaning Blessed Francis, who was called by the other brothers *The Brother,* as it were par excellence) , there is a certain region called Germany, where there are devout Christian people, who, as you know, often pass through our country, perspiring under the heat of the sun, bearing large staves and wearing large boots,[35] singing praises to God and the Saints, and visit the shrines of the Saints. And because once the brothers who were sent to them were treated badly and returned, *The Brother* does not compel anyone to go to them; but to those who, inspired by zeal for God and for souls, may wish to go, he desires to give the same obedience that he gives to those who go beyond the sea, and even a broader one. If there are any who wish to go, let them rise and gather in a group aside." And there arose about ninety brothers inflamed with such a desire, offering themselves to death; and, gathering in a group

---

34. He had contracted an eye disease in the East and suffered too the effects of malaria. Cf. Celano, *Vita I,* 98, 101, 105, etc., and *Vita II,* 44, 51, 64, etc.
35. The manuscripts have *cereis* here (candles), but Glassberger and Wadding have *ocreis* (leggings, boots). This latter seems preferable. Cf. *Archivum Franciscanum Historicum,* Vol. II, 1909; a critical review of Boehmer's edition of Jordan's Chronicle; pp. 647-650.

aside, as they were commanded, they awaited the answer who, how many, in what manner, and when they were to go.

18.   There was at that time a certain brother in the chapter who was accustomed to ask God in his prayers that his faith should not be corrupted by the heretics of Lombardy and that he should not be moved from his faith by the ferocity of the Germans, and that the Lord should deign in His mercy to keep him free from both of these peoples. Seeing now the many brothers who arose ready to go to Germany, he thought they would be immediately martyred by the Germans; and remembering with regret that he had not known by name the brothers who had been sent to Spain[36] and there been martyred, this brother, not wishing the same thing to happen to him with regard to the former as had happened to him with regard to the latter, arose from the midst of all the brothers and went to them; and as he went from one to the other, he asked, "Who are you and where do you come from?" For he thought it would be a great glory for himself, if, in case they were martyred, he would be able to say, "I knew this one, and I knew that one."

Amongst them there was a certain brother by the name of Palmerius, a deacon, who afterwards became the guardian at Magdeburg; he was an amiable and cheerful man from the neighborhood of Monte Gargano in the province of Apulia. When that inquisitive brother came to this brother and asked, "Who are you and by what name are you called?" this brother answered, "I am called Palmerius." Then putting his hand upon that brother, he added, "And you too are one of us and shall

---

36. Morocco, to be exact.

go with us," wanting to take him with him to Germany, about which this brother had so often asked the Lord that He might send him wherever He wished but not to the Germans. And holding even the name of the Germans in abhorrence, that brother answered, "I am not one of you, but I came to you wanting to know you, but not with the desire of going with you." But the other, prevailing by reason of his cheerfulness, detained him; and though he struggled both by word and action, drew him to the ground beside him and made him sit with him among the others.

Meanwhile, while these things were going on and that inquisitive brother was being detained among the others, he was assigned to another province and it was announced: "This brother will go to this place." Then, while those ninety brothers were awaiting their answer, Brother Caesar, the German, who was born in Speyer, as was said before, was appointed minister of Germany, with the authority to choose whomever he wished from among those ninety. And when he found that inquisitive brother among the others, he was urged by the others to take him with him. But since this brother was unwilling to go among the Germans and continued to say, "I am not one of you, because I did not rise with the desire of going with these others," he was led to Brother Elias. Now when the brothers of that province to which he had been assigned heard about these things, they strove to keep him amongst them, especially since he was weak and the land to which he would go was cold. But Brother Caesar was anxious to take him with him by all means.

Brother Elias solved the dispute in this way, saying: "I command you, Brother, in holy obedience, to decide finally whether you wish to go or to be released." But the brother,

constrained thus by obedience, still hesitated what he should
do; he feared to choose because of his conscience, lest, if he
chose, it would seem that he were following his own will; and
he feared to go because of the cruelty of the Germans, lest he
should lose his patience amid sufferings and imperil his soul.
And thus, perplexed between the two choices and not finding
any counsel within himself, he approached a brother who had
been proved by many tribulations, namely, the brother who,
as was said before, lost his breeches six times in Hungary,[37] and
asked advice of him. "My dear Brother," he said, "this is what
is commanded me, and I fear to choose, and I do not know
what to do." But he replied: "Go to Brother Elias and say to
him: 'Brother, I neither wish to go nor to stay behind, but
whatever you command me, that will I do.' Thus you will free
yourself from your perplexity." And this he did. And when
Brother Elias heard this, he commanded him by virtue of holy
obedience to go with Brother Caesar to Germany. Now this
brother is Brother Jordan of Giano who writes this down for
you, who came to Germany under these circumstances, who escaped the fury of the Germans which he had dreaded, and who,
together with Brother Caesar and the other brothers, first
planted the Order of Minors in Germany.

19.　　The first minister of Germany was Brother Caesar,
who, solicitous to carry out in a useful manner the obedience
placed upon him, took with him the following brothers: John

---

37. See the earlier paragraph 6 where the number is given as fifteen
　　times.

of Pian di Carpine,[38] a preacher in the Latin language and in that of the Lombards; Barnabas, a German, a renowned preacher in the language of the Lombards and in German; Thomas of Celano[39] who later wrote both a first and a second *Legenda* of St. Francis; Joseph of Treviso; Abraham, a Hungarian; Simon, a Tuscan, the son of the countess of Colazon; Conrad, a German cleric; Peter, a priest from Camerino; James and Walter, both priests; Palmerius, a deacon; Brother Jordan of Giano, a deacon; and several lay brothers, namely, Benedict of Soest, a German, and Henry, a Swabian, and a number of others whose names I do not remember. There were in all,

---

38. The present day Magione near Perugia. John played an extensive role in the spread of the Order as can be seen from this chronicle. He established the Order in Saxony, then in Bohemia, Poland, Hungary, Denmark and Norway. In 1245 Pope Innocent IV sent him as a legate to the Tartars; he was successful in winning over the Grand Khan; he returned to Europe in 1247, accomplished a mission to Louis IX, King of France, then died in Italy on August 1, 1252.

39. Thomas of Celano came from the region of Abruzzi in central Italy. He entered the Order in 1215 or perhaps as early as 1213. In 1221 he went with Caesar of Speyer to Germany, and in 1223, when Caesar returned to Italy, he acted as vicar provincial until a new provincial should arrive. He was back in Assisi at least in 1228 (if not earlier) for the cannonization of St. Francis and again in 1230 for the translation of the remains of the saint. He died about 1260 or shortly thereafter. At the command of Pope Gregory IX he undertook to write a biography of St. Francis. He finished this *Vita Prima* by 1229 or 1230. In 1244 the minister general Crescentius of Jesi issued an order that all the friars should set down in writing their recollections of St. Francis. After these documents had been received, the minister general ordered Thomas of Celano to write a new life of St. Francis, the *Vita Secunda*. This life was approved by the general chapter in 1247. He also wrote a *Tractatus de Miraculis* and he is known also for the famous sequence of the Mass, the *Dies Irae*.

however, twelve clerics and thirteen lay brothers. After Brother Caesar had chosen these, being a devoted person, he was reluctant to leave Blessed Francis and the holy brothers; with the permission of Blessed Francis, therefore, he dispersed the companions given to him among the houses in Lombardy to await word from him there; he himself then remained in the Spoleto valley for about three months. Then, when he was ready to undertake the journey to Germany, he summoned his brothers and sent Brother John of Pian di Carpine, Brother Barnabas, and certain other brothers ahead to prepare a place for him and his brother in Trent, and the rest of the brothers followed in groups of three and four.

20.   The brothers traveling thus in separate groups were reunited in Trent before the feast of the Blessed Michael,[40] and during the six days they thus arrived in separate groups they were received kindly by the lord bishop of Trent. But on the feast of St. Michael Brother Caesar delivered a sermon to the clergy and Brother Barnabas to the people. At their preaching a certain citizen of Trent, a wealthy man, skilled in the German language and the language of Lombardy, Peregrine by name, clothed the brothers in new outer and under tunics and then sold the rest of his goods, distributed the money among the poor, and was received into the Order.

21.   Brother Caesar, then, after he had called together his brothers in Trent, admonished them to be humble and to

---

40. September 19. The bishop of Trent was Adelbert of Ravenstein, 1219-1223.

preserve their patience. Then, leaving some of the brothers there for the edification of the people, he grouped them in twos and threes, placed one of them in charge of temporal things and another in charge of spiritual things, and he sent them on ahead to Bozen. And there the lord bishop of Trent provided for the brothers as they arrived separately over several days and gave them permission to preach in his diocese. From Bozen they went to Brixen and were received kindly by the bishop of that place. From Brixen they entered the mountainous regions and arrived at Sterzing after the luncheon hour of the people. And since the people did not have any bread on hand and the brothers did not know how to ask for it, they hoped that they would come in the evening to a place where they would be refreshed through the piety of the people. They then came to Mittenwald, where, amid the greatest scarcity, they satisfied miserably, or indeed rather increased, the discomfort of their hunger with two small pieces of bread and seven turnips and quenched their thirst with joy in their hearts. Then, after discussing amongst themselves how they might fill their empty stomachs so that they might pass a peaceful night after the toil of their seven-mile walk, they decided to drink water of a clear stream that flowed by, so that their empty stomachs would not growl.

When morning came, they got up, starved and empty, and continued the journey they had begun. After they had gone about five hundred paces, their eyes began to fail, their limbs gave way, their knees grew unsteady from the fast, and their entire bodies became weak. Wherefore, because of their hunger, they plucked fruit from the thorns and from the different kinds of trees and herbs they found along the way. But, since it was Friday, they were afraid to break the fast. However, they seemed to be refreshed a little by the very fact that they carried with them the fruits of various trees and brambles, so that, if extreme necessity forced them to it, they would have something to eat. And thus, now pausing, now going on slowly, they came with difficulty to Matrey.[41] And behold, God, to whom the poor are committed, solicitous for His poor, provided that, as they entered the town, they met two hospitable men who bought for them two deniers[42] worth of bread. But what was this among so many? But because this was the season for turnips, they begged turnips and thus supplied with turnips what was wanting in bread.

22.   After their meal, more full than satisfied, they continued on their journey and thus, passing by villages and towns and monasteries, they came to Augsburg, where they were charitably received by the bishop of Augsburg[43] and by his nephew, the vicar and canon of the principal church. The lord bishop of Augsburg was moved by such great affection for the brothers, that he received each one with a kiss and dismissed him with a kiss. The vicar too received them with such great affection that he moved out of his palace and put up the brothers in it. In addition, they were received kindly and greeted reverently both by the clergy and by the people.

---

41. On the Brenner.
42. A very small coin.
43. Some manuscripts insert the name Siboto as the name of the bishop. If indeed Jordan did put in that name, he was in error, for Siboto did not become bishop until May 1228. Siegfried III was bishop from 1209-1227.

23. In the year of our Lord 1221, about the feast of St. Gall,[44] Brother Caesar, the first minister provincial of Germany, called together his brothers in Augsburg, thirty-one in number, for the first chapter since their entry into Germany, and from it he sent brothers to the various provinces of the country. He sent Brother John of Pian di Carpine and Brother Barnabas as preachers to Würzburg. From there they passed over to Mainz, Worms, Speyer, Strassburg, and Cologne, appearing before the people and preaching the word of penance and preparing hospices for the brothers who were to follow.

24. In this same chapter Brother Caesar sent Brother Jordan of Giano with two companions, namely, Abraham and Constantine, to Salzburg. They were received kindly by the bishop[45] of that place. Three other brothers he sent to Regensburg with Brother Joseph; and Brother Caesar, following in the footsteps of those who had gone on ahead, confirmed the brothers in good both by word and example.

25. In the same year, when Brother Caesar came to Würzburg, he received into the Order a capable and educated young man named Hartmuth; the Italians did not know how to pronounce his name, so they called him Andrew since he was received into the Order on the feast of St. Andrew.[46] In a short time he was ordained priest and became a preacher; later he was made custos of Saxony. Likewise, he received a certain lay brother named Rodiger who later became guardian

---

44. October 16.
45. Eberhard II, 1200-1246.
46. November 30.

in Halberstadt and the spiritual director of Elizabeth,[47] teaching her to observe chastity, humility, and patience, to keep watch in prayer, and to spend herself in works of mercy. Similarly, he received also a brother named Rudolph.

26.   In the year of our Lord 1222 Brother Caesar had received so many brothers, both clerics and lay brothers, that he called together the brothers from the neighboring cities and held the first provincial chapter at Worms. And, because the place in which the brothers had been received was small and not suited for the celebration of Mass and for preaching when such numbers were present, after consulting the bishop[48] and the canons, they convened in a larger church for the celebration of Mass and for preaching; the canons restricted themselves to one choir and left the other for the brothers. One of the brothers of the Order celebrated Mass, and with one choir chanting with zeal against the other choir, they performed the Divine Office with great solemnity.

27.   From this chapter Brother Caesar sent two brothers with a letter for the brothers in Salzburg[49] who had not come to the chapter, inviting them to come to him, if they so wished. These, however, since they had given themselves completely to obedience, so much so that they wished to do nothing of their own will, were not a little disturbed over the condition placed in the letter, namely, "If they wished to come," and they

---

47. St. Elizabeth of Hungary.
48. Henry II, 1213-1234.
49. Jordan, Abraham, and Constantine. See number 24. There were others too.

said: "Let us go and find out why he wrote thus to us, since we wish nothing but what he wishes." Along the way, when they came to a certain village for the sake of a meal, they went two by two through the village begging; and they were answered with the German expression *God berad,* which translated[50] means *May God provide for you,* and even more, *Let God provide for you.* One of the brothers, seeing that at these words nothing was given them, thought and even said: "This *God berad* will be the death of us today." And going on ahead of his brother who was used to begging daily,[51] he began to beg in Latin. The Germans replied: "We do not understand Latin; speak to us in German." And the brother said with a very bad pronunciation *Nicht diutisch,* since in Latin one says *Nihil theutonici,* understanding *scio,* I know no German. And he added in German *"Brot durch Gott*—bread for God's sake." But they answered: "It is remarkable that you speak German when you say you do not know German." And they added, *God berad.* And the brother, rejoicing in spirit and smiling to himself and pretending not to understand what they had said, sat down on a bench. Then a man and a woman, glancing at each other and smiling to themselves at his audacity, gave him bread, eggs, and milk. Therefore, seeing that by such pretense he could be useful to himself and to the brothers, he went to twelve homes doing the same thing and begging what was needed for the seven brothers.

Proceeding along this same road, they came on the holy day of Pentecost to a certain village before Mass. There they

---

50. Literally, *which means in Latin.*
51. The meaning probably is that the other brother was used to begging in German.

heard Mass, and one of them received Holy Communion.[52] And the people of the village were so touched when they saw the simplicity and humility of the brothers that they knelt before the brothers and venerated their very footprints. From there they went on through Würzburg, Mainz, and Worms and came to Speyer. There they found Brother Caesar and several of the brothers gathered together and they were received very charitably by them, as was the custom, and these latter rejoiced greatly over their coming. Brother Caesar, when asked by the brothers why he had written to them in that manner, excused himself and explaining his intentions, satisfied them.

28. In the same year, which was the second year since the brothers had come to Germany, after Brother Caesar, the minister of Germany, had placed brothers in Cologne and in the aforementioned cities, there was a scarcity of priests, so much so that one novice priest celebrated Mass on solemn occasions for the brothers in Speyer and in Worms and heard their confessions. Wherefore, that same year, he had three brothers raised to the priesthood, namely, Palmerius, of whom we spoke before, Abraham the Hungarian, and Andrew the German, who had been known before as Hartmuth.

29. In the year of our Lord 1223, on the third day before the calends of December,[53] the Rule of the Friars Minor was confirmed by the lord Pope Honorius III.

---

52. In those days it was not customary to receive Holy Communion very often.
53. November 29.

30. The same year, on the fifteenth day before the calends of April, Brother Caesar had a fourth brother[54] in the group promoted to the priesthood, namely, Brother Jordan of Giano in the Spoleto valley, who for almost the whole of one summer was alone alternately in Worms, Mainz, and Speyer. And the same year he appointed Brother Thomas of Celano custos for Mainz, Worms, Cologne, and Speyer.

31. In the same year, Brother Caesar, a man wholly contemplative in spirit and greatly zealous for the Gospel and for poverty—in fact he was so highly regarded by the brothers that they venerated him as the most holy brother after Blessed Francis—this Brother Caesar, worn out and desirous of seeing Blessed Francis and the brothers in the Spoleto valley, now that the Order was established in Germany, took with him Brother Simon, who is now called a saint in Spoleto, and some other worthy and devoted brothers, leaving Brother Thomas, who at the time was the only custos, to be his vicar in Germany, and proceeded to Blessed Francis or to Brother Elias and was kindly received by him and by the other brothers. And in the chapter that was held that same year at St. Mary of the Portiuncula, Brother Caesar was released from the office of minister which he had held for two years, and Brother Albert of Pisa was put in his place.[55]

---

54. The other three were mentioned in no. 28. The date was March 18.
55. Brother Albert of Pisa may have entered the Order as early as 1212. He held the office of minister provincial in Germany from 1223-1227 and successively in various other places (Hungary, Bologna, the Marches of Ancona, and in England). In 1239 he was elected minister general of the whole Order, the first priest to hold this office.

32.   Along with Brother Albert of Pisa some worthy and educated brothers were sent from Italy, namely, Brother Mark of Milan, Brother James of Treviso, Brother Anglicus, a lawyer, and a number of others.

33.   Brother Albert of Pisa, therefore, the second minister of Germany, after he had come to Germany, called together the senior brothers of Germany, namely, Brother John of Pian di Carpine and Brother Thomas, the vicar and sole custos, and certain others, and celebrated a chapter on the feast of the Nativity of the Blessed Virgin[56] at Speyer at the leprosarium outside the walls. Brother Jordan was the guardian there at this time, and he sang the solemn Mass at this chapter. In this chapter, solicitously considering the state of the Order and its spread, they appointed Brother Mark custos of Franconia, Brother Angelus of Worms custos of Bavaria and Swabia, Brother James custos of Alsace, and Brother John of Pian di Carpine, custos of Saxony.

34.   The following went to Saxony with Brother John of Pian di Carpine: Brother John and Brother William, both Englishmen; Brother Giles, a Lombard cleric; Brother Palmerius, a priest; Brother Raynald, a priest from Spoleto; Brother Rodiger, a German lay brother; Brother Rokkerus, a lay brother; Brother Benedict, a German lay brother; Brother Tichmar, a lay brother; and Brother Emmanuel of Verona, a tailor.

---

56. September 8.

35.　These all came to Hildesheim and were received and pleasantly entertained by the first canon, Henry of Tossem. Then they presented themselves to the lord bishop Conrad, a great preacher and theologian,[57] and were received by him with great honor. This bishop, I say, after he had gathered together the clergy of his city, had Brother John of Pian di Carpine, the first custos of Saxony, preach in the presence of a great crowd of clerics. After the sermon, the lord bishop commended Brother John and the brothers of his Order to the clergy and the people, and gave them the faculty to preach and hear confessions in his diocese. At the preaching of the brothers and by reason of their good example many were led to penance and they entered the Order. One of these was Bernard, the son of the countess of Poppenburg, a canon of the cathedral; another was Albert, a teacher of children and an educated man; a third was a certain Ludolph; and another, a certain soldier. When, however, there arose in this place a disturbance over the fact that certain brothers had left the Order, the favor of the people toward the brother grew cool, so much so that they gave them alms only angrily and seemed to turn away their faces when they saw them begging. Of a sudden, however, by the providence of God, the lost favor was rekindled, and the people returned to their first love for the brothers.

36.　In the year of our Lord 1223 Brother John of Pian di Carpine, extending the Order still further, sent several prudent brothers to Hildesheim, Brunswick, Goslar, Magdeburg, and Halberstadt.

---

57. Conrad II, bishop from 1221 to 1246. He was the master of Brother Caesar of Speyer. See no. 9 of this chronicle.

37. In the year of our Lord 1224, at the provincial chapter held at Würzburg on the feast of the Assumption of the Blessed Virgin,[58] the custodes, guardians, and preachers having been called together, they released Brother John from his office and sent him to Cologne; they also appointed Brother James, who had been custos of Alsace, and who was a gracious, kind, modest, and pious man, to be the second custos of Saxony, and they sent with him some of the older brothers of the Order, both clerics and lay brothers, who by their humility and by the example of their lives grew greatly in the esteem of both the clergy and the people.

38. In the same year Brother Albert of Pisa, minister of Germany, seeing the progress in Saxony, and seeing that from Saxony there was a way open through Thuringia to the Rhine, sent Brother Jordan, the guardian of Mainz, with seven brothers to obtain houses in Thuringia and to place brothers in suitable places.

39. Brother Jordan started on the journey from Mainz to Thuringia with his brothers on the sixth day before the calends of November[59] and arrived at Erfurt on the feast of St. Martin.[60] Since it was winter and not a time for building, at the advice of the people of the city and some of the clergy, he placed the brothers in the house of a priest who was in charge of the lepers outside the walls, until the people could make some better arrangement for the welfare of the brothers.

---

58. August 15.
59. October 27.
60. November 11.

40. Now the brothers who were sent with Brother Jordan were these: Brother Hermann of Weissensee, a priest, novice, and preacher; Brother Conrad of Würzburg, a subdeacon and novice; Brother Henry of Würzburg, a subdeacon and novice; Brother Arnold, a cleric and novice; and the lay brothers, Brother Henry of Cologne, Brother Gernot of Worms, Brother Conrad of Swabia. And Brother John of Cologne[61] and Brother Henry of Hildesheim[62] followed these later.

41. In the year of our Lord 1225 Brother Jordan sent lay brothers through Thuringia to find out the conditions of the cities. Brother Hermann, a priest, novice, and preacher, followed them and sometimes went on ahead of them. When he came to Eisenach, where he formerly had been chaplain and from where he had joined the brothers of the German house,[63]

---

61. The name in the edition of the *Analecta Franciscana*, (Vol. I, p. 13) is incomplete: Jo....de Colonia. Glassberger (Chronicle, *Analecta Franiscana*, Vol. II, p. 32) has: Johannes de Coridua.

62. In the *Analecta Franciscana* edition Brother Jordan has: Henricus de Hilden (Vol. I, p. 13). Glassberger has: de Hildesia (Vol. II, p. 32, *Analecta Franciscana*).

63. Brother Hermann had been chaplain of the Teutonic Knights in Eisenach before his entry into the Franciscan Order. The passage of the chronicle in the version contained in the *Analecta Franciscana*, Vol. I, reads: Qui veniens in Isenacum, ubi olim cappellanus fuit et unde reddiderat se ad fratres domus theutonicae, cum populo. ... Glassberger, who quotes verbatim much of Brother Jordan's chronicle and uses a more perfect copy has this reading: ... ubi olim cappellanus Dominorum domus Theutonicae existens, Ordini se tradiderat, cum pluries. ... The translators and critics interpret the domini domus Theutonicae as the Teutonic Knights, and this interpretation seems likely. These knights were founded

Continued on page 50

and after he had preached a number of times to the people, at his preaching and because of the good example of his life, in as much as he had left the great convenience he had had in the house of the German brothers and had humbled himself to enter so lowly and austere an Order, the people were not a little moved and they flocked to whatever place he announced he would preach. For which reason, the priests of the city feared that if the brothers favored one of them, the people of the other would be drawn away; consequently, one of them offered the brothers two churches, and the other offered one, so that they might choose at whichever one they wished to stay. But Brother Hermann did not presume to choose without the advice of his brothers; so he asked Brother Jordan to bring with him a prudent companion and to come to Eisenach and to choose with the advice of that companion whatever place it would please him to choose. And coming, he chose with the advice of that other brother the place in which the brothers now live.

42.   The same year the brothers received during Lent a place in Gotha where two brothers lived for twenty-five[64] years, and with great generosity, performed over and above what they could conveniently perform various works of mercy and hos-

---

Continued from page 49

toward the end of the 12th century, about 1190, in Palestine. After they had contributed greatly to the capture of Damietta by the crusaders in 1219, they were given large tracts of land in Prussia and they undertook the task of protecting the Christians of that region from their pagan neighbors. They founded many cities, like Thorn, Culm, Marienwerder, Koenigsberg, and others. (T.N.)

64. Brother Jordan, in the version of the *Analecta Franciscana*, omits the number of years. Glassberger adds the number.

pitality both for our own brothers and for the Friars Preachers and for all other religious.

43. In the same year, at the advice of the lord Henry, priest of St. Bartholomew's, and of Gunther, the assistant, and of the citizens of Erfurt, the brothers moved to the church of the Holy Spirit, which was deserted at that time, but which had been occupied by the women religious of the Order of the Blessed Augustine, and here the brothers remained for six full years. The man who was appointed by the people to be the procurator for the brothers asked Brother Jordan if he wished to have a house built after the fashion of a cloister; but he, since he had never seen a cloister in the Order, answered. "I do not know what a cloister is; just build us a house near the water so that we can go down to it to wash our feet." And this was done.

44. In the same year brothers were sent to Nord-hausen around the feast of the Apostles Peter and Paul.[65] There they were well received by the people and they were established for their convenience in a certain garden in which there was a house conveniently located for them to go to the church frequently. They paid an annual rent of four solidi[66] for this place. And because the brothers sent there were only lay brothers and the custos[67] grew tired of going there as often as was necessary to hear their confessions, after they had been

---

65. June 29.
66. About $12.00.
67. Brother Jordan himself.

there three years, he recalled them for their own peace of mind and placed them in other houses. But in the year of our Lord 1230, when a certain virgin gave the brothers a building site, they returned there.

45.   That same year, at the petition of Count Ernest,[68] four lay brothers were sent to Mühlhausen. He assigned to them a certain new house that was not as yet roofed over and an adjoining small garden, and until they could put a roof on the house and a wall around the garden he put them up in a cellar in the castle. Here these brothers prayed, ate, received visitors, and slept. And because the lay brothers, being content with the cellar, had not been able to roof over the house or to wall in the garden within a year and a half, the count, seeing no progress in them, began to withdraw his help from them. Thus the brothers, having nothing with which to roof the house or to wall the garden, were compelled by necessity to withdraw and they were lodged in other houses. But in the year of our Lord 1231 the brothers returned there, and, by permission of King Henry, were lodged in the hospital. The master of the hospital, however, believing that whatever was given to the brothers would be withdrawn from himself, began to be annoying and captious toward them. The brothers could not put up with this, and when a certain soldier gave

---

68. Ernest III, who is mentioned a number of times in early documents of the villages of Erfurt and Mühlhausen. According to one legend, he went to the Orient around 1228, was made captive by the Saracens, but obtained his deliverance through the intercession of a certain beautiful maiden. According to the legend, he obtained papal permission to marry her even though his first wife was still living. The legend, however, has little intrinsic value.

them a plot of ground they began to build on it, and they have remained there to this day.

46. In the same year[69] the brothers who were living outside the walls came into Erfurt.

47. In the same year, Brother Nicholas of the Rhine,[70] a priest and lawyer, who was called Nicholas the humble because this virtue shone so conspicuously in him, was sent by Brother Albert of Pisa, the minister of Germany, to Brother Jordan, then the custos of Thuringia, for his comfort and assistance. Brother Nicholas died at Bologna with abundant testimony to his sanctity. When Brother Jordan met him between Gotha and Eisenach, they saluted each other reverently and fraternally with a kiss and then sat down together. But as Brother Nicholas, a humble man with the simplicity of a dove, was sitting reverently in silence before Brother Jordan, Brother Peter of Eisenach, the companion of Brother Nicholas and a cheerful and joyous person, knowing the humility of Brother Nicholas, said to him: "Brother Nicholas, do you not recognize our king and our master?" And he, joining his hands· replied humbly: "Willingly I recognize and serve my lord." And Brother Peter added: "He is your custos." Hearing this, he arose and proclaimed his fault with a profound bow that he had greeted him so irreverently. And rising, in all humility he knelt and presented his letters of obedience to Brother Jordan.

---

69. That is, 1225 again, not the 1231 that was just mentioned.
70. Some identify this Nicholas as Nicholas of Montefeltro. He was at one time or another minister provincial of Hungary, Slavonia, and Dalmatia. He died in Bologna.

But Brother Jordan sent him to the house at Erfurt to await his command. After three weeks Brother Jordan sent him letters of obedience appointing him guardian in that place. Receiving them reverently, he said: "What has our father done to me!" But Brother Jordan was so disturbed by the humility of Brother Nicholas that he could hardly put up with him and for six weeks he did not dare to go to Erfurt. Brother Nicholas, however, kept the brothers within discipline by his presence better than others could by their reproofs and commands.

48.   Also that same year, Brother James, custos of Saxony, founded a church of the Friars Minor in the new city of Magdeburg, and this church was consecrated on the feast of the Exaltation of the Cross[71] by the lord Albert, archbishop of that place. When it had been consecrated, the lord archbishop generously left all the altar ornaments to the brothers. But the aforesaid Brother James, when one day within the octave of the Dedication he was saying Mass in the church of the brothers, became so weak at the end of the Mass that he was carried to the guest house which the brothers had at that time in the old city near St. Peter's—at this time the brothers did not yet have any buildings in the new city except the church—and there on the twelfth day before the calends of October,[72] which is the vigil of St. Matthew, he departed to the Lord. But the brothers hardly had a place to bury him and they had no established practice relating to burial;[73] so, after

---

71. September 14.
72. September 20.
73. Burials were often an occasion of conflict between the brothers and the secular clergy

they had consulted together, above all because of the council which was about to be held on the feast of St. Maurice,[74] for which a great number of bishops had already assembled, they decided to approach the bishop of Hildesheim[75] since he had venerated Brother James as a father. The bishop had given orders to his household that whether he was sleeping or doing anything else they should tell him if the brothers wished to speak with him. Now the bishop was already asleep, but he was awakened and told that Brother James had died. When he heard this he was filled with grief and said. "Behold, this is the dream I have had"; and he added: "I will come and bury him." For he had seen in his sleep a certain dead person clothed and bound with white cloths, and it was said to him: "Go and loose him!" The body was brought to the church of the brothers in the new city, which Brother James himself had founded and had caused to be consecrated; and in it he was buried with honor. But in the year 1238 his bones and the bones of Brother Simon, the Englishman, the first lector at Magdeburg and the third minister, were removed when the brothers moved to the old city where they now dwell and buried there.

49. After the death of Brother James of blessed memory, the brothers of Saxony were not a little disturbed and they asked Brother Albert of Pisa, the minister of Germany, to provide them kindly with a custos. But the minister proposed to send them Brother Nicholas, the guardian of Erfurt, for their custos. But, knowing well his humility, he did not presume to

---

74. September 22.
75. Conrad of Speyer.

send him letters of obedience, fearing that he would not accept the office because of his humility; but he preferred to go to him personally in the hope that by talking to him in a familiar way he could move him to accept the office. Accordingly, the minister came to Erfurt, after he had summoned Brother Jordan on this business, and he began to speak with Brother Nicholas about accepting the office of custos of Saxony. But he excused himself humbly, affirming that he was incompetent for all offices because one who does not know how to count or to reckon accounts should be neither lord nor prelate. The minister then caught him up at this word and, as though indignant, said to him: "You do not know how to be a lord—but since when are we lords who hold offices in the Order? Acknowledge your fault, therefore, quickly, in as much as you have called the offices of the Order lordships and prelacies when they can be called no more than burdens and liabilities." When he had humbly acknowledged his fault, the minister imposed upon him as his penance the custody of Saxony; and he, as was always his custom, gave his submission kneeling down. The brothers rejoiced over this obedience and they celebrated it solemnly in the church of the Holy Spirit where they were staying at the time. Brother Nicholas sang the Mass, but he did so in the ferial tone and with great depression of spirit. Thus appointed the third custos of Saxony, Brother Nicholas did not abandon in his office the humility he had before, but he was always the most humble and the first to perform the duties of the kitchen and to wash the feet of the brothers. And if in atonement for a fault he imposed upon a brother the penance of sitting upon the ground or of taking discipline, he performed the same penance with him in the greatest humility. And though he preserved humility and obedience in all things himself, he was still such an avenger and punisher of obstinate disobedience that he would receive back to favor a brother who was obstinately disobedient only with difficulty, even if he were penitent; for he considered disobedience in a brother so great an evil and obedience so great a good, that he showed both by deed and example that the brothers simply had to obey in all things.

50.   In the year of our Lord 1226, on the fourth day of October,[76] the founder of the Order of Friars Minor, Blessed Father Francis, departed to the Lord at St. Mary of the Portiuncula. And though our Blessed Father Francis wished to be buried in that church, the people of the district and the citizens of Assisi, fearing that he might be snatched away violently by the Perugians because of the miracles God had deigned to work through him in life and after death, bore away his body and buried it with honor in the church of St. George near the walls of Assisi where he had first learned his letters and where he later first began to preach. After the death of Blessed Francis, Brother Elias, the vicar of Blessed Francis, addressed a letter of consolation to the brothers throughout the Order who were so dismayed over the death of so great a father. In the letter he announced to each and all that on the part of Blessed Francis he blessed them and absolved them from every fault. Furthermore, he made known to them the stigmata and the other miracles which the Most High God had deigned to perform through Blessed Francis after his death, and he com-

---

76. St. Francis died on Saturday evening about one hour after sunset. According to the reckoning of that time this was already October 4, since the calendar day was reckoned from sunset to sunset.

manded the ministers of the Order to come together for the election of a minister general.

51.   In the year of our Lord 1227, on the second day of the February after the death of Blessed Francis, Brother Albert of Pisa, the minister of Germany, when he was about to leave for the general chapter for the election of the first minister general, called together all the custodes, preachers, and guardians of Germany and held a chapter in Mainz. In this chapter [Brother Nicholas was released from the office of custos of Saxony, and was appointed Vicar, and Brother Leonard the Lombard succeeded him. Things being arranged in this way, Brother Albert with the brothers he had chosen proceeded to the general chapter].[77] In this chapter Brother John Parenti, a Roman citizen and a master of laws, born in the city of Citta di Castello,[78] was elected the first minister general in the Order.

52.   The new minister general, on the advice of the minister of France,[79] released Brother Albert of Pisa from the

---

77. The words in brackets are not in Brother Jordan's chronicle, though obviously they should be to make sense in this paragraph. They are supplied here from Nicholas Glassberger's chronicle, p. 43-44.

78. This seems to be an error. He was born at Carmignano, near Pistoia. He was a doctor of laws on the faculty of the university of Bologna before he received the habit of the Order. He was minister provincial in Spain at the time he was elected minister general. He filled this office until 1232. He was in reality the first minister general after St. Francis since Peter of Catania and Brother Elias acted as vicars of St. Francis.

79. Brother Gregory of Naples.

administration of Germany and put in his place the English-man Brother Simon, custos of Normandy, a scholar, and a great theologian.

53. Brother Simon, therefore, coming to Germany with Brother Julian, who later wrote the offices of Blessed Francis and of Blessed Anthony in a lofty style and beautiful meter, ordered a provincial chapter to be held in Cologne on the feast of the Apostles Simon and Jude.[80]

54. In the year of our Lord 1228 Blessed Francis was canonized.[81] And the same year Brother Simon, minister of Germany, celebrated a provincial chapter at Cologne between Easter and Pentecost.

The same year Brother John Parenti, the minister general, hearing that Germany did not have a lector in theology, released Brother Simon from the office of minister of Germany and appointed him lector, and he appointed Brother John of Pian di Carpine minister of Germany. He called a provincial chapter at Worms, and there he presented the letters concerning the release of Brother Simon and his own appointment.

In the same chapter the canonization of Blessed Francis was announced to the brothers.

---

80. October 28. The chapter, however, was not held at that time, as is evident from the following paragraph. Glassberger adds here: but for some reason the chapter was held the following year. See his chronicle, *Analecta Franciscana,* Vol. II, p. 47.

81. July 16. The office of lector mentioned immediately hereafter is the office of teacher, especially of theology and philosophy.

Brother John of Pian di Carpine, wanting to honor Saxony and give it greater strength, sent Brother Simon as the first lector to Magdeburg and with him some excellent men, the respected and educated Brother Marquard the Long from Aschenburg, Brother Marquard the Short from Mainz, Brother Conrad of Worms and some others.

55. This Brother John, because he was fat, was carried upon an ass, and the people of the time, on account of the newness of the Order and the humility of the rider, and having before their minds the example of Christ riding on an ass rather than on a horse, were moved with greater devotion toward that ass than they now show to the person of the ministers after they had grown accustomed to associating with them. This brother was great for his spreading of the Order. For after he had been made minister, he sent brothers to Bohemia, Hungary, Poland, Dacia, and Norway. He also accepted a house at Metz and planted the Order in Lorraine. He was also a staunch defender of his Order, for he constantly stood up for his Order in person before bishops and princes. He cherished and ruled over all his brothers as a mother her sons and a hen her chicks in peace and charity and in all consolation.

56. In the year of our Lord 1229 Brother John the Englishman was sent as the first visitator to Germany.[82]

---

82. In the Order the minister general has the obligation to visit periodically either in person or by a delegate all the provinces of the Order to make sure that the Order is living up to its ideals.

57. In the year of our Lord 1230 Brother John, minister of Germany, celebrated his last provincial chapter of Germany in Cologne. In this chapter he appointed the English Brother John as his vicar and then proceeded to the general chapter. In this chapter Brother John of Pian di Carpine was released from office and transferred to Spain as minister there, and Brother Simon, the first lector in Germany, was put in his place. But before the letters of obedience came to him, he died on the vigil of the Blessed Vitus[83] and was buried at Magdeburg. In the same general chapter the administration of Germany was divided into two provinces, one for the Rhine and the other for Saxony. For the Rhine Brother Otto, a lawyer from Lombardy, was made minister; and Brother Simon for Saxony, as was said before. In the same general chapter breviaries and antiphonaries according to the usage of the Order were sent to the provinces.[84]

58. After the death of Brother Simon, the first lector and first minister of Saxony, Brother Leonard, the custos of Saxony, and Brother Jordan, the custos of Thuringia, who were the only two custodes of the province of Saxony, went to the chapter of the Rhine in Worms. In this chapter, in as much as there had been but one administration which had been but recently divided, and in as much as Brother Simon had been forestalled by death from entering upon his office as minister, the province was still as it were one, and the brothers were admitted as belonging to the capitular body. There then, at

---

83. The feast today is celebrated on June 15.
84. Cf. Van Dijk, "Some manuscripts of the Earliest Franciscan Liturgy," apud *Franciscan Studies*, new series, Vol. 14, pp. 225-264.

the advice of the minister, the vicar, and the other brothers, Brother Jordan, after entrusting his custody to the custos of Saxony, set out with letters of obedience, from the minister of the Rhine and with one companion to go to the minister general to ask for a minister and a lector. But while the minister general was deliberating who should be sent, Brother Jordan asked for the English Brother John who earlier was visitator of Germany, and he got him. The minister general therefore wrote to the minister of France that he should send the English Brother John to be minister of Saxony and Brother Bartholomew, also an Englishman, to be lector.[85]

59.   But Brother Jordan, returning to Germany, went to Brother Thomas of Celano,[86] who, gave him some relics of Blessed Francis. When Brother Jordan came to Würzburg, he told the brothers of his custody that if they found it necessary to speak with him they should meet him at Eisenach because he was about to go there. Rejoicing, the brothers went to the designated place, and they told the porter not to admit Brother Jordan when he came, but first to come and tell them. When Brother Jordan therefore came to the door and knocked, he was not admitted, but the porter ran to the brothers and informed them that Brother Jordan was standing before the door. They then told him he could not enter by that door,

---

85. He entered the Order in France, studied at Oxford, was a lector at Paris. About 1250 he wrote *De Proprietatibus Rerum,* a veritable encyclopedia of the learning of the day. Cf. Thomas Plassmann, "Bartholomaeus Anglicus," apud *Archivum Franciscanum Historicum,* Vol. XII, 1919, pp. 68-109.
86. Glassberger says the relics were of the hair and garments. Celano was living in Assisi.

but through the church. The brothers then, rejoicing in spirit, entered the choir, carrying in their hands crosses, a censer, palm branches, and lighted candles, and then proceeded in procession, two by two, into the church outside of the choir. And lining up, they opened the doors of the church and admitted Brother Jordan, receiving him with great excitement and joy, and they sang the responsory: "This is he who loves the brothers."[87] But Brother Jordan was astonished at the new way of receiving him and motioned with his hands for them to be silent; but they finished what they had begun with rejoicing. While Brother Jordan marvelled at this in his astonishment, it came into his mind that he had with him the relics of Blessed Francis, which he had forgotten in his astonishment. And rejoicing in spirit, he said at the end of the chant: "Rejoice, brothers, because I know that it is not I whom you praise, but rather our Father Blessed Francis in me; while I kept silence, he, whose relics I have with me, kindled your spirits." And taking the relics from his bosom, he laid them on the altar. And from then on Brother Jordan began to hold in greater reverence and honor Blessed Francis, whom he had seen in life and for this reason something of whose humanity had struck him,[88] since he saw that God, by inflaming the hearts of the brothers with the Holy Spirit, did not wish his

---

87. II Mach. 15, 14.
88. This is a difficult passage, but the meaning seems to be that, since Brother Jordan had known St. Francis in life and had therefore been very conscious of his human frailties, he did not hold him in sufficient reverence and honor; but seeing the hand of God in the reception he received on this occasion when he was bearing the relics of St. Francis, he was deeply moved and as a result held him ever after in great reverence and honor. See Glassberger, *Analecta Franciscana,* Vol. II, p. 54. (T.N.)

relics in his keeping to remain concealed.

60. In the year of our Lord 1231 Brother Jordan, custos of Thuringia, returning to Saxony, sent Brother John of Penna with Brother Adeodatus to Paris for the English Brother John, the minister, and Brother Bartholomew, the lector, to bring them to Saxony with all honors.

61. In the year of our Lord 1232, in the general chapter celebrated at Rome,[89] Brother John Parenti, the minister general, was released from office, and Brother Elias was put in his place. In the same chapter Brother John the Englishman from Reading, the minister of Saxony, was released from office and Brother John of Pian di Carpine was put in his place. Brother Leonard, the custos of Saxony, died on the way back from the chapter in his native city of Cremona, and Brother Berthold of Hoexter was put in his place. But Brother Elias, having been elected minister general, wishing to complete the building he had begun at Assisi in honor of St. Francis, ordered levies upon the whole Order to complete the work. For he had the whole Order in his power, just as Blessed Francis had had it and also Brother John Parenti who had preceded him; whence he arranged many things according to his own will rather than for the good of the Order. For seven years he did not hold a general chapter as prescribed by the Rule and he dispersed hither and thither the brothers who resisted him.

---

89. The *Speculum Vitae* puts this chapter at Assisi. Thomas of Eccleston places it at Rieti. But Pope Gregory IX was residing at Rieti and this is the more likely place.

After taking counsel, therefore, the brothers decided to provide as a community for the Order. Foremost among these in the counsel were Brother Alexander[90] and Brother John of Rupella, masters at the University of Paris at that time.

62.   In the year of our Lord 1237 Brother Elias sent visitators to the various provinces with the intention of furthering his own plans; and because of these irregular visitations the brothers were even more incensed against him than they were before.

63.   In the year of our Lord 1238 the brothers of Saxony appealed to the minister general against these visitators; they sent messengers to him, but they gained nothing at all thereby. They were forced therefore to appeal to the lord Pope. When Brother Jordan came to him, having greeted him, he was commanded to go away; but Brother Jordan did not wish to leave; instead he ran joyfully to the couch of the lord Pope, drew forth his bare foot and, kissing it, exclaimed to his companion: "Behold, we do not have such relics in Saxony." The lord Pope, however, still wished them to leave; but Brother Jordan said: "No, lord, we do not have anything to ask of you now, for we have an abundance of good things and we are happy; for you are the father of our Order, its protector and corrector; we have simply come to see you." And thus at last the lord Pope became cheerful, arose, and seated himself on

---

90. Alexander of Hales already held a chair at the University when he entered the Order. He was received at Paris in 1236. John of Rupella or de la Rochelle was a disciple of Alexander and succeeded to his chair.

the couch and, asking why he had come, added: "I know you have appealed; Brother Elias, however, coming to me, said that you appealed by going over his head, and I replied to him that an appeal made to me absorbs all other appeals." After Brother Jordan had made clear to the Pope the points about which the appeal had been made, the Pope replied that the brothers had done well to appeal.[91] When therefore the various brothers were come together to the curia to pursue the appeal they had made, and after a long discussion had been carried on, in the end the advice of the majority was that nothing should be done except to put their hand to the root, namely, to proceed directly against Elias.

64.   And the brothers sat down together and, after a scrutiny among the brothers who had gathered, they set down in writing whatever they could know and prove from fact or report against Elias. When these things had been read before the Pope, discussions were had concerning the question. The lord Pope quieted the disagreement, saying: "Go and carry on the discussion among yourselves and write down both the objections and the answers to these objections and present them to me, and I will pass judgment." This was done. Then, when the lord Pope had heard and read thoroughly the objections and the answers, he decreed that the brothers there assembled should return to their provinces and that from the various provinces, and especially from those which had moved the question of reformation of the Order, twenty mature and discreet brothers should be sent to converse at Rome four

---

91. It is obvious that Brother Jordan did some embellishing in the account of his visit to the Pope.

weeks before the general chapter and frame regulations for the welfare and reformation of the Order.

65. In the year of our Lord 1239, therefore, in accordance with what was said above, discreet brothers from the various provinces came to Rome and on the advice and according to the will of the lord Pope and subject to the approbation of the general chapter ordained that there should be elections of the ministers, custodes, and guardians, and certain other things which are still observed today. In addition, they ordained that the individual ministers should hold a chapter in their provinces, and the subjects, two chapters.[92]

66. In the same chapter, Brother Elias, after he had been at the head of the Order seven years, was released from office and Brother Albert of Pisa was put in his place and confirmed by the lord Pope.

67. In the same chapter the provinces were defined.[93]

68. In the same chapter Brother John of Pian di Carpine, minister of Saxony, was released from office, and Brother Conrad of Worms was put in his place. But he, since he did not receive an obedience, did not accept the office. And Sister

---

92. This was changed again later.
93. Brother Elias wanted to raise the number of provinces to 72 in honor of the 72 disciples of Christ. The chapter reduced the number to 32: 16 cismontane and 16 ultramontane.

Agnes of Prague,[94] hearing this, sent a message to the Pope and this election of Brother Conrad was recalled.

69.   In the same year after the chapter at Rome the brothers of Saxony held a provincial chapter at Magdeburg on the feast of the nativity of the Blessed Virgin Mary,[95] and elected Brother Marquard the Short as minister. As minister he was a great champion of his Order and of the austere life. He was kind to the good, stern with the evil, and severe to the incorrigible. He incurred a permanent infirmity in carrying on the business of the Order against Elias, but despite this infirmity he was elected minister. Yet, because of this infirmity, since he was not able to give an example of the austerity he demanded of others, he had to be released from office. But before he was released, he held three chapters, at Erfurt, at Hildesheim, and at Altenburg. In this latter he was released from office.[96]

70.   In the year of our Lord 1240, on January 23, Brother Albert, the third minister general, died. He had governed

---

94. She was the sister of King Wenceslaus I of Bohemia and was canonized later.

95. September 8.

96. The last two sentences here are missing in Brother Jordan's chronicle as it occurs in some versions. They are supplied here from Glassberger's chronicle, *Analecta Franciscana*, Vol. II, p. 62.

the Order for eight months and some days. He was succeeded by Haymo the Englishman.[97]

71. In the year of our Lord 1242, Brother Haymo held a chapter in Altenburg on the feast of St. Michael,[98] and in that chapter he released Brother Marquard from office. That chapter confided the appointment of the new provincial to the minister general. He left after he had appointed Brother Jordan vicar and Brother Godfrey minister provincial.

72. In the year of our Lord 1243, Brother Godfrey came to the province. He was a man very temperate in the use of food and drink. He loved the common life very much and he punished singularities. He was kind to the good and severe to the evil. He pursued the way Brother Marquard had started and he ruled the province laudably for three years and some months.

73. In the year of our Lord 1244 Brother Haymo died; and in the same year Brother Crescentius succeeded him.[99]

---

97. Haymo was the first non-Italian to be minister general. He was from Haversham in England. He entered the Order in 1224, attended the University of Paris, was lector at Tours, Bologna, and Padua, was custos of Paris. See the account of his life in Thomas of Eccleston's chronicle, Chapter 6.
98. September 29.
99. Crescentius was a celebrated doctor and jurist and minister provincial of the Marches of Ancona. During his generalate, studies flourished, new buildings were erected, the apostolate was expanded, and many privileges were granted the friars by the Pope.

He called two brothers from each province to the convent at Rome so that all who would come to the curia would find brothers of their own nation with whom they could take counsel. But since the curia remained a long time at Lyons,[100] the brothers who were thus sent were sent back to their provinces. But at that time the brothers were greatly troubled by Frederick who had been deposed from his rule by a decree of the Council of Lyons[101] and in many provinces they were ejected from their houses amid great confusion, many being held prisoner, many killed, in as much as they, in obedience to the commands of the Church, had manfully stood by their mother as good children, something that no other religious but the Friars Minor did.

74.   At that time Siegried, Archbishop of Mainz, caused much annoyance to the brothers.[102]

75.   In the year of our Lord 1247 Brother Godfrey, minister of Saxony, after he had been in office for three years and some months, was released from office in the chapter of Lyons and Brother Conrad, lector at Hildesheim, was appointed vicar. And the same year in the chapter at Halle on the feast of the nativity of the Blessed Virgin Mary he was elected minister of Saxony and confirmed about the feast of Blessed Martin. He ruled the province amid the peace he inherited

---

100. Innocent IV resided at Lyons from November 29, 1244 to April 19, 1251.
101. July 17, 1245.
102. Archbishop Siegfried had put an interdict upon the village of Erfurt. This is probably what Brother Jordan is referring to.

from his predecessors with discipline and firmness, with great maturity and observance of the Rule. And after he had ruled for almost sixteen years, fatigued and worn out by work, he obtained his release by great and constant importunity to the sorrow of many of his brothers.

76. In the year of our Lord 1248, in the chapter at Lyons, Brother Crescentius was released from office after he and Brother Haymo had ruled for seven years. And the same year Brother John of Parma[103] was put in his place.

77. In the year of our Lord 1257, in the chapter celebrated at Rome on the feast of the Purification,[104] Brother John of Parma, the minister general, was released from office; he had governed the Order for ten years. Brother Bonaventure,[105] a lector at Paris, replaced him.

78. In the year of our Lord 1262, Brother Conrad of Brunswick, minister of Saxony, was released from his office in the chapter at Halberstadt and in the same chapter, on

---

103. He was born at Parma in 1208 and entered the Order in 1233. He is venerated as blessed. The chapter, however, was 1247.
104. February 2.
105. Bonaventure (John Fidanza) was born in 1221 at Bagnorea in Tuscany. At the age of 17 (or as some say, 22), he entered the Franciscan Order. He studied at the University of Paris and was admitted to the faculty of Theology in 1257. He served for 18 years as minister general, and in 1273 he was created Cardinal-Bishop of Albano. He is a canonized saint and doctor of the Church.

April 29, Brother Bartholomew, the former minister provincial of Austria, was unanimously elected on the first ballot to the office of minister of Saxony and confirmed by Brother Conrad on the authority of the minister general. And after he was summoned, since he was absent when he was elected, he consented, though reluctantly, to the petition of the brothers and presided at the chapter and brought it to a conclusion to the consolation of the brothers.

LETTERS[1]

I

Brother Jordan, of the Order of Friars Minor, vicar of the province of Poland, with all the other brothers of the convent of Prague, greetings to the very dear faithful of Christ to whom this letter will come.

The sins of men are producing their fruit: for, while they multiply themselves throughout the world, a calamity, foreseen and predicted for a long time, is come and, all of a sudden, has let itself loose upon us. The Friars Preachers, our brothers, and the other faithful have been thrust back by the people of Tartary, a race that comes from the bottom of Tartarus.[2] You

---

1. Three letters have come down to us (see the general introduction to Brother Jordan's chronicle). It may well be that all three can be traced to Brother Jordan of Giano. Two are given here. The third, headed "Brother R. of the Order of Preachers and Brother I. of the Order of Minors," treats pretty much the same subject matter, but it is omitted here.
2. That is, hel!.

know that their ferocity was already foretold by the testimony of Holy Scripture; how many people they have already destroyed we do not know, but we do know that they are also ravaging Russia and it is said that they have seven leaders. Ah, how sad! They are destroying the progress of the Church. They are rushing past with incredible speed even the swiftest rivers and the deepest forests. They have occupied the greater part of the kingdom of Hungary. We are too far away to calculate with certainty what has happened, but we are able to describe exactly the events within our province. Almost all of Poland has been cruelly destroyed by these barbarians who do not care either for the age or the condition or the sex of the people but who put the people to the sword and profane the places consecrated to God. They are already at the frontiers of Germany and Bohemia; they will soon be upon you and upon the other Christians if God does not fight with us. What is more, Christendom is a prey to internal wars, to schisms, and it seems that it is not their intention to concern themselves about their common interests and the peace of all.

Troubled by such dangers, we ask you to pray for us and we exhort all the faithful to do the same. Know that five convents of Friars Preachers and two custodies of the Friars Minor have been completely destroyed. Now, in these northern countries, the custodies had a greater prosperity even than Tuscany and Lombardy. The enemies are let loose; only three custodies survive; one custody, or rather two are almost completely abandoned. In the third, that of Bohemia, the king[3] has gone to meet the enemy with a very large army. But victory is from God alone.

Given at Prague, on the 10 day of April, 1241

_____

3. Wencelaus III.

II

Brother Jordan, vice-minister provincial of the Friars Minor of the kingdoms of Bohemia and Poland, and Brother A, custos of Prague and guardian of that convent, send to the illustrious Prince H[enry], duke of Brabant, assurance of their humble and devout prayers.

The eminent grandeur of your generosity has not disdained to interest itself kindly in the well-being of our Order and it has proved, by actions, your benevolent dispositions. Knowing how much zeal you have for God and for the public good, we approach you to make known to your Serenity how the barbarians, whom we call Tartars, have audaciously broken loose, encouraged by the disagreements and carelessness of princes and prelates. They have ravaged with the sword the whole kingdom of Hungary and the five duchies of Poland. They have driven out the king of Hungary[1] and have slain the grand duke of Poland,[2] together with several thousand inhabitants who were found defenseless. In a short time, they have perpetrated the greatest massacres, not only in these countries but also in the Marches and especially in the kingdom of Bohemia.

They owe their victory more to a ruse than to courage. In reality, when they know that the adversary is armed, often and even always, they simulate flight or retreat, then, a little later, they return, attacking and fighting furiously. They have

1. Bela IV.
2. Henry II of Silesia.

no regard for sex, nor for age, nor for condition; they profane the places consecrated to God; there they encamp with their women, attach their mares to the tombs of the saints, disinter their bodies and expose them to the beasts of the earth and to the birds of the heavens. The fear alone of their name makes the multitude flee. In as much as God is enraged against us, their trickery makes their entry seem miraculous and their number increases every day. They make combatants out of those they conquer; they unite those who are submissive to them, that is to say, the pagans, the heretics and the great multitude of pseudo-Christians. It is feared that all Christendom will suffer total ruin, unless God is appeased; it is feared too that the Christians are not united by love in the bonds of peace, that the wrath of the Lord may not be averted and that the Tartars, accomplices of the devil, may not be extirpated from the land of the living.

In such peril we turn to your Eminence and ask of you boldly that you, the other princes, the prelates, and all faithful Christians take the initiative against these misfortunes that threaten us, by your prayers, by fasts, and also by means of arms. We ask that, armed with spiritual and temporal arms, you make us free from this imminent calamity and make it possible for Christian freedom to breathe again.

They who are called Tartars have already devasted India, both greater and lesser,[3] the kingdom of Persia, seventy-two principalities of Russia, Hungary, Poland. In these countries they have massacred the leaders and countless multitudes of

---

3. The reference undoubtedly is to China, conquered in 1206, and India, conquered in 1222.

the people. A little before Ascension[4] they entered Moravia and they are still there. Their women ride in arms and they spare no one. The one who fights the best is considered by them to be the most desirable, while in our countries the one who knows best how to weave and to sew is sought after as much as the one who is most beautiful.

Farewell.

---

4. This was the ninth of May, 1241. The letter is otherwise undated, but this gives a good indication that it was written just after that date.

THE CHRONICLE

OF

BROTHER THOMAS

OF ECCLESTON

THE COMING

OF THE FRIARS MINOR

TO ENGLAND

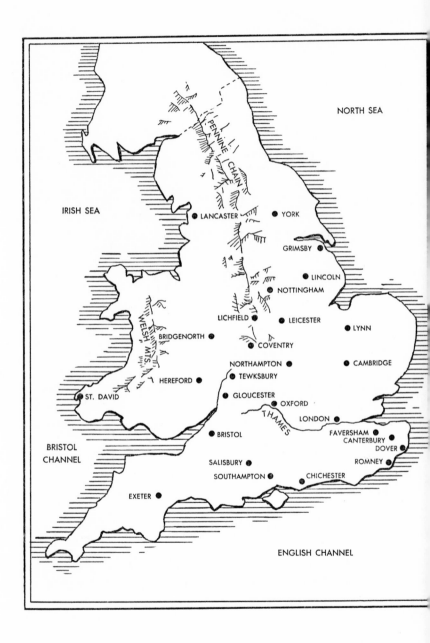

NORTH SEA

IRISH SEA

PENNINE CHAIN

LANCASTER ● ● YORK

GRIMSBY ●

● LINCOLN

● NOTTINGHAM

LICHFIELD ● ● LEICESTER ● LYNN

WELSH MTS.

BRIDGENORTH ● ● COVENTRY

NORTHAMPTON ● ● CAMBRIDGE

HEREFORD ● ● TEWKSBURY

ST. DAVID ● ● GLOUCESTER ● OXFORD

THAMES ● LONDON

● BRISTOL

FAVERSHAM ●
CANTERBURY ●
DOVER ●

BRISTOL
CHANNEL

SALISBURY ● ● ROMNEY

SOUTHAMPTON ● ● CHICHESTER

EXETER ●

ENGLISH CHANNEL

INTRODUCTION

1. THE AUTHOR

Brother Jordan of Giano wrote his chronicle in this style: "Brother Jordan said this or that ..." Brother Salimbene degli Adami, more vain, wrote like this: "I, Brother Salimbene, did this ..." On the other hand, their confrere, Thomas of Eccleston, merely gives his name *Thomas* in the prologue, and he does not use the pronoun *I* more than two or three times in the course of his chronicle. This extreme modesty, however, is quite annoying to the historian for he is thereby obliged to acknowledge that he knows very little about the author of the treatise entitled *The Coming of the Friars Minor to England.*

The chronicler presents himself to us in the prologue in these words: "In the sweetness of our Lord and Savior Jesus

81

Christ, his brother Thomas to his beloved father, Brother Simon of Ashby, the consolation of the Holy Spirit." This is just about all, and the name *Eccleston* by which he is known was added by a later hand, perhaps of the seventeenth century, on the title page of one of the four manuscripts of the chronicle that are known.

One cannot learn very much about Brother Simon of Ashby to whom Brother Thomas dedicated his work. He was probably a superior of some kind in the Order.

The date and the place of birth of Brother Thomas remain unknown, and the circumstances of his entry into the Order are equally a mystery. The best and most recent in time among the editors of Brother Thomas, Andrew George Little, has noted that the chronicler mentions very few of the convents of the north of England and these he knows very badly. Perhaps one must conclude that he is not from the north of England, nor from the east either, since he passes over in silence the founding of particular important convents in that region.

We get one glimpse of Brother Thomas, when, while he himself still wore secular clothing, he enters almost by accident into the scene where several brothers who had entered the Order in Paris are setting out for England.[1] This departure from the University of Paris took place in 1229. On the other hand, the author tells us that he spent twenty-six years in assembling the materials of his chronicle. When did he finish his narrative? He mentions the end of John of Parma's term of office as minister general in 1257, but he does not say anything of his successor, St. Bonaventure. He speaks of the nuncio Mansue-

---

1. Chapter VI.

tus, who was named in 1257 and who was in England in 1258. The last minister provincial he names is Brother Peter of Tewkesbury who was succeeded by John of Stamford in 1258. He tells us quite a bit about Adam Marsh, but he makes no allusion to his death in November 1258. The chronicle therefore was finished in 1257 or at the beginning of 1258. And, since Brother Thomas says he was busy gathering materials for twenty-six years, this would indicate that he began work on it in 1231 or 1232. The entry into the Order of this chronicler then would be placed between 1229 and 1232. Any greater precision in the matter is not possible.

Brother Thomas studied at Oxford and he belonged to the convent of London, for, telling an ancedote about that convent, he says, "I saw the brothers . . ." and "I frequently ate . . ." He does not tell us that he exercised any office in the Order and we do not know if he received the order of priesthood, though it is quite possible that he did. He uses some phrases that resemble those of the Roman curia, so that it is possible that he received a legal training; but these hypotheses are at best only vague.

The character of the author is more difficult to determine than that of Brother Jordan. The one trait that we notice most is that he was a true Englishman. He is deeply persuaded of the superiority of the brothers of the English province. He is very proud of the fact that the minister general Haymo of Faversham was English. The way he uses the phrase "Very sweet Jesus" and the terms he uses when he speaks of the Blessed Eucharist show that he was a deeply pious man. Brother Thomas did not have, unfortunately, a personality so well defined as Brother Jordan of Giano; and he does not have the vanity and aplomb of Brother Salimbene. As a result we know much less about him than we know about his confreres.

2. The Manuscripts and Editions

We know actually four manuscripts of Brother Thomas, though two of them are only fragments.

One manuscript, formerly owned by Sir Charles Isham of Lamport Hall, near Northampton, and called by the different editors and translators of the text *Manuscript L,* is today in the British Museum: Ms. Egerton 3133.

The manuscript of the British Museum, Cotton Nero A. IX, is called *Manuscript C.*

The Phillipps Manuscript 3119 at Thirlestaine House, Cheltenham, is called *Manuscript P.*

Lastly, a manuscript of the cathedral of York (In Latin: Eboracum) , Manuscript XVI.K.4., is called *Manuscript E.*

These manuscripts pose fewer problems of textual reconstruction than the manuscripts of the chronicle of Brother Jordan. All of them are copies. *E* and *P* are complete; *L* and *C* are fragments.

The chronicle of Brother Thomas was edited for the first time in 1858 by J. S. Brewer.[2] He based his edition on manuscripts *E* and *C.* Manuscript *E,* dating from the XIV century, gives a rather complete text of the chronicle, except for a few omissions. The copyist evidently transcribed one word for another at times. Manuscript *C* begins with Chapter IX and runs to the end. It is found with numerous marginal notes in the same handwriting as the handwriting

---

2. Thomas of Eccleston, *Fragmentum Libri Thomae de Eccleston, De Adventu Minorum in Angliam,* Monumenta Franciscana, edited by J. S. Brewer, I, London, Longman, 1858, pp. 1-28.

of the text. This handwriting is of the type characteristic of the latter half of the thirteenth century. The edition put out by Brewer adjusts the uncertainties in the reading.

In 1882, Richard Howlett edited manuscript L^3 which is a very brief fragment in the handwriting characteristic of the end of the thirteenth century; it gives us chapters I to VI. Unfortunately, this manuscript was lost thereafter for some years, but it was found again recently and is now in the British Museum.

In 1885, the Franciscan Fathers of the College of St. Bonaventure, at Quaracchi, re-edited the chronicle,[4] but they based their edition on the editions of Brewer and Howlett without reference to the other manuscripts.

A fragmentary edition was made in 1888 in the German collection *Monumenta Germaniae Historica*.[5] The author, Dr. Liebermann, collated manuscripts *C* and *E*, but the edition is still only a fragment.

In 1883, a Dominican, Fr. Heinrich Denifle,[6] pointed out the existence of manuscript *P*, which the English scholar Andrew George Little later studied. This discovery opened the way to new possibilities. The manuscript is a collection

---

3. Thomas of Eccleston, *Fragmentum Libri Thomae de Eccleston De Adventu Minorum in Angliam*, Monumenta Franciscana, edited by Richard Howlett, II, London, Longman, 1882, pp. 3-28.
4. Thomas of Eccleston, *Liber de Adventu fratrum Minorum in Angliam*, edited by PP. Collegii S. Bonaventurae, *Analecta Franciscana*, I, 1885, pp. 215-256.
5. Thomas of Eccleston, *Ex Thomae de Eccleston Libro de Adventu fratrum Minorum in Angliam*, edited by F. Liebermann, Monumenta Germaniae Historica, Scriptores XXVIII, pp. 560-569.
6. P. Heinrich Denifle, *Die Universitaeten des Mittelalters bis 1400*, I Bd. Die Entstehung der Universitaeten des Mittelalters bis 1400, Berlin, Weidmann, 1885, p. 811.

of different texts which belonged for a long time to Queen's College at Oxford and, very probably, belonged before that to the convent of the Friars Minor in that city. The text of the chronicle of Brother Thomas is a complete copy made in the fourteenth century. A detailed examination of the text establishes the fact that the manuscript is a copy from manuscripts *L* and *C,* which are really fragments of the same manuscript; the copyist incorporated into his text the notes that are on the margin of the two texts and in other interpolations.

Being acquainted with three manuscripts and a copy of a fourth, A. G. Little, who was teaching paleography at the time, published in 1909 an edition far superior to any of the preceding ones, since he utilized manuscripts *C* and *E* and, for the first time, *P*; but he was not able to use manuscript *L*, which was lost after Howlett had made his copy of it.

The rediscovery of manuscript *L*, after it had come to the British Museum, spurred A. G. Little to publish a second edition of the chronicle of Brother Thomas. This redaction was almost finished when he died in 1945. His son-in-law, the Reverend J. R. H. Moorman finished the work.[7]

3. The Style and Historical Value of the Chronicle of Brother Thomas

Although this chronicle is almost twice as long as that of Brother Jordan, it has less value than Brother Jordan's; but it is far from being uninteresting. Its author is not indeed a writer of particular talent, and his narrative is at times

---

7. Thomas of Eccleston, *Fratris Thomae, vulgo dicti de Eccleston Tractatus De Adventu fratrum Minorum in Angliam,* edited by A. G. Little and J. R. H. Moorman, Manchester, University Press, 1951.

confused. The different manuscripts often give a different sequence of the paragraphs, and the plan of the author shows up so unclearly that it is not possible today to assign the fragments to their proper places. As to some of the notations, we do not know if they are notations of the author or of a copyist; but it would be foolhardy to suppress them since they have the appearance of having been made by Brother Thomas. These notations give the narrative the appearance at times of being without form. The chronicle seems to be in an unfinished state; historical facts, anecdotes, and reflections follow one another without any special method.[8] We may add that the author does not always have a feeling for what is valuable and for what is just a pleasantry, and that aside of the narratives of historical interest he brings in narratives of apparitions, visions, and miracles, more or less authentic, and mixes in anecdotes naively exaggerated for the purpose of glorifying the province of England.

The style is frequently quite ordinary, in spite of some passages that are quite bombastic. The Latin is not as imperfect as that of Brother Jordan of Giano, but one cannot consider it a model for imitation.

But if the style of Brother Thomas is rather ordinary, if he mixed into his chronicle narratives of visions, apparitions, and miracles that are at times difficult to accept, he does not fail to give us an excellent document that can almost always be verified by means of other contemporaneous sources, at least where there is question of events in England. All that he writes about the founding of convents in England, about the construction of buildings, the donations of benefactors, can

---

8. This is particularly noticeable in chapter XV which is a jumble of anecdotes.

be verified through numerous public and private documents. Brother Thomas is almost always well informed, and one can seldom catch him in error.

He is perhaps less sure of himself when he speaks about events outside of the province of England. He was not a direct witness to these events, or at least we have no evidence to show that he ever went outside of his province. He may, therefore, be confused about some of the events he narrates. One finds him in error once or twice at least. Thus he tells us that Brother Crescentius of Jesi had been minister of Verona at the time when he was actually minister of the Marches of Ancona; but this could be the mistake of the copyist.[9] The narrative he gives of the deposition of Brother Elias, the minister general, is confused;[10] he mixes up the events of 1230, 1232, and 1239.

The fact that Brother Thomas gets confused occasionally should not lead us to neglect his testimony. One cannot write a history of the Order of Friars Minor in England from the year 1224 to the year 1258 without using his chronicle. We do have other sources, to be sure, but these are all very fragmentary. When a document tells us that on a certain date a benefactor made a donation in favor of a convent, we are forced to conclude that Brother Thomas was very well informed indeed in telling us that on that date the convent had been founded by such and such brothers. His testimony is reliable and it is found to be quite accurate when compared with other available documents.

His testimony is equally important for the history of the Order outside of England. However, he tells us very little

---

9. Chapter XIII.
10. Chapter XIII.

about St. Francis, just two or three anecdotes and the moving testimony of one brother concerning the stigmata: "These sinful eyes beheld them, and these sinful hands touched them."[11] He shows us above all the exalted place the glorious figure of their founder held in the hearts of the Friars Minor of England.

If his narrative of the events that brought about the deposition of Brother Elias, the minister general, is confused and demands verification, it is still certain that Brother Thomas, who probably relied on a written document, gives us facts that are not known to us from the *Speculum Vitae* and the *Chronica XXIV Generalium*.

The narrative of Brother Thomas permits us also to complete and correct certain points in the biography of the minister general Haymo of Faversham,[12] and what he tells us of the general chapters of Metz and Genoa has led us to revise the chronology of the general chapters.

The most interesting passages are perhaps the ones where Brother Thomas shows us with great intimacy, at times with naivete, the brothers suffering from hunger and cold; and he moves us when he tells us in what strict poverty the Friars Minor of England lived that they might remain faithful to the ideal of their founder.

English translations of the chronicle of Brother Thomas exist, but none was made after the publication of the edition based on the four manuscripts. Only one German translation has been made since the appearance of the second edition of A. G. Little. Similarly, the only French edition available to the reading public is that of Marie-Thérèse Laureilhe which

---

11. Chapter XIII.
12. Chapters VI and XIII.

too was made after Little's second edition of the chronicle.[13] The present English translation makes use of this French version along with other available sources.[14]

---

13. Translator's addition.
14. See the bibliography and the Translator's Foreword.

THE COMING
TO ENGLAND
OF THE FRIARS MINOR

Prologue

Here begins the Treatise concerning the Coming of the
Friars Minor to England and their Spread and their Increase
in that Country.

Here begins the Prologue.

*In the sweetness of our Lord and Savior Jesus Christ,
his brother Thomas to his beloved father, Brother Simon of
Ashby, the consolation of the Holy Spirit.*

Every just man must judge his own life according to the
examples of the better ones, because generally examples prod
more than do the words of reason. In order that you may have
something for your own with which you may comfort your
most dear sons; that they too who have left behind so many
and such great things and even their own selves in entering

into our state and our Order, when they read or hear the wonders of the other Orders, may have something from which they may be strengthened in their own vocation, and that they may give unceasing thanks to Him who called them, the sweet Jesus: behold, beloved father in the sweet Jesus, I send you the accounts which it has been my pleasure to gather together from my most dear fathers and confreres during twenty-six years. To the honor of Him, therefore, in whom God the Father was well pleased, Jesus Christ, the most sweet God and our Lord, I send you this little book.

1. The First Coming of the Friars Minor to England

In the year of our Lord 1224, at the time of the lord Pope Honorius, that is, in the same year in which the Rule of Blessed Francis was confirmed by him,[1] in the eighth year of the lord King Henry, the son of John,[2] on the Tuesday after the feast of the Nativity of the Blessed Virgin,[3] which that year fell on a Sunday,[4] the Friars Minor first touched shore in England at Dover, namely, four clerics and five lay brothers. The clerics were these: the first was Brother Agnellus of Pisa,[5] a deacon in orders, about thirty years of age, who was destined by Blessed Francis in the recent general chapter to be minister

---

1. Honorius III, 1216-1227, confirmed the Rule on November 29, 1223. The year was sometimes reckoned from March 25; sometimes from the beginning of Advent.
2. Henry III, 1216-1272.
3. September 10, 1224. The chronicle of Lanercost, in part at least the work of a Friar Minor, says that the brothers disembarked "after the feast of the Nativity of the Blessed Virgin," though it also gives the date as the feast of St. Bartholomew, August 24. Chronicon de Lanercost, 1201-1346, ed. by Joseph Stevenson, Edinburgh, 1839.
4. Brother Thomas' dating is so precise that it is hard not to accept it as correct, though there is still some uncertainty as to the year 1224 for their first coming to England.
5. Minister general from 1239 to 1240.

provincial in England;[6] he had indeed been custos of Paris and had conducted himself with such prudence that he deservedly enjoyed a reputation for great sanctity both among the brothers and among the seculars.

The second was Brother Richard of Ingworth, an Englishman by nationality, a priest and preacher and a man of more advanced age, who was the first in the Order to preach to the people on this side of the mountains; and in the course of time, under Brother John Parenti[7] of blessed memory, he was sent to Ireland as minister provincial; for he had been the vicar of Brother Agnellus in England, while the latter went to the general chapter in which the remains of St. Francis were translated,[8] and he had given outstanding examples of great sanctity. When therefore he had completed a term of ministry that was faithful and acceptable to God, he was released from office among the brothers in the general chapter[9] by Brother Albert[10] of blessed memory, and, filled with zeal for the faith, he went to Syria and there died peacefully.

The third was Brother Richard of Devon, likewise an Englishman by nationality, an acolyte in orders, a youth in age, who left behind for us numerous examples of forebearance and obedience. For, after he had traversed various provinces out of obedience, he dwelt for eleven years continuously at Romney,[11] where however he was frequently worn down by the quartan fevers.

---

6. The general chapter of 1223.
7. Minister general from 1227 to 1232, the first friar to be elected to this office.
8. General chapter of 1230.
9. General chapter of 1239.
10. Minister general from 1239-1240.
11. This Franciscan house in Kent seems not to have lasted long.

The fourth was William of Ashby, who was still a novice with the caperon[12] of probation; he also was an Englishman, young in age as well as in the Order. He held various offices[13] over a long period of time and, assisted by the spirit of Jesus Christ, showed us examples of humility and poverty, charity and meekness, obedience and patience and every perfection. When, however, Brother Gregory,[14] the minister of France, asked him if he wished to go to England, he replied that he did not know if he wished to go. And when the minister wondered at this answer, Brother William finally said that he did know what he wished because his will was not his own but the minister's; wherefore, whatever the latter willed that was what he himself wished to will. Concerning him Brother William of Nottingham testified that he was a most obedient man; for when he gave him the option of choosing the place where he would live, he said that that place suited him best to which it pleased him to assign him.

And because he was especially endowed with charms and was therefore most pleasingly gentle, he aroused the affection of many seculars for the Order. Moreover, he brought many suitable persons of various dignities, ages, and ranks to the way of salvation; and in many ways he showed convincingly that the sweet Jesus knew how to

---

12. The caperon was part of the clothing of the novices to distinguish them from the professed brothers. Today the novices wear a bit of cloth attached to their capuch or cowl, which is also called the caperon.
13. He was guardian at Oxford even while yet a novice; and, among other offices, he held also that of custos of Oxford and visitator of Ireland.
14. Of Naples, provincial of France from 1223-1233.

accomplish striking things and how to conquer giants with locusts.[15]

Once when he was tempted to sins of the flesh, he mutilated himself in his zeal for chastity; having done this, he made a request to the pope, and, after being severely rebuked by him, he merited a dispensation to celebrate the divine mysteries. This same William died at London many years later.[16]

The lay brothers were these: the first Brother Henry of Treviso, a Lombard by nationality, who by reason of his holiness and outstanding discretion was later made guardian of London,[17] and who, after finishing the course of his work in England and after the number of brothers had already been increased, returned to his fatherland.

The second was Brother Lawrence of Beauvais, who at first worked with his hands, according to the decree of the Rule,[18] and later, having returned to the Blessed Francis, he merited to see him often and to be consoled by conversation with him; finally the holy father most generously gave him his tunic[19] and with his most sweet blessing sent him back to England happy. After many labors, through the merits of that same father, as I think, he reached the haven of peace in London, where now, laid low with desperate illness, he awaits the end of so long a weariness.

---

15. See Numbers 13, 33.
16. We follow the practice of A. G. Little and inset these two paragraphs and others in the course of the text. He considers them marginalia contemporary with the text but not incorporated into it.
17. First guardian there, 1224-1231.
18. Regula Bullata, Chapter V.
19. Cf. Thomas of Celano, *Vita II*, Pars II, no. 181 and the footnote page 234, apud *Analecta Franciscana*, Vol. X.

The third was Brother William of Florence, who after the brothers had been received went quickly back to France.

The fourth was Brother Melioratus.

The fifth was Brother James, from the other side of the mountains, who was still a novice with the caperon of probation.

These nine were charitably transported to England and courteously provided for by the monks of Fecamp. When they had come to Canterbury, they remained for two days at the priory of the Holy Trinity.[20] Immediately four of them went to London, namely, Brother Richard of Ingworth, Brother Richard of Devon, Brother Henry and Brother Melioratus. The other five, however, went to the priests' hospital[21] where they remained until they could provide a place for themselves. Very shortly thereafter a small room was given to them within a school house[22] where they remained almost continuously shut in day after day. But when the students had returned home in the evening, they went into the schoolhouse where they sat and built a fire for themselves; and they sat next to it and sometimes, when they had to have their collation,[23] they put on the fire a little pot containing the dregs of beer, and they dipped a cup into the pot and each drank in turn and

---

20. The Benedictine abbey mentioned had two priories in England. The priory of the Holy Trinity at Canterbury is Christ Church Cathedral.

21. This was the Hospital of Poor Priests, St. Mary's.

22. The ancient grammar school of Canterbury. The Chronicle of Lanercost says the brothers remained indoors because they had been ill-treated at Dover.

23. In the evening on fast days it was the custom to have a reading or conference. Is the Latin phrase *cum collationem bibere deberent* a technical phrase of the time, or a humorous phrase, to cover the custom of having a drink along with it?

spoke some word of edification. And, as one testified who was their companion in this sincere simplicity and holy poverty and who was permitted to share therein, their drink was sometimes so thick that when the cups had to be heated they poured in water and thus drank with joy. In a similiar way it frequently happened at Salisbury,[24] where the brothers drank these dregs with so much happiness and joy around the fire in the kitchen at the hour of collation, that he would consider himself fortunate who could snatch away the dregs from another in a friendly way.

At Shrewsbury[25] when the brothers first came to that place, old Brother Martin, who founded that place, boasted how he had done the same thing.

In those days the brothers avoided contracting debts so strictly that hardly even in extreme necessities were they permitted to contract a debt. Whence it happened that Brother Agnellus, along with Brother Solomon, the guardian, wished to audit the account of the brothers of London, how much, namely, they had spent within the period of one year; when he had heard how sumptuously they had carried on, though the outward appearance of the brothers was frugal enough, he threw away all the tallies and counters and, striking himself in the face, he exclaimed, "Woe is me!"[26] and never afterwards would he again audit an account. It happened also that two brothers came to a certain place of the brothers much upset; since there was no beer in the house, the guardian, after taking counsel with the older brothers, caused a flagon of beer to be accepted on credit, in such a way, however, that the

---

24. Founded probably about 1230.
25. This house was not founded until about 1246.
26. *Ay me captivum*, which can hardly be rendered literally.

brothers of the convent, who were with the guests, did not drink from it, but only pretended to drink out of charity.

Incident.[27] Up to the time of the formation of the Order[28] the brothers were accustomed to have a collation every day, and, those who wished, to drink in common; also to hold a chapter every day. Neither were they restricted in receiving various dishes or wine; but they did not accept food[29] that was offered except three days a week in many places. In the same convent in London, at the time of Brother William, the minister, of pious memory, and of Brother Hugh, the guardian, I saw the brothers drink beer that was so sour that some preferred to drink water, and I saw them eat bread that is commonly called *torta*. In addition, in the absence of bread, I have long eaten other things[30] in the presence of that same minister and of the guests in the guest house.

---

27. Some manuscripts omit the word *incident*, Latin *incidens*. These were apparently marginalia, but contemporary with the text. We follow A. G. Little's method of inserting these incidents.
28. Probably is meant the reformation after Elias was deposed.
29. The Latin is *pitancia* which seems to mean the portions of fish or meat allotted to the individual monks or friars. *Food* seems to be the easiest way to translate it.
30. The Latin text has *alia*. Some have proposed *alicam* instead, that is, spelt.

2. The First Dispersion of the Brothers

When the four brothers named above had come to London, they turned aside to the Friars Preachers[1] and were received kindly by them; and they remained with them for fifteen days, eating and drinking what was placed before them as would those belonging to the community. Afterwards they rented a house for themselves in Cornhill and they built cells in it, filling up the chinks in the cells with grass. They continued to live there in simplicity without a chapel of their own until the following summer, because as yet they did not have the privilege of erecting altars and of celebrating the divine mysteries in their places.[2]

Immediately before the feast of All Saints[3] and even before Brother Agnellus had come to London, Brother Richard of Ingworth and Brother Richard of Devon went to Oxford, and there too they were received by the Friars Preachers[4] in a most hospitable manner; they ate in their refectory and

---

1. The Friars Preachers had come to London in 1221.
2. Pope Honorius III granted the Friars Minor the privilege of celebrating Mass in their chapels on a portable altar by the decree *Quia populares tumultus* of December 3, 1224. Innocent IV by the bull *Cum tanquam veri* made their chapels conventual churches and they were allowed to have fixed altars, 1249.
3. November 1.
4. The Friars Preachers had come to Oxford August 15, 1221.

slept in their dormitory like members of the convent for eight days. Afterwards they rented a house for themselves in the parish of St. Ebbe[5] and they remained there without a chapel until the following summer. There the sweet Jesus planted the grain of mustard seed which later grew into the greatest of all trees.[6]

From that place Brother Richard of Ingworth and Brother Richard of Devon went to Northampton and were received there at the hospital.[7] Later they rented a house for themselves in the parish of St. Giles, where the first guardian was Brother Peter the Spaniard who wore an iron cilice next to his flesh and showed forth many other examples of perfection.

The first guardian at Oxford was Brother William of Ashby, who was still a novice; the habit of profession, however, was given to him.

The first guardian at Cambridge[8] was Brother Thomas of Spain.

The first guardian at Lincoln[9] was Brother Henry Misericorde, a lay brother; [under him there was in the convent Brother John of Yarmouth, a man of great sanctity, who died later at Nottingham and lies buried among the canons of Shelford.[10]][11]

---

5. A. G. Little says this house had belonged to a Richard le Marcer. See his *Grey Friars in Oxford.*
6. Cf. Matthew 13,32.
7. Probably that of St. John which was for both the poor and the sick, though there was also one for lepers.
8. The first house at Cambridge was probably established before 1230.
9. The Friars Minor came to Lincoln by 1231 at least.
10. These were Augustinian canons. The Friars Minor came to Nottingham by 1230.
11. The section in brackets is added in the Phillipps manuscript in the margin, but is in a contemporary hand. Sic, A. G. Little.

Incident. Sir John Travers[12] first received the brothers at Cornhill and rented them a house; and a certain lay brother from Lombardy, Henry by name, was made guardian; he then first learned letters at night in the church of St. Peter at Cornhill, and later was made vicar of England, during the time when Brother Agnellus was gone to the general chapter. In this office of vicar he had, however, Brother Richard of Ingworth as companion. Toward the end, however, not being able to bear such good fortune, but being rather demoralized by the honors and becoming a stranger to himself, he apostatized miserably from the Order.[13]

Incident. Worthy of memory is the fact that in the second year of the administration of Brother Peter, the fifth minister of England, that is, in the thirty-second year[14] from the coming of the brothers to England, there were one thousand two hundred and forty-two brothers living in England in forty-nine places.[15]

_____

12. He was sheriff of London from 1223-1225.

13. In the Phillipps manuscript this incident is inserted in the middle of the first section of this chapter.

14. Probably 1256. Peter of Tewkesbury became provincial in 1254, succeeding William of Nottingham. Manuscripts L and P have *quinto anno* (5th); this is probably a scribe's error. A. G. Little cites contemporary evidence that tends to back up the figures given here. See the 1951 edition of the *De Adventu,* footnote, p. 11.

15. This incident is variously located by the manuscripts. L has it in the margin; E as given here. P puts it at the end of the next chapter. A. G. Little suggests that it would fit more naturally at the end of chapter four. P. 11 of his 1951 edition.

3. The Reception of Novices

Therefore, when the brothers who had first come to England had split up and had gone to different places, certain men whom the spirit of Jesus led to it came and asked to be admitted to the Order.

Of these the first who was received was a young man of good disposition and elegant appearance, the very renowned Brother Solomon; he was wont to tell me that while he was still a novice he was made procurator and came to the house of his sister to beg alms. But she, when she brought him bread, turned her face away, saying: "May the hour be cursed in which I ever saw you." And he accepted the bread with gladness and departed. So strictly did he adhere to the established form of poverty that he at times carried in his caperon some meal or salt or small figs for some sick brother and under his arm some wood to build a fire; he very diligently took care that he would not accept or retain anything above the limits of the most pressing necessity. Whence it happened once that he suffered so intensely from the cold that he thought he would surely die. But since the brothers did not have anything wherewith they could warm him, holy charity showed them a kindly remedy. All the brothers gathered closely around him and warmed him by huddling up against him as pigs are wont to warm each other.

When the time came for him to be promoted to the order of acolyte, he was sent to the venerable father of blessed memory, the archbishop Stephen,[1] and was presented to him by a certain senior brother; the archbishop received him most graciously and promoted him to the desired order under this form: "Let Brother Solomon of the Order of the Apostles come forward."[2] I make mention of this so that it might be known with what great reverence the early simplicity of the brothers was regarded amongst the wise. But after they had eaten at the table of the archbishop, they returned to Canterbury barefooted in the snow, which was very deep and frightening to those who saw it. Afterwards Brother Solomon's foot became inflamed, and he suffered from this for two years at London, so much so that he could hardly move except he were carried. In this infirmity he merited to be visited by Brother Jordan, of holy memory,[3] the master of the whole Order of Preachers, who said to him: "Brother, be not ashamed if the Lord Jesus Christ draws you to Himself by the foot." Therefore, after he had lain so long in his cell, where he did not hear the solemnities of the Holy Masses—for the brothers did not celebrate in their own places, but went to the parochial church to hear the divine services and to celebrate Mass—his illness became so desperate that in the opinion of the physician his foot had to be amputated. When the axe was brought and the foot had been uncovered, a kind of matter flowed from it and gave promise of some hope; for that reason the painful judgment was put off for that time.

1 Stephen Langton, who died July 9, 1228.
2. According to Wadding this formula was also used at the ordination of Brother Agnellus of Pisa: ad annum 1220, *Annales Minorum*.
3. Jordan of Saxony, master general of the Friars Preachers from 1222 to 1236. He was in England probably in 1230.

Meanwhile, he conceived a certain hope that if he were taken to St. Eloy[4] he would surely recover his foot and his health. Accordingly, when Brother Agnellus came, he commanded that he should be taken without delay and in whatever manner it could be most conveniently done to St. Eloy across the sea. This was done. Neither did his faith deceive him. But indeed he afterwards recovered to such an extent that he walked without a cane and celebrated Mass and functioned as guardian of London and general confessor of the whole city.

Nevertheless, because he had begged of the sweet Jesus that He would cleanse him of his sins in this life, He sent him an infirmity that bent his spinal column so that he became hunchbacked and bent; He sent him a feverish dropsy and frequent bleeding from hemorrhoids that lasted until his death.

In the end, morever, on the day before he went to Him, the sweet Jesus sent him such great sorrow of heart, the cause of which sorrow he did not know, that all the preceding sufferings he considered as nothing in comparison with this one. Therefore, when he had called three brothers who were his close friends, he told them of his agony and asked earnestly that they would pray unceasingly for his condition. While these brothers, therefore, were persevering together in prayer, the most sweet Jesus Christ appeared to him together with the Blessed Apostle Peter, standing before his bed and looking upon him; he, however, as soon as he recognized the Savior, cried out: "Have mercy on me, Lord, have mercy on me." And the Lord Jesus answered him: "Because you always asked me to afflict and purify you to the fullest extent in this

---

4. A shrine at Noyon in Flanders. St. Eloy or St. Eligius.

life, I sent you the present suffering, and above all because you left your first love and did not perform, as was fitting your vocation, worthy fruits of penance, and because you spared the very rich in imposing penance upom them." And Blessed Peter added: "Besides, know that you sinned gravely in judging Brother John of Chichester who died recently. And now ask God to grant you an end such as he had." And crying out, Brother Solomon said. "Have mercy on me, most sweet Lord; have mercy on me, sweet Jesus." Who smiling, looked upon him with so serene a countenance that all the suffering that had been there before disappeared, and he, filled with spiritual joy, conceived a most certain hope of salvation; and immediately he told what he had seen to the brothers he had called; for which reason they were not a little consoled.

> *Incident.* It is worth remembering that when the brothers were in their place at Cornhill,[5] the devil came visibly and said to Brother Gilbert of Wyke while he was sitting alone: "Do you believe you can escape me? Behold, you will have this yet"; and he threw over him a handful of lice and then disappeared.[6]

The second brother who was received by Brother Agnellus was Brother William of London, who was at one time dumb, but at Barking, through the merits of St. Ethelburga, as he told me, he recovered his speech. He also, when he was in the household of the Lord Justiciar of England, Sir Hubert de Burgh, though he lived like a lay brother and a scholar,

---

5. The Friars left Cornhill in 1225.
6. This incident seems to have been added by a later hand. According to A. G. Little it does not appear in the Phillipps manuscript. See his latest edition of the *De Adventu*, p. 14.

as it was thought, and was famous in the art of carving,[7] was clothed in the habit of the Order at London before the brothers had land or a chapel there.[8]

The third was a noble and delicate young man of excellent disposition, who was born in the city of London itself, Brother Joyce of Cornhill, a cleric. After many labors which he bore there, he went to Spain to live and he died there happily.[9]

The fourth was Brother John, a cleric, a young man about eighteen years of age and of good dispositions and

---

7. There is no easy way out in translating this phrase here. The Latin reads: licet laicus et latinus, ut putabatur, existeret et in arte scissoria famosus ... All the manuscripts read *latinus*. In his edition J. S. Brewer substitutes *latius;* and the editors of the *Analecta Franciscana* substitute *lascivus,* but hesitantly. Accordingly, the English translations vary. Fr. Cuthbert follows the *Analecta* and renders it: "by repute a man of loose life." Others give: "a layman and a scholar," or "a scholarly layman." The word *laicus* is used often in these chronicles and always in the meaning of lay brother. It would hardly be used here to indicate that William was a layman before entering the Order since that is self-evident from what else is said. Perhaps the best way is to say that "he lived like a lay brother," indicating a way of life rather that a status. *Latinus* could hardly mean *lascivus* in that case; hence, it might more properly be given as "and a scholar." The phrase *in arte scissoria* also gives trouble. Fr. Cuthbert renders it: "he was moreover a renowned tailor." There was a William the Tailor, a benefactor of the Friars; but he was certainly not a Franciscan between 1226 and 1236 (see A.G. Little's *De Adventu*, p. 14). Edward Hutton renders it: "very famous for his skill in carving at table." The term does mean carving, but it does not necessarily mean carving at table; it may mean wood carving too. Hence we have rendered the whole section: "though he lived like a lay brother and a scholar, as it was thought, and was famous in the art of carving." We do not suggest, however, that this is a definitive interpretation. (T.N.)

8. This must have been before 1225.

9. Manuscript P adds: he was a very old man.

excellent manners, who, completing quickly the course of his life, went to the Lord Jesus Christ. He persuaded Sir Philip, a priest who was suffering unbearably from his teeth, to send bread and beer to the Friars Minor and promised that the Lord Jesus would cure him.[10] As a result, both of them shortly thereafter offered themselves and entered the Order of Friars Minor.

The fifth was Brother Philip, born at London and a priest in orders, who, having been made guardian of Bridgenorth later,[11] and having obtained the office of preaching, gained many souls. Toward the end, he was sent to Ireland and there he passed peacefully to the Lord.

After these there entered the Order certain masters[12] who added greatly to the fame of the brothers, namely, Brother Walter de Burgh, concerning whom one brother had an extraordinary vision, this, namely, that the Lord Jesus, descending from heaven, gave him a scroll on which was written: "The time of your harvest is not here but elsewhere." To him the Lord revealed the deception[13] of a certain religious woman who led astray a certain discreet brother by her imagined visions, to the extent that he wrote them down. But Brother Agnellus, not believing her, enjoined upon the convent to pray that God would reveal to him a certain matter about which he was concerned. And behold, that night it seemed to Brother Walter that he saw a certain doe ascend quickly to the top of a certain high mountain and that two black dogs followed her and turned her back into the valley and there

10. Manuscript E adds: and so it happened.
11. In Shropshire.
12. Of the university.
13. A word is missing in the Latin text. A. G. Little supplies *dolum.*

strangled here; but when Brother Walter ran to the spot where he thought he would find her, he found only a sack full of blood. When therefore he told Brother Agnellus this vision, he saw immediately that she had been led astray by her hypocrisy, and he sent two discreet brothers to her, who reconciled her to the truth after she had finally confessed that she had made up what she had said.

Another master entered too, namely, Brother Richard, a Norman, who, when he was asked for a word of edification by the aforementioned Brother Walter, replied after long deliberation: "Let him who wishes to be in peace keep silent."[14]

Also at this time there entered the master Vincent of Coventry, who not long thereafter, through his own diligence and with the help of the grace of Jesus Christ, prevailed upon his brother, master Henry, to enter the Order. He entered on the day of the conversion of St. Paul,[15] along with the master Adam of Oxford[16] and Sir William of York with the degree of bachelor. This master Adam, famous over the whole world, vowed that whatever should be asked of him for love of the Blessed Mary he would do; and this he told to a certain cloistered nun he knew. But she revealed his secret to her friends, namely, a certain monk of Reading and another of the Cistercian Order and a certain Friar Preacher, telling them that they could gain a worthy man in this way, for she did not want him to become a Friar Minor. But, though one would have him in his company, the Blessed Virgin did not permit that he

---

14. "Ki vout estre en pes tenge sey en pes." See A. G. Little's edition of the *De Adventu*, p. 16.
15. January 25. The year is not given.
16. Manuscript E has Oxonia; the others Exonia. Adam may be the Adam Rufus who was a friend of Bishop Grosseteste.

should ask for love of her, but he would put if off to another time. In a dream, it seemed to him that one night he had to cross a certain bridge where there were men setting nets in the water to catch him; he, however, escaped and came to a most restful place, but only with great difficulty. Therefore, when by the will of God he had escaped these others, he came by chance to see some Friars Minor; and when Brother William of Coleville the elder,[17] a man of extraordinary holiness, spoke to him, he said among other things: "My most dear master, for the love of the mother of God enter our Order and enhance our simplicity." Immediately, as though he had heard this word from the mouth of the mother of God, he agreed, and, as it is said, he entered the Order to the very great edification of the clergy.

He was at that time the companion of the master Adam Marsh[18] and one of his followers; not long thereafter he wisely induced him, with the help of God's grace, to enter the Order. Brother Adam Marsh saw one night in a dream that they came together to a certain castle, and over the door was painted a crucifix of the Lord, and whoever wished to enter had to kiss the crucifix. First Brother Adam of Oxford entered, after kissing the crucifix; and the other Brother Adam after kissing the crucifix, followed immediately after him. But the former found the stairs and ascended so quickly that

---

17. Brother William came to England with Haymo of Faversham not long after the first brothers arrived.

18. Adam Marsh was a nephew of Richard Marsh, the bishop of Durham. He was a priest when he entered the Order, perhaps as early as 1226 or as late as 1232. He was a close friend of Bishop Grosseteste, the early teacher of the Franciscans in England. He died in 1257 or 1258 and was buried beside Bishop Grosseteste in the cathedral of Lincoln.

he was swiftly snatched from the sight of the brother who was following. The latter therefore cried out: "Go more slowly, go more slowly." But the other was never found again. And indeed, this vision could be understood by the brothers who were in England at that time: for Brother Adam of Oxford, after his entry into the Order, went to Pope Gregory IX, by whom, in accordance with what he wished, he was sent to preach to the Saracens; but at Barletta,[19] after predicting his death to his companion, he died, and afterwards, as it is said, became well known for his miracles. Brother Adam Marsh, however, entered the Order at Worcester, led on by the fervor of his love for poverty.

After these Brother John of Reading, abbot of Osney, entered the Order.[20] He left us examples of every perfection. After him came the master Richard Rufus, renowned both at Oxford and at Paris.

Some knights also entered the Order, namely, Sir Richard Gubiun,[21] Sir Giles de Merc, Sir Thomas the Spaniard, Sir Henry of Walpole; concerning their entry into the Order the lord king said: "If you had wished to be discreet in receiving brothers, if you had not procured privileges to oppress men, and above all if you had not been importunate in begging, you might have ruled over the princes."

---

19. North of Bari in Italy.
20. Entered the Order in 1235 at Northampton.
21. Gubiun or Gobion.

4. The Acquisition of Places

Thereafter, as the number of the brothers grew and their holiness became known, the devotion of the faithful toward them also grew; wherefore they took care to provide suitable places for them.

At Canterbury, Sir Alexander, the master of the Priests' Hospital, gave them a plot of ground and built a chapel that was sufficiently becoming for the time; and because the brothers wished to appropriate nothing at all to themselves, it was made the property of the corporation of the city and lent to the brothers at the pleasure of the citizens.[1] In a very special way their welfare was promoted by the lord Simon Langton, archdeacon of Canterbury,[2] and Sir Henry Sandwich, and the noble countess, the recluse of Hackington,[3] who cherished them in all things as a mother does her children, by wisely gaining for them the favor of the princes and prelates whose respect she had won to an extraordinary degree.

At London, Sir John Iwyn befriended the brothers; he

---

1. Innocent IV made the houses of the friars the property of the Holy See by his Bull *Ordinem vestrum* of November 14, 1245.
2. Brother of Stephen Langton, archbishop of Canterbury 1227-1248.
3. Loretta, countess of Leicester. After her husband, Robert of Beaumont, died, she became a recluse.

assigned ownership of a plot of ground for the brothers to the corporation of citizens, but very devotedly assigned the usufruct of it to the brothers at the pleasure of the owners. Later he himself entered the Order as a lay brother and left us examples of the most perfect penance and of the highest devotion. Sir Joyce,[4] however, the son of Peter, added to this plot of ground; his son, a man of excellent parts, later devoutly entered the Order and more devoutly persevered to the end. Sir William Joynier[5] built a chapel out of his own funds and donated, at various times, about two hundred pounds toward the erection of other houses; he continued indefatigably in his spiritual friendship for the brothers until his death, bestowing upon them uninterrupted kindnesses. Toward the building of an infirmary, Sir Peter of Elvyland[6] left a hundred pounds at his death. Sir Henry of Frowik[7] and a young man of excellent disposition, Salekin of Basing, by their joint gifts, provided for the most part the aqueduct, though the king helped out too in a most generous manner.[8]

I have seen in my time at London many other gifts too, both buildings and books and other gifts to enlarge the lands and to mitigate the needs of the brothers, gifts so many and so great and so diverse as to arouse the admiration of all living people, gifts that were provided for the brothers by the most sweet Jesus Himself, so that it is only proper that

---

4. A sheriff of London at one time.
5. A wealthy merchant and also sheriff at one time.
6. Elvyland in Kent.
7. The Frowiks and Basings had several of their family function as sheriff at one time or another.
8. A. G. Little records that the king gave the friars 14½ marks toward the aqueduct in 1256. *Op. cit.*, p. 21.

they should love and honor Him in a special way, more than all others do, for all eternity.

At Oxford Robert le Mercer first received the brothers and rented them a house, where many worthy bachelors from the university and many nobles entered the Order. Later they rented a house on the plot of ground where they are now from Richard le Molenir, who within the year gave over the land and the house to the corporation of the village for the use of the brothers. The plot of ground, however, was small and too restricted.

At Cambridge the burgesses of the town first received the brothers and they made over to them an old synagogue that was next to the jail. But because the neighborhood of the jail was unbearable to the brothers for the reason that both the prisoners and the brothers had the same entrance, the lord king gave them ten marks to buy the lease from the court of the exchequer, and thus the brothers built a chapel that was so very poor that the carpenter made and set up in one day fifteen[9] pairs of rafters. But on the feast of St. Lawrence,[10] when there was no one there but three brothers who were clerics, namely, Brother William of Ashby, Brother Hugh of Bugden, and a novice by the name of Brother Elias, who was so lame that he was carried to the chapel, they sang the office solemnly with music, and the novice wept so much that the tears could be seen running down his face as he sang. Therefore, after he had died a most holy death at York, he appeared to Brother William of Ashby at Northampton and, when the latter asked how it went with him, he replied: "I am well; pray for me."

---

9. Another manuscript says fourteen.
10. August 10.

At Shrewsbury the lord king gave the brothers a piece of land; a certain burgher by the name of Richard Pride built a church, and another by the name of Lawrence Cox built the rest of the buildings. The latter removed the stone walls of the dormitory, because the minister, Brother William, so decreed in his zeal for poverty, and he built walls of mud with remarkable devotion and gentleness and at great expense.

At Northampton Sir Richard Gubiun, a knight, first housed the brothers outside the eastern gate on a piece of land he had inherited near the church of St. Edmund, where a little later the son of this patron, John by name, received the habit; his parents, however, took this hard and the said knight commanded the brothers to go away and vacate his land. The guardian replied with great maturity to them: "Let the young man be placed in our midst, and whatever he chooses, let that stand." They consented. The young man was therefore placed in the middle of the choir, the parents standing on one side, and the brothers on the other. When the guardian had put the choice to him, Brother John ran to the side of the brothers, put his arms around the pulpit, and cried out: "Here I wish to remain." The brothers then prepared to leave, while the said lord stood outside the door waiting for their departure; they came out as in procession and, when they had gone out, an old and weak brother followed carrying a psalter in his hand. When the lord saw their simplicity and humility, moved to compunction, he broke out in tears, and he cried out urgently and devoutly, asking them to forgive him and to go back in. This they did. Ever after, this lord conducted himself as a father to the brothers. Later

they were brought into the town by the villagers and
located where they now remain.[11]

---

11. This whole passage is found in the Phillipps manuscript, and
there it is inserted in the lower margin, as A. G. Little tells us.

5. The Early Zeal of the Brothers

The brothers of that time, having the first-fruits of the Holy Spirit, served the Lord not by means of constitutions made by men, but by the free affections of their devotion, being satisfied with the Rule alone and the very few statutes that had been first published within the year after the confirmation of the Rule. This was the first constitution that St. Francis made after the Rule confirmed by papal Bull,[1] as Brother Albert of blessed memory said, namely, that the brothers should not eat among seculars, except for three morsels of meat for the sake of observance of the Gospel,[2] because the rumor had come to him that the brothers were eating avidly.

The brothers were accustomed to keeping silence until tierce[3] and to being so assiduous in prayer that there was hardly an hour during the whole night in which there were not some brothers in prayer in the oratory. Likewise, on the main feast days they sang with such great fervor that at times their vigils continued throughout the night; and even if there were no more than three or four, or at most six, they

---

1. The Regula Bullata of 1223.
2. A reference to Luke 10, 8: "eat what is set before you."
3. The second of the small hours of the office.

sang solemnly with music. So great also was their simplicity and so great their purity that if any defilement happened to them at night they confessed their faults in the chapter before all. There also grew up among them the very religious custom never to swear to anything but simply to say, "Know that it is so." As soon as any of them was reprimanded either by a superior or by a confrere, he would immediately answer, "*Mea culpa,* I am at fault," and, frequently, he would even prostrate himself. For this reason, the master of the Preachers, Brother Jordan of happy memory,[4] said that the devil told him when he appeared to him once, that the *mea culpa* took away from him whatever he thought to gain amongst the Friars Minor, because they confessed their faults one to the other if one had offended against the other.

The brothers, however, were at all times so joyous and happy amongst themselves that they could hardly keep from laughing when they saw one another. Wherefore, since the young brothers of Oxford were all too frequently given to laughter, it was enjoined upon one of them that he would receive the discipline as many times as he would laugh in choir or at table. It happened, however, that, after he had received the discipline eleven times in one day, and still could not restrain himself from laughing, he saw in a dream one night that the whole convent was standing as usual in the choir and the brothers were tempted to laugh as usual; and behold, the crucifix that was standing at the entrance to the choir turned toward them as though alive and said: "They are the sons of Core who laugh and sleep in the hour of the cross."[5] It seemed to him then that the crucified tried to free

---

4. He died in 1237.
5. A reference to Numbers 16.

its hands from the cross, as though wishing to descend and depart; and behold, the custos of the place immediately went up and made the nails fast so that it did not descend. When therefore this vision was made public, the brothers were frightened and they conducted themselves more maturely and without too much laughter. They were also so zealous for the truth that they hardly dared to speak with exaggeration or to hide their own faults, even though they knew they would be punished if they confessed them.

In taking over places or in remaining where they already were, there was no difficulty for them, or in anything else whatsoever, so long as they knew it was so ordered by their superiors. Wherefore it happened that brothers of noble birth and of noteworthy conditions in the world and those most beloved in the Order allowed themselves to be put without murmur in places that are called nowadays wildernesses. This alone seemed to sadden the sweetest affection of their hearts that they would have to be separated from one another. For which reason, the brothers would often accompany those who were sent to remote places, and, in leaving, they would show their mutual affection by shedding tears in abundance.

6. The Promotion of Preachers

Although the brothers sought above all in all things the greatest simplicity and purity of conscience, they were nevertheless so fervent in attending the lectures in sacred theology and in scholastic exercises that they went daily to the schools of theology, no matter how far away they were, and they went with bare feet in the bitter cold and were not held back by any depth of mud. Wherefore, with the help of the grace of the Holy Spirit, many of them were promoted to the office of preaching in a short time. Amongst these the first were Brother Hugh of Baldock, Brother Philip of London, and Brother William of Ashby; the latter preached the word of God to the people not only by word but also by the example of his devotion.

However, the coming of Brother Haymo of Faversham increased the number of preachers considerably and increased their influence by reason of his authority and his fame; a priest and a famous preacher, he entered the Order with three other masters at St. Denis on Good Friday.[1] While he was still in the world, he wore a hair-shirt down to his knees,

---

1. Haymo entered the Order therefore in Paris, probably in 1224. See number 70 of Brother Jordan's chronicle.

and he gave many other examples of penance. For this reason
he became at last so weak and delicate that he could hardly
live without using soft and warm garments. A vision came
to him in which it seemed that he was at Faversham and was
praying in the church before Christ crucified; and behold,
a cord came down from heaven and he seized it and held on
to it and was drawn up to heaven by it. When therefore he
saw the Friars Minor at Paris, mindful of this vision, he
summoned up his courage and, setting himself against himself, he wisely induced his fellow master Simon of Sandwich
and two other famous masters to ask the Lord Jesus Christ,
while he himself was celebrating Mass, what would be most
conducive toward their salvation. Since the profession of
the way of life of the Friars Minor seemed good to all of
them at the same time, they went for greater security to
Brother Jordan of blessed memory, the master of the Order
of Preachers, and obliged him in conscience to give them
his advice faithfully. He, as one truly inspired, confirmed
their proposal by his advice. These four therefore went to
the minister, namely, Brother Gregory of Naples, and were
received by him at St. Denis; after Brother Haymo had
preached on Good Friday on this verse: *When the Lord
brought back the captives of Sion, we were like men dream-
ing,*[2] they were clothed with the habit amid great rejoicing.
On Easter, when Brother Haymo saw such a great number
of people in the parish church in which the brothers attended
divine service—for they did not yet have a chapel—he said to
the custos, who was a lay brother, Beneventus by name,
that, if he might dare to do so, he would gladly preach to the
people, lest perhaps they should receive Holy Communion

2. Psalm 125, 1.

in mortal sin. The custos, therefore, commanded him on the part of the Holy Spirit to preach. He preached, therefore, so movingly that many put off going to Holy Communion until they had gone to confession. Accordingly, he sat in the church for three days and heard confessions and comforted the people in no small way.

As was said, when the brothers first came to England, this brother came with them, and he gave much support to the first brothers in their simplicity, both by reason of his preaching and his disputations and more especially by reason of the favor he gained with the prelates. For he was so gracious and eloquent that he found favor with and was accepted by even those who were opposed to the Order. Wherefore he was first made custos of Paris, and later lector at Tours, Bologna, and Padua. He was also sent by Pope Gregory of pious memory as a legate to Vatatzes[3] in Greece, along with Brother Ralph of Rheims of happy memory. He also caused Brother Gregory of Naples, one time minister of France, to be removed from office, as his merits demanded, and, by a just judgment of God, imprisoned him after those were freed whom he had unjustly imprisoned. Brother Elias too, who was minister general, he deposed with wonderful zeal for God, because of the scandals he had wrought and the tyranny he had exercised against the zealous members of the Order, for it was Brother Haymo who brought it about that many of the provinces appealed against Brother Elias in the presence of our father Pope Gregory. Who indeed could presume on his own merits, who could feel safe about himself, when he knows that such great persons have come

---

3. The emperor who was so anxious to bring about re-union of the Greeks with the Roman Church.

upon so great a calamity? For who in the University of Paris or amongst the clergy of the whole of France was comparable to Brother Gregory in preaching or as a prelate? Who in the whole Christian world was more gracious or more famous than Elias? And yet, one merited in the end perpetual incarceration; the other, because of his disobedience and apostasy, excommunication from the Supreme Pontiff. Both, however, repented, though late in life.

Now there came to England with Brother Haymo Brother William of Coleville the elder, a man of the utmost simplicity and of outstanding charity. His sister was later most cruelly strangled in the cathedral of Chichester for preserving her chastity. For a certain young man who, because of her beauty, had long desired to find her alone and to seduce her, since he could by no means bend her to his will, proved how evil carnal desire can be by killing her in the church. For with those who love carnally it often happens that in the end their hatred becomes as great as was their love in the beginning.

Later there came to England many other very worthy brothers, who, though English by birth, had entered the Order in Paris; I saw these myself while I was still in secular clothing, namely, Brother Richard Rufus,[4] a renowned lector, who later, in his zeal for the reform of the Order against Brother Elias, went to the curia on behalf of France with Brother Haymo. He also related that a certain novice had told him that when he had suffered a continual thirst and could not sleep at night, there appeared to him a certain handsome

---

4. There is considerable confusion in Brother Thomas' account of Brother Richard Rufus on various occasions. But it would seem that he entered the Order in 1229.

young man in the habit of the brothers and commanded him to rise and follow him; when he had done this, he led him to a most pleasant place and took him into a very beautiful palace and gave him a very sweet drink, saying to him: "Son, whenever you are thirsty, come here to me and I will give you drink." And the novice asked him who he was. He said that he was Brother Francis. Then the novice returned to himself and never after did he suffer the temptation of thirst; but watching constantly, he felt himself refreshed and comforted in heart and body.

Also at that time there came Brother Ralph of Rochester,[5] who, having become very close to the lord king of England because of the charm of his preaching, proved by his end how inimical to God is the friendship of this world and how contrary to the purity of the Order of Friars Minor it is to be exalted by the favors of the great and to dwell in the courts of princes.

There came also Brother Henry of Burford, who, while he was still a novice and a chanter of the brothers at Paris, composed during meditation the following verses against the temptations which he had to bear:

Do thou, oh Friar Minor, never laugh,
For tears alone become one such as you.
Be thou in actions what thou art in name:
In name a minor, be so too in deed;
Shirk not to work, but let thy patience prove
The greatness of thy mind. And if thy heart
Reprove thy deeds, thy patience then will cleanse
What guilt perhaps weighs down upon thy heart.

---

5. The Latin is Rosa, but all render it Rochester.

If someone offers thee correction, he
It is who guards thee close; not thee he hates,
But what thou dost of wrong. And what, indeed,
Will be thy gain from thy rough garb, thy food,
Thy squalid, lowly cell? In truth, thy all
Will come to naught, if thou in very deed
Beliest what thou art in humble dress.
A shadow only art thou of a Friar,
If that thou art in name but not in fact.

This brother later, because of his great honesty, merited to be the special companion of four ministers general and of four ministers provincial in England. Likewise he acted first as interpreter and preacher for the patriarch of Antioch when he was legate in Lombardy,[6] and later as the penitentiary of the lord pope Gregory IX, custos of Venice, and at one time vicar of the custos of London.

Likewise there came Brother Henry of Reresby,[7] who afterwards was appointed minister of Scotland while he was vicar of Oxford, but he was prevented from taking office by death. After his death he appeared to the custos, saying that, although the brothers were not damned for their excesses in the matter of buildings, still they would be punished severely; and he added that if the brothers said their Divine Office well, they would be the sheep of the apostles.

There also came to England at that time Brother Martin of Barton, who merited to see Blessed Francis frequently; afterwards he was vicar of the minister of England, and he conducted himself excellently in many other offices too. He related that

---

6. Albert, who was legate in Lombardy in 1235.
7. In Leicestershire.

in the general chapter in which St. Francis ordered a house
to be torn down which had been built for the chapter there
were five thousand brothers present.[8] His brother according
to the flesh was seneschal of the chapter and he defended the
house on the part of the community. And through him,[9] Blessed Francis, standing in the open in the rain, but without getting wet, wrote in his own hand a letter to the minister and
brothers of France that, seeing his letter, they should rejoice
and sing praises to the Triune God, saying: "We bless Thee,
Father, Son, and Holy Ghost."[10] On that same day the same
father saved a brother unharmed, who had fallen into a well,
by fleeing to the church when he heard about it and pouring
out his heart in prayer. He told us also that a certain brother
who was standing at prayer at Brescia on Christmas day was
found unhurt under a ruin of stones when an earthquake
struck and the church collapsed; an earthquake that Francis
had foretold and by a letter in which there was bad Latin had
caused to be announced through all the schools of Bologna.[11]
This earthquake happened before the war of Frederick and
lasted for forty days, so that all the mountains of Lombardy
were shaken.

There came also to England Brother Peter the Spaniard,
who was later the guardian at Northampton; he wore an iron
corselet to overcome the temptations of the flesh. He had a
certain novice in his convent who was tempted to leave the
order; he finally persuaded him to go with him to the minis-

---

8. Probably the so-called Chapter of Mats of 1221. See also Thomas
   of Celano, *Vita II,* Pars II, Chapter XXVII.
9. That is, Brother Martin.
10. This letter is not extant.
11. This happened in 1222. Many chroniclers record it. Nothing more,
    however, is known of this letter of St. Francis.

ter. When therefore they were going along the way, Brother Peter began to preach to him on the virtue of holy obedience; and behold, a certain woodland bird went before them walking in the road. The novice therefore, Stephen by name, said: "If it is as you say, Father, command me in the virtue of obedience to capture this woodland bird, and that it wait for me." When he had done this, the bird immediately stood still, and the novice went up and took it and treated it as he wished; and immediately the whole temptation was subdued, and God gave him a new heart, and he immediately returned to Northampton, was professed with the intention of persevering, and later became a great preacher, as I myself have seen.

7. The Division of the Province into Custodies

After this, when the number of places had already grown and the brothers had greatly increased both in merits and in number, it seemed expedient to divide the province into custodies. The province was therefore divided into custodies[1] at the first provincial chapter at London,[2] and each of these custodies was noted for some particular mark of sanctity.

In the custody of London, over which Brother Gilbert ruled, the one to whom the Blessed Virgin appeared at his death, there flourished especially fervor, reverence, and devotion in the Divine Office.

In the custody of Oxford, at the head of which was Brother William of Ashby, study flourished in a special way.

In the same custody of Oxford, over which Brother Peter ruled,[3] the brothers did not use pillows up to the time of the minister Brother Albert. Wherefore, when Brother Albert said in chapter[4] that the brothers were unfittingly making little pillows to elevate their heads,

---

1. The Phillipps manuscript adds an arabic 4 before custodies. But it is ill-formed and the reading is doubtful.
2. The date of this chapter is uncertain, but probably before 1230.
3. Peter of Tewkesbury, 1236 to about 1248.
4. The provincial chapter at Oxford, probably in 1237.

the custos replied that the brothers knew well enough that they were carnal and it was not necessary to tell them this. But the brothers did not use sandals, unless they were sick and weak, and then only with permission. It happened, however, that Brother Walter of Madeley[5] found two sandals, and, when he went to Matins, he wore them. He stood therefore at Matins, as it seemed to him much more comfortably than he was accustomed to stand. But afterwards, when he came to his bed and went to sleep, he dreamed that he had to go along a certain dangerous road between Oxford and Gloucester, which is called Baisaliz,[6] where there were usually robbers; and when he had come down into a deep valley, they came running out from both sides of the road and shouting and saying: "Kill him, kill him." Very much frightened, therefore, he said that he was a Friar Minor. But they said: "You lie; you do not go without shoes." But, thinking that he was without shoes as was the custom, he said: "But indeed, I do go without shoes." But when he confidently put out his foot, he found that he was wearing before them the aforesaid sandals; and being aroused immediately from sleep by exceedingly great confusion, he threw the sandals into the middle of the field.[7]

In the custody of Cambridge, over which Brother Richard of Ingworth ruled, there flourished especially a strictness with regard to money, so much so that up to that time when Brother

---

5. In Shropshire or in Staffordshire.
6. An unidentified name. A. G. Little suggests that it might be Besselsleigh, about 4½ miles from Oxford on the road to Gloucester.
7. The Phillipps manuscript locates this whole passage as given here. Manuscript E has it at the end of the chapter.

Albert visited England the brothers of that custody did not use mantles, as that same father related.

In the custody of York, over which Brother Martin of Barton ruled, zeal for poverty flourished; for he did not permit more brothers to be in any place than could be supported by begging alone, without incurring debts.[8]

In the custody of Salisbury, over which Brother Stephen ruled, mutual charity flourished in a special way. He himself was a man of such sweetness, such joyfulness, and of such extraordinary charity, that he would permit no one, to the best of his ability, to be sad. Wherefore when it came time for him to die and he was offered the saving host, he saw in the host the gateway through which he was to pass, and singing in a loud voice, "Hail, Queen of mercy," he died a happy death at Salisbury.

In the custody of Worcester, over which Brother Robert of Leicester ruled, there flourished especially straightforward simplicity; for he himself, a man small of body but large of heart, always practiced the highest simplicity and brought many men known for simplicity into the Order. At length, with a loud cry and with tears he gave back his holy and simple soul to the Lord at Worcester.

---

8. This was according to the wish of St. Francis.

8. The Chapters of the Visitators

It happened after this that special visitators[1] were sent to England who celebrated chapters as part of the visitation. The first visitator of England was Brother William of Coleville the elder, who celebrated his chapter at London under Brother Agnellus,[2] where Sir William Joynier had built a chapel at his own expense; and he celebrated at this time the entry into it with memorable pomp.

And in the same chapter of the visitation of Brother William of Coleville a certain brother preached against contracting debts, and he said that it was the same with the procurators[3] as it was with a certain priest who was accustomed each year to celebrate the feast of St. Nicholas. And behold, it happened that he became so poor that he could not celebrate the accustomed feast or have the banquet. When the day approached and the bell announced Matins, he lay on his bed and thought what he should do. As the one bell rang, it seemed to say: "How will I pay; how will I pay"; and the second bell seemed to reply:

---

1. The visitators sent by Elias were intended to further his own schemes.
2. Not later than 1229.
3. Laymen appointed to manage the business affairs of the Friars.

"By credit; by credit"; and while he thought how he should pay for the celebration, both bells rang together, and it seemed to him that they said: "Borrow this, borrow that; borrow this, borrow that." And rising, he held the feast by borrowing. The sermon was approved by the chapter.[4]

After this there came Brother John of Malvern, who then for the first time brought the exposition of the Rule by the lord pope Gregory IX.[5] He called together for visitation the brothers and also the novices in great numbers under Brother Agnellus in London, Leicester, and Bristol. And indeed, so strict was the conscience of the brothers at this time about erecting buildings and having pictures that he took the strongest measures because of the windows in the chapel of the place at Gloucester; and because of the pulpit which a certain brother had painted himself, he took the capuch away from him; and he did the same thing to the guardian of the place also, because he had permitted the painting.

The third visitator came from the minister general, Brother Elias, under Brother Albert; this visitator was Brother Wygerius, a German, a man very renowned for his legal knowledge, conspicuous for his integrity of conduct, and a close friend of the lord cardinal Otto, who was at that time legate in England.[6] He had received very strict and subtle instructions from the minister general, and especially that those should be immediately excommunicated who in any way what-

---

4. The phrases used in the Latin text are these: "Ieo ke fray, ieo ke fray." "A crey, a crey." "Ke del un, ke del el, ke del un, ke del el."

5. The Bull *Quo elongati* of September 28, 1230.

6. He came to England in late June of 1237, appointed by Gregory IX.

soever hid anything from him or revealed what he had said;[7] from this sentence no one but himself could absolve; moreover, that he should bring all accusations to the minister general. As a result, there was such a commotion among the brothers everywhere that nothing like it had ever been seen in the Order before. For after he had called together the brothers at London, Southampton, Gloucester, and Oxford, they came in great numbers and protracted their stay unduly; and because of the mutual accusations within the Order and the suspicions of the seculars without, an intolerable storm suddenly arose throughout the province. In the end, when the visitation was somehow completed, the provincial chapter was celebrated at Oxford, and a unanimous appeal was made against Brother Elias. Over and above the visitation, however, the visitator had the power, and in his mandate he had received instructions, to do certain things that would result in a notable injury to the brothers.

He went, therefore, to the province of Scotland, and after calling a chapter, he wanted to make the visitation. But the brothers made up their appeal and presented it when it was ready, saying that since they had already been visited by the minister of Ireland on the authority of the general chapter they did not want another visitation. Therefore, since everywhere everyone was upset, the visitator himself became not a little upset and returned to Germany, taking with him the report of his visitation. But Brother William of Ashby, whom he had sent to make the visitation in Ireland, after he had accomplished what he could, went to join him in Cologne.

---

7. Some manuscripts have *velarent*; manuscript E has *revelarent*, and that undoubtedly is what it should be.

Therefore, when the brothers had come to Rome,[8] they asked that the brothers be visited in their places through the general chapter in accordance with the constitution concerning visitators. Brother Arnulph, the penitentiary of the lord Pope, said that if the devil were incarnate he could not find a more subtle or a more forceful snare to catch souls than the visitation just completed.

In the chapter of the visitation of Brother Wygerius, Brother Eustace de Merc of blessed memory was accused repeatedly and he was excluded from the chapter for a day and a half. A certain other brother, however, about whom less was believed, was cleared immediately, and that brother said: "Miserable me! That that man of such well-known sanctity and of such proved religious spirit and of such outstanding discretion should be thus visited; and I have thus escaped! Who will ever in the future grant any credence to the judgments of men?"[9]

---

8. Those sent to carry the appeal to Rome.
9. This occurs a few sentences earlier in manuscript P.

9. The Division of the Administration of England

Not long after the coming of the brothers to England, it was commanded by the minister general Brother Elias that the English province should be divided into two provinces: that there should be, namely, a province for Scotland, and the other, as before, for England. He wished, as it is said, that just as the Order of Friars Preachers had twelve priors provincial throughout the world, as there were twelve apostles, so he wished to have under him seventy-two ministers, as there were seventy-two disciples.

Brother Henry of Reresby was made minister of Scotland; but before the obedience came to him, he died. Brother John of Kethene, the guardian of London, succeeded him; he it was who caused all the places north of York to be included in his province; afterwards he received many upright and useful persons into the Order. Practicing unusual zeal for the Divine Office, he showed himself an example of devotion. He received our venerable father Brother Albert with proper reverence in the place at Leicester and humbly asked him to explain the Rule to the brothers. Therefore after he had ruled the province of Scotland laudably for many years, he was made minister of Ireland at the time when the province of Scotland was rejoined to that of England.

Incident. At the time of Brother John, Brother Elias commanded that the brothers themselves should wash their *femoralia;* the brothers of the English administration therefore washed theirs, according to what was commanded; the brothers, however, of the administration of Scotland waited for their rescript.[1]

Brother John also, and this I think is worth remembering, stood unwaveringly by Brother William of Nottingham of blessed memory, the minister of England, along with Brother Gregory of Bossells, in the general chapter of Genoa,[2] where happily they won their case against almost the entire general chapter, that the privilege granted by the lord pope concerning the receiving of money through procurators should be completely annulled and that the exposition of the Rule according to the lord Innocent, in those things in which it is more lenient than that of Gregory, should be suspended. He also spoke with all the definitors general of the chapter in favor of the reconciliation of Brother Elias, and he obtained that he should be admonished by the brothers not to put off his return to the obedience of the Church and of the Order.

Besides, he was so zealous for the promotion of studies that he caused a Bible thoroughly annotated throughout to be bought at Paris and sent to Ireland. Finally, he was so filled with zeal for comforting the brothers that many from other provinces who were desolate came to him and seemed to prosper under him. When therefore he had been minister for about twenty years, he was released from office in the chapter

---

1. This incident is inserted here by the Phillipps manuscript.
2. Most probably in 1251.

of Metz,[3] in which also Brother William, the minister of England, was released.

> *Incident.* When Brother Elias was deposed from office,[4] it was provided that there should be only thirty-two administrations in the Order, sixteen, namely, ultramontane, and sixteen cismontane; for this reason, namely, that, since the election of the minister general pertains to the ministers and custodes, if there were too many votes in an election or in making laws, since such a multitude is the cause of confusion, anything that required the consent of so many persons could hardly be settled at all.[5]

---

3. In 1254. More recent research has inverted the chronology of the chapter of Genoa and Metz. Formerly that of Genoa was put in 1254. See *Archivum Franciscanum Historicum*, Vol. III and IV.
4. In 1239.
5. In manuscripts C and P this paragraph is in the margin; in E it is at the end as here.

10. Changes in the Places

With the day by day increase in the number of brothers, the houses and lands that had sufficed for a few could not suffice for so many. Besides, by the providence of God, such persons frequently entered the Order for whom it seemed only right to provide in a more munificent manner. In some places, also, the simplicity of the brothers had so inconsiderately situated them that the land could not be increased, and it became necessary to move their houses elsewhere. Therefore it happened that while Brother Agnellus of blessed memory was still living there was a great expansion of houses and places. Yet, so great was his zeal for poverty that he would scarce permit either the lands to be increased or houses to be built, except unavoidable necessity demanded it. This was very evident with regard to the infirmary at Oxford, which he had built so humbly that the height of the walls did not exceed by much the height of a man, and up to the time of Brother Albert the house itself lacked a guest room. In the same way he strengthened the dormitory at London by removing the mud walls and putting up stone walls, but leaving the roof unchanged.[1] Also, under Brother Albert the place at North-

---

1. This is the reverse of what William of Nottingham did at Shrewsbury. And at Southampton he destroyed the stone cloister.

ampton was changed and so was the place at Worcester and that at Hereford.

Under Brother Haymo, likewise, an increase was brought about in the lands in many places; for he said that he preferred that the brothers would have more ample grounds and cultivate them, so that they could have their own food at home, rather than that they should beg it from others. This he said on the occasion of the expansion of the grounds at Gloucester, where the brothers had once, at the order of Brother Agnellus, disposed of part of it, and later with great difficulty recovered that part from Sir Thomas of Berkeley through the clever devotion of his wife.

Under Brother William the place at York was changed, and also the place at Bristol and that at Bridgewater. But both the place at Grimsby and the place at Oxford were amply enlarged. But when a certain brother said to him, moved by too great familiarity, by reason of which he was also called the soul of Brother William by some brothers—because the latter had deigned to write to him in his own hand with inestimable affection when he was in desolation—when this brother told him that he would accuse him to the minister general because the place at London was not enclosed, he replied with burning zeal: "And I will reply to the general that I did not enter the Order to build walls." With this same zeal he had the roof of the church at London taken down and had the embossments of the cloister scraped away. Once, however, he said to that brother who was his friend that it was necessary to erect buildings that were somewhat large lest the future brothers would make them too big.

Incident. Brother Robert of Slapton said to me that while the brothers were in a certain place that was loaned to them, before they had a piece of land, it seemed to the brother guardian in a dream that St. Francis came to that place; and when the brothers met him, they led him into the solarium, and he sat down looking about him for a long time in silence. And the brothers being astonished, the guardian said: "Father, what are you thinking?" And Francis said to him: "Look around at the house." And he looked around; and behold, the whole house was made of twigs, mud, and mire. And he said to the brothers: "That is the way the houses of the Friars Minor should be." And the guardian took water and washed the feet of Francis and kissed the stigmata in his feet. These things, I think, happened to Brother Robert himself. I myself saw, however, a certain famous preacher who confessed publicly that because of his concern about building the houses of a certain place he had lost his liking for preaching and the devotion he used to have.

Brother John also, the visitator of the Order of Friars Preachers in England, said of Brother William of Abingdon that before he built the houses at Gloucester, he had an incomparable gift of preaching, and that a preacher like that and one so pleasing should never be occupied about buildings. For, that Brother John said, he had so degraded himself by soliciting alms that the king of England told him: "Brother William, you used to speak so spiritually; but now your whole speech is: give, give, give." And another time, when he used flattery on the king in his begging something from him, that prince called him a serpent.[2]

---

2. Manuscripts P and E omit the above incident.

The lord abbot of Chertsey[3] told me that, when a certain very close friend of his in the Order of Preachers asked him for some wood, he gave him one piece; and when he said it seemed to him quite burdensome to be put to so much trouble for one piece of wood, the abbot gave him another piece; and when he said that there were three persons in one God and that therefore he ought to give him three pieces, the abbot replied: "By God who is one alone, you shall now have but one piece."

When Brother Henry of Burford was clothed at Paris, there were only thirty brothers in that convent. They were building at that time in a place which was called Valvert[4] where they built a long and high house which seemed to many brothers to be contrary to the state of poverty of the Order. Wherefore some of the brothers, and in particular Brother Angeler,[5] begged St. Francis to destroy it. And behold, when the brothers were about to go into it, by divine disposition no one took up his abode there, for the roof and the walls collapsed to the very basement. These verses were found written in that place:

God's grace doth teach us by this very ruin
That man should be content with smaller houses.

And so they gave up the place.[6]

---

3. A Benedictine abbey in Surrey; the abbot was called Alan.
4. Near the Luxemburg gardens.
5. All the manuscripts give Angeler. Perhaps Agnellus is meant. The building collapsed in 1229 most probably.
6. The last two paragraphs are in the margin in manuscript C in another hand.

11. The Promotion of Lectors

After the place had been enlarged where the principal seat of studies flourished in England[1] and where scholars from all over were wont to gather, Brother Agnellus had a sufficiently suitable school built at the place of the brothers, and he asked the master Robert Grosseteste of saintly memory to lecture to the brothers there.[2] Under him they progressed immeasurably within a short time both in theological matters and in preaching with suitable and subtle moral examples. Now after he had been transferred by divine providence from the chair of teaching to the episcopal chair, the master Peter lectured to the brothers; he later was promoted to the episcopacy in Scotland.[3] Succeeding him was the master Roger of Weseam,[4] who first was deacon of Lincoln Cathedral and later was made bishop of Coventry. Likewise, too, the master Tho-

---

1. That is, Oxford.
2. He was chancellor of the University of Oxford and a renowned master. He lectured to the brothers up to about 1235, in which year he was made bishop of Lincoln. He died in 1253.
3. Most probably Peter of Ramsay who became bishop of Aberdeen in 1247.
4. Roger of Weseam or Weasenham was archdeacon of Oxford 1236 to 1241, deacon of Lincoln about 1240, and bishop of Lichfield and Coventry in 1245.

mas Wallensis,[5] after he had lectured in a praiseworthy manner to the brothers in that place, was chosen bishop of St. David in Wales.

These masters, therefore, being always favorably inclined toward the brothers in all things, promoted their deeds and their fame very much. Therefore, so greatly did the fame of the brothers of England and their progress in studies become known also in other provinces, that the minister general Brother Elias sent for Brother Philip of Wales and Brother Adam of York, who then lectured at Lyons. When Brother Albert came, he appointed Brother Vincent of Coventry lector at London and this one's brother, Brother Henry, lector at Cambridge. And thus gradually lectors were placed in various other places, namely, Brother William of Leicester at Hereford; Brother Gregory of Bossells at Leicester; Brother Gilbert of Cranford at Bristol; Brother John of Westun at Cambridge; Brother Adam Marsh at Oxford. And the gift of wisdom so flooded the English province that before Brother William of Nottingham was released from office there were thirty lectors who engaged in solemn disputations and three or four who lectured without engaging in these disputations. For he had assigned students in the universities for the single places, who would succeed the lectors who died or who would be removed from office. Therefore, omitting other things, we will speak briefly of the succession of lectors in the universities.

For some begin as masters, others lecture as bachelors. At Oxford the first to lecture was Brother Adam Marsh. The

5. Thomas Wallensis was canon of Lincoln in 1235, regent master at Paris in 1238, archdeacon of Lincoln, and then bishop of St. David in 1247. He died in 1255.

second, Brother Ralph of Corbridge,[6] who, while at Paris, where he presided earlier in a praiseworthy manner—in fact he entered the Order while he was regent in theology—was appointed by the minister general to preside at Oxford, where he lectured while he was still a novice. The third was Brother Eustace of Normanville [who formerly had been a noble and rich, a master of arts and of laws and chancellor of Oxford].[7]

Brother Peter, minister of England, said that Brother Eustace of Normanville was a source of greater edification than others with regard to his entrance into the Order, because he was a noble and rich and had presided in a praiseworthy manner in arts and laws and had been chancellor of Oxford and adept at learning theology.[8]

The fourth was Brother Thomas of York.[9] The fifth Brother Richard [Rufus][10] of Cornwall who at the time when Brother Elias was disturbing the whole Order, entered at Paris and during that disturbance, while the appeal was still pending, made his profession in England with courage and devotion. Afterwards he gave a course of lectures on the *Sentences*[11] at Paris, where he was acclaimed a great and admirable philosopher.

When this Richard came to England he told in the chapter at Oxford how, when a brother at Paris was

---

6. Corbridge in Northumberland. A. G. Little notes that he has left us a beautifully written copy of St. Paul's Epistles.
7. The last clause is omitted in manuscript E but is in C and P.
8. The Latin phrase *promptus ad incipiendum in theologia* seems to imply some such idea as ease in studying or in getting a degree. The Phillipps manuscript places this paragraph here; manuscript E puts it at the end of the chapter; C in the margin.
9. Wrote a monumental work on metaphysics, still unpublished.
10. *Rufus* is added in the margin in C; in the text in P.
11. The *Sentences* of Peter Lombard.

caught up in ecstasy, it seemed to him that Brother Giles, a lay brother but a contemplative, sat and lectured on the seven authentic petitions of the Lord's prayer, all his hearers being brothers who were lectors in the Order. But St. Francis, entering, first stood silent, then exclaimed in these words: "Oh how shameful it is for you that such a lay brother should exceed your merits in heaven above. And because," he went on, "knowledge puffs up, but charity edifies,[12] many brothers clerics are counted as nothing in the eternal kingdom of God."[13]

Incident. A certain renowned lector, who studied with me at Oxford,[14] was wont always to give his attention in school to other things than the lecture during the master's lectures or disputations, such as compiling original material of his own. And behold, when he himself was made lector, his own students were so inattentive that he used to say he would gladly close his book each day and leave rather than lecture; and with regret, he said: "By the just judgment of God no one wants to hear me because I never wanted to listen to any teacher." He also, because he was much too intimate with seculars and because of this familiarity was with the brothers less than had been the custom, became an example to others that only in silence and quiet are the words of wisdom learned, that the commandments of God too, as the holy one says, cannot be pondered on except the mind be at rest. Afterwards, however, having returned to himself, he sought

---

12. I Corinthians 8, 1.
13. This preceding paragraph occurs only as a marginal note by a contemporary hand in manuscript P, as Little tells us.
14. Perhaps Stephen the Englishman, mentioned by Salimbene.

quiet and made such excellent progress that the lord bishop of Lincoln said that he would not know how to give the lecture that brother gave. Wherefore, later, as the fame of his upright life spread, he was called to Lombardy by the minister general and he dwelt in the curia of the pope with the reputation of being a great man. In the end, in his death agony, the Mother of God, to whom he had always been devoted, appeared to him, and the evil spirits having fled from him, he merited to pass happily to the pains of Purgatory, as he later revealed to a certain friend of his. For he said he was in Purgatory and that he suffered severely in his feet, because only too often he had been accustomed to go to a certain religious woman to console her, when he should have attended to his lectures and other more necessary occupations; and he asked that Masses be celebrated for his soul. His friend did this for two years continuously and offered many other suffrages besides.[15]

The following, however, lectured at Cambridge and not at Oxford. Brother Vincent of Coventry, Brother John of Westun, Brother William of Poitiers, Brother Humphrey. The latter once, when he became sick at Cambridge, as he himself told me, heard a voice saying to him: "May you feel that you are a stone." Therefore, as he lay immobile like a stone, two demons came and

---

15. This preceding incident is in the margin in manuscripts C and P; in the text in manuscript E. There follows here a list of Franciscan lectors at Oxford which very obviously is a compilation by a later writer. There are sixty-two names given in addition to the five given by Brother Thomas. Of note especially is John Pecham, later archbishop of Canterbury. We omit the list here. It can be found in various places, including A. G. Little's edition of the *De Adventu.*

sat at his left, and one good angel stood at his right. And
the demons began to irritate him by calumnies; the good
angel, however, was silent for a long time. Finally, the
two demons said: "When the brothers sit gossiping over
their drinks at the hour of Compline, that is when we
are busy with them; when they leave, then we have
things to do elsewhere." And the good angel said: "See
how great is the malice of the devils; they want to kill
you with boredom, so that you will not be able to praise
the name of your Creator any more." Comforted, therefore, by this, he began to sweat and was made whole
again.[16]

---

16. This last paragraph is in the margin in manuscripts C and P.
There follows here a list of Franciscan lectors at the University
of Cambridge, again in a later hand. It contains seventy-three
names, repeating also the four mentioned by Brother Thomas.
Again we omit it; it too can be found in Little's *De Adventu.*

12. The Appointment of Confessors

There were also many brothers, who, though they did not have the office of preaching or of teaching, did, however, by the most gracious favor of the prelates and by obedience and the command of their minister provincial, hear confessions in various places both of religious and of seculars. Amongst these there was especially Brother Solomon at London, who was the general confessor of the citizens and of the members of the court. From him while he was guardian at London after his illness, as was said above, the lord Roger of blessed memory, bishop of London,[1] demanded canonical obedience; but Brother Solomon opposed him in a friendly way because of his long-standing friendship with him and asked for a delay for a time. Now the lord bishop held the Order in such reverence, that he would arise when the individual brothers would greet him. Therefore Brother Agnellus, on this occasion, immediately sent to the Roman curia and obtained for the brothers the decree that is entitled *Nimis iniqua*.[2]

---

1. Bishop from 1229 to 1241.
2. Of August 21, 1231. It gave the Friars a virtual exemption from the jurisdiction of the bishops, except in the founding of houses and in preaching.

There also flourished in the office of confessor Brother Maurice of Dereham,[3] who, when he discovered a certain boy who had been wasting away for a long time with a desperate illness, after hearing his confession, imposed upon him the penance of reciting each day three *Hail Marys* and asking that the Blessed Virgin would obtain for him his health so that he could become a Friar Minor; when he did this, he was cured completely. When he was about fifteen years of age, therefore, he bound himself and lived amongst the brothers as one of them until he should have the required age;[4] when he had attained this age, he was clothed with the habit without delay under Brother Agnellus.

There flourished also at Gloucester Brother Vincent of Worcester, father to the whole country, who practiced such great abstinence and such great rigor toward himself, and such kindness and affability toward his subjects, that he was loved by all as though he were an angel; wherefore, because of the graveness of his character and his extraordinary prudence, he was later promoted to the office of preaching and he became the confessor of Roger, the lord bishop of Coventry.[5]

At Lynn there flourished a man of very renowned sanctity, Brother Geoffrey of Salisbury, who by the austerity of his life showed himself, if it might be said, another Francis, and by his practice of virtue and by reason of his kindness and sympathy, a second Anthony. For he was a man of such great love and compassion in hearing confessions, that, when he did not see the penitents manifesting proper signs of contrition,

---

3. In Norfolk.
4. Eighteen seems to have been the ordinary age. This was incorporated into the Constitutiones Narbonnenses under St. Bonaventure.
5. Roger of Wesham, bishop of Lichfield and Coventry 1245-1256.

he moved them to tears by his own tears and sobs; as happened to the nobleman Sir Alexander of Bassingbourn;[6] for when he was confessing as though he were telling some story, Brother Geoffrey wept bitterly and forced him to weep too and moved him by his merits and his salutary counsels to form the resolution to enter the Order of Minors; and in this resolution he died a most holy death. He appeared later to a friend of his, Brother John of Stamford,[7] and to the latter's question how it fared with him, replied: "My soul is a creature that is obedient to its Creator; and he is at rest who obeys with his whole heart."[8] He instructed him also about faith in the sacrament of the Eucharist so sublimely that no other mortal could have done it so well.

There flourished also at Oxford Brother Eustace de Merc, who later was made guardian and finally custos of York. He used to tell how the holy Lanfranc, wishing to enter religion when he was already a very great theologian, put on the garment of a fool and went to various monasteries to try out the state of the monks. And he came and knocked at the door of the choir with his wand, and when he saw the monks look toward the door and laugh, he said: "God is not here." And when he came to Bec Herluin,[9] and no monk paid any attention to his knocking, he entered there and took the habit of a lay brother. And when Pope Nicholas celebrated the council against Berengarius, he obtained permission to go with his abbot, and

---

6. He held various public offices and was employed also in various capacities by Church authorities.
7. Custos of Oxford 1253; minister provincial 1257.
8. "La meye alme le fet cum creature que est obeysant a sun Creatour; et repose est en celi ke la par ducour."
9. In Normandy.

there, when all were thrown into confusion over the statements of the heretic, he asked to be heard; and he set forth
his arguments so clearly that Berengarius said: "Either you
are Lanfranc or you are the devil." And thus he was recognized
by the council.[10]

---

10. The Lateran Council 1059. The pope was Nicholas II. Berengarius
    had denied the doctrine of transubstantiation.

13. The Ministers General of the Order

The first minister general after Blessed Francis was Brother Elias, who had been a notary at Bologna. Brother John Parenti[1] succeeded him; he was minister of Spain, a wise and deeply religious man and a man of great austerity. He was dismissed from office by the partisans of Brother Elias, and Brother Elias was made general again.[2] In the chapter held at the time of the translation of St. Francis' remains,[3] the partisans of Brother Elias, whom he had permitted to come to the chapter—for he granted this permission to all who wished to come—wanted to make him general in opposition to the ministers provincial. Wherefore they carried him on their arms from his cell to the door of the chapter room, and there, after they had broken down the door, they wanted to put him in the place of the minister general. When the good Brother John saw this, he stripped himself before the whole chapter; and thus finally they were confounded and gave up after a very

---

1. St. Francis appointed Peter of Catania in 1220 to act as Vicar General of the Order. But he died in the spring of 1221. Brother Elias was then appointed to act as Vicar General, an office that he held until the first election of a Minister General at the chapter of 1227 when Brother John Parenti was elected.
2. The date of this chapter was 1232.
3. This was in 1230.

great disturbance. For they did not listen to St. Anthony or to any minister provincial. The people, however, thought that the discord arose because the body of St. Francis had been translated already on the third day before the fathers had convened. Five novices, who had been soldiers and who were present at the chapter, saw everything, and they wept and said that this disturbance would work great good for the Order, because an Order could not put up with such disorder. And thus it happened that all of these disturbers were scattered amongst the various provinces to do penance.

But Brother Elias, going apart to a certain hermitage, let his hair and beard grow, and by this pretense at holiness was reconciled to the Order and to the brothers.[4]

From this chapter a solemn delegation was sent with the minister general to Pope Gregory to obtain an exposition of the Rule, namely, St. Anthony, Brother Gerard Rusinol, penitentiary of the lord pope, Brother Haymo,[5] who later became minister general, Brother Leo, who later was made archbishop of Milan,[6] Brother Gerard of Modena, and Brother Peter of Brescia.[7] They told the pope what great scandal Brother Elias had caused because the minister general had revoked his decree so that not all the brothers could come to the chapter who wished; and also how he became indignant about this and had the body of St. Francis translated before the chapter convened. The pope, already greatly moved by all this, became very angry toward him, until he heard of the unusual life he was

---

4. There is some confusion about the date of this retirement; the *Speculum Vitae*, for instance, gives 1239. But 1230 seems the correct date.
5. Minister general from 1240 to 1244.
6. In 1241.
7. The result was the Bull *Quo Elongati*.

leading at the hermitage. As a result of this, he granted in the general chapter at Rieti,[8] after Brother Parenti had been released from office, that Elias might become minister general, above all because of the friendship he had had with Blessed Francis.

Afterwards, because Elias had upset the whole Order by his worldly living and his cruelty, Brother Haymo moved an appeal against him at Paris; and though Elias was unwilling, many ministers provincial and many of the best brothers from the Cismontane provinces gathered to celebrate a general chapter, Brother Arnulph, the penitentiary of the lord pope Gregory IX, acting on behalf of the Order at the Roman curia. Therefore, after a long consultation, brothers were chosen from the whole Order to provide for the reformation of the Order. When this was done, an account thereof was given in the general chapter before the pope, at which seven cardinals were in attendance too.

After the sermon preached by the pope, which dealt with the golden statue seen by Nabuchodonosor and the theme of which was, *Thou, O king, didst begin to think in thy bed what should come to pass hereafter*,[9] Brother Elias began to make excuses, saying that the brothers, when they elected him to the office of minister general, said that they wanted him to eat gold and to have a horse, if his weakness demanded it; but now they were offended and scandalized in him. And when Brother Haymo wanted to reply to him, the pope did not allow it until the lord cardinal Robert of Somercote[10] said to him:

---

8. Rieti was probably the place of the chapter, though Jordan of Giano places it at Rome and the *Speculum Vitae* at Assisi.

9. Daniel 2, 29.

10. Created cardinal 1239; died 1241.

"Lord, he is an old man; it is good that you hear him, for he is sparing in words."

Brother Haymo, therefore, stood timid and trembling; but Brother Elias sat completely unshaken, as it seemed, and unafraid. Brother Haymo began by briefly praising the words of Brother Elias as the words of a revered father, and then made the point against him that, though the brothers said they wanted him to eat gold, they did not say that they wanted him to have a treasure. Moreover, though they said they wanted him to have a horse, they did not say they wanted him to have a palfrey or a charger. And immediately Brother Elias, losing patience, said openly that he was lying; and his followers began likewise to make like charges and to raise a tumult; and those of the other party began to do likewise against them. Then the pope, much moved, commanded them to be silent, saying: "This is not the way of religious." Then the pope remained seated for a long time, as though in silence and meditation he would turn them to shame. Meanwhile, the lord Reginald, protector of the Order,[11] suggested openly to Brother Elias that he give his resignation into the hands of the pope; he publicly replied that he would not. Then the pope, first commending his person and the friendship he had had with St. Francis, concluded that it seemed to him that his ministry had been acceptable to the brothers; but since it did not now please them, as was just shown, he decreed that he should be removed from office. And immediately he released him from the office of minister general. There was then such immense and inexpressible joy that those who merited to be present said they had never seen anything like it.

---

11. Cardinal bishop of Ostia who became Alexander IV.

Therefore the pope went alone into one of the cells and called the ministers and custodes for an election; and before they wrote down their votes, he heard the votes of each one;[12] and since Brother Albert of Pisa, the minister of England was canonically elected, Brother Arnulph, the penitientiary, who in particular had forwarded the whole business, announced the election and began the *Te Deum Laudamus*. And because Brother Elias, it was said, had never made profession of the *Regula Bullata*,[13] and for which reason his conscience permitted him to receive money, it was immediately arranged that he should make profession of this Rule and then under the same formula the whole chapter, and the whole Order. And so it was done. Therefore after the minister general had said Mass, the pope said to the brothers who had not been part of the chapter: "You have now heard the first Mass ever celebrated by a minister general of your Order.[14] Go now with the blessing of Jesus Christ to your places." In this chapter Brother Haymo was made minister of all England, and Brother John of Kethene, who had been minister of Scotland, was made minister of Ireland.

After this, Brother Elias, having chosen the place of Cortona for his dwelling place, went without permission and against the general prohibition of the minister general to visit the houses of the Poor Ladies; for this reason he seems to have incurred the sentence of excommunication decreed by the pope. But Brother Albert commanded him to come to him to obtain absolution or at least to meet him at some intermediate place. When he declined to do this, the pope heard

---

12. Salimbene says he heard the votes to speed up the election.
13. The Rule of 1223.
14. He was the first priest to hold the office of minister general.

about it; and, when he saw that the pope wanted him to obey the minister general like any other brother, not being able to bear the humiliation in as much as he had not learned to obey, he betook himself to the neighborhood of Arezzo.[15] Wherefore, not undeservedly, he was publicly excommunicated by the pope.

Therefore Brother Albert, conducting himself in a praiseworthy manner in the office of minister general by correcting the excesses of his predecessor, occupied himself beyond the mountains where the greater deformation of the Order had taken place. He died happily at Rome, commending the English above all for their zeal for the Order.[16]

But Brother Haymo the Englishman succeeded him;[17] he took care to carry on what Brother Albert had begun. Under him was held the first and the last general chapter of definitors[18] that was ever held in the Order because of the insolence of certain of them; they wanted by all means to send away from the place all the ministers provincial who were at the chapter along with the minister general. And this was done. Therefore, the ordinance that was made about such a chapter before the pope at the time of the absolution of Brother Elias and about the canonical election of custodes and guardians was abrogated in the next general chapter because of the insolence of these subjects. For certain brothers wanted the custodes eliminated entirely from the Order, saying that their office was superfluous.

---

15. Manuscripts P and E add "to the territory of the emperor Frederick."
16. He ruled less than a year and died probably on January 23, 1240.
17. Elected some time after the death of Brother Albert in 1240.
18. They were delegates of the brothers from various provinces.

Once, when Brother Haymo was on this side of the mountains, he was summoned in the middle of winter by the protector of the Order and other cardinals; he answered so excellently before them to the objections made against him that he gained the greatest respect.

While he was minister general, the order came from the chapter[19] that brothers be elected throughout the provinces of the Order to take note of the doubts that would arise concerning the Rule and to send these to the minister general. For this, therefore, there were elected in England Brother Adam Marsh, Brother Peter, the custos of Oxford,[20] Brother Henry of Burford, and certain other brothers. In that very night St. Francis appeared to Brother John Bannister and showed him a deep well; Brother John said to him: "Father, behold, the fathers want to explain the Rule; much better would it be for you to explain it to us." The saint replied; "Son, go to the lay brothers and let them explain the Rule for you."

Therefore, when certain doubts had been noted down, the brothers sent them to the general in a document without a seal, and they begged him, by the shedding of the blood of Jesus Christ, to let the Rule stand as it had been set down by St. Francis at the dictation of the Holy Spirit. This mandate greatly pleased both the protector of the Order and also the brothers beyond the sea; and it confirmed the testimony Brother Albert had given concerning the English brothers. But Brother Haymo died at Anagni;[21] on his deathbed, the lord pope Innocent IV deigned to visit him.

---

19. The chapter of the definitors just mentioned, 1241.
20. Brother Peter of Tewkesbury.
21. Most probably in 1244.

Incident. Brother Haymo said that the brothers who did not wish to return to the convent after an illness before they were sufficiently strong, lest they be not able to go to the recreation, were like the little boy who had to be taught his letters even though he was unwilling, and when he had said *A,* said that he would not say *B* even though he knew it equally as well as he knew *A,* for, if he said *B,* the master would command him to say *C,* and so on.

He also said that when he was still a secular, he was so delicate that he could not live without a multiplicity of remedies in clothing and shoes, but that later he became stronger without such things.

When Brother Haymo returned from the general chapter in which he had been made minister provincial, fearing his weakness, he thought that if he could get beyond the mountains, he would not thereafter be afraid; it happened, however, that he grew stronger where he had been most in fear, and in France, weaker.[22]

Brother Crescentius succeeded Brother Haymo.[23] He was a famous doctor and minister of Verona; his charity inflamed his zeal; his knowledge molded it; and his constancy confirmed it. For the brothers of his province were so opposed to him that on the very night before the general chapter in which he was elected, after the complaint he had lodged against them before the zealous brothers of the Order concerning the rebellion of his brothers, one of the brothers saw him in a vision with shaven head and a beard reaching to his cord, and he heard a voice coming from heaven upon him, saying: "This

---

22. A. G. Little notes that this passage is in the margin of manuscript C and within the text in P.
23. Elected in 1244.

is Mardochaeus." Therefore, when Brother Ralph of Rheims heard of this vision, he immediately said: "It is certain that he will be elected general today." When, however, he had carried out his office faithfully and prudently for a time, he asked to be released from office; he was later made bishop of the city of his birth.[24]

> *Incident.* Brother Ralph of Rheims, an Englishman, after lengthy labors, came to England, and after he had spent a long time in contemplation at Salisbury, he died a happy death. He related that when St. Francis had been walking along the way in a cold wind and was growing weak of resolution, he roused his spirits and went up on a mountain and stripped off his garments, and turning himself toward the wind, he said to himself that now it would indeed be good for him if he had even one tunic.[25]

After Crescentius came Brother John of Parma as minister general.[26] He was a lector and had given courses at Paris[27] on the *Sentences;* he was also outstanding for his zeal for the Order. He came to England at the time of Brother William of Nottingham and celebrated a provincial chapter at Oxford. He brought back to unity of practice the brothers who had begun to outrun the others by the singularity of their opinions. He made known throughout all the provinces the obedience and uprightness of the English brothers. He quieted the unrest of the brothers at Paris by personally reminding them at the university of the simplicity of their profession and pre-

---

24. He was released from office in August, 1247 and later became bishop of Jesi, 1252 to about 1263.
25. This incident is variously located in the different manuscripts.
26. John of Parma became general in 1247 and resigned in 1257; he suggested that Brother Bonaventure succeed him.
27. 1245-1247.

vailed upon them to revoke their appeal.[28] He made the ruling that the general chapter should be held alternately beyond the mountains and on this side of the mountains. Finally, not being able any longer to carry the weight of the office of minister general, he obtained permission to resign from the lord pope Alexander IV. The same father said, however, that the edifice of the Order was built upon two walls, namely, upon holiness of life and upon learning, and that the brothers had raised the wall of learning beyond the heavens and heavenly things in that they were posing the question whether God existed; the wall of holiness of life, however, they permitted to remain so low that it was said with great praise of a brother, "He is an untroubled brother." They therefore seemed not to be building properly. He wished, however, that the brothers should safeguard the reverence for their way of life against prelates and princes by their merits before the people rather than by any apostolic privileges, and that they should be the least amongst all by their humility and meekness.

Incident. Brother John of Parma, the minister general, in the full general chapter at Genoa,[29] ordered Brother Bonitius, who had been a companion of St. Francis, to tell the brothers the truth about the stigmata of the saint, because many in the world were doubting this matter. And he replied with tears: "These sinful eyes have seen them; and these sinful hands touched them."[30]

But Brother Leo, the companion of St. Francis, told

28. An appeal seems to have been made to the pope in the quarrel the brothers were having over the number of chairs they were entitled to at the university.
29. 1249 or 1251.
30. Manuscripts P and E omit this incident.

Brother Peter, the minister of England,[31] that the apparition of the Seraphim came to St. Francis while he was rapt up in contemplation and more clearly even than was written in his life;[32] and that many things were revealed to him at that time that he did not communicate to any living person.[33] But he did tell Brother Rufinus, his companion,[34] that when he saw the angel from afar, he was greatly afraid, and that the angel had treated him harshly; and he told him that his Order would continue to the end of the world, that no one of evil will would remain long in the Order, that no one who hated the Order would live long, and that no one who truly loved the Order would come to a bad end. But Saint Francis commanded Brother Rufinus to wash and anoint with oil the stone on which the angel had stood; this he did. These things Brother Warin of Sedenefeld wrote down from the lips of Brother Leo.

---

31. Peter of Tewkesbury.
32. See I Celano, II, 3.
33. See the *Legenda Major* of St. Bonaventure, Chapter 13, 4.
34. Brother Rufinus of Assisi was one of the three companions.

14. The Ministers Provincial of England

The first minister of England, therefore, was Brother Agnellus of Pisa,[1] as was said above; he was a man outstandingly endowed with natural prudence and was conspicuous for every virtue, for regularity and uprightness of life. After he had successfully completed the mission at the Roman curia which he had undertaken along with Brother Peter of Tewkesbury, who at that time was guardian of London, for the prelates of England and the Friars Preachers, he became ill of dysentery at Oxford, the result, it was said, of the cold and the labor which he had to bear when he went to make peace between the lord king and his earl marshal in the marches of Wales[2] and in his travels through England. However, after his dysentery had been checked with medicines, he was afflicted with an intestinal pain and a pain in the side, because of which he could hardly restrain himself from crying out. For three days in succession before he died, he cried out almost continuously: "Come, sweetest Jesus!" Therefore, after he had properly received the sacraments of the Church and was asked to give advice concerning his successor, he advised

---

1. Probably entered the Order in 1211 along with Albert of Pisa.
2. In 1223. The mission, however, was unsuccessful.

that Brother Hugh of Wells be sent to Brother Elias and that the brothers should ask that they be given as minister Brother Albert of Pisa, or Brother Haymo, or Brother Ralph of Rheims. He appointed, however, in so far as he had the power to do so, Brother Peter of Tewkesbury to be his vicar; and thus, after asking the prayers of the brothers individually, and after the prayers for the dying, in which he himself joined with the community, had been finished, he died in peace.[3] It seemed, however, to his companion, Brother Walter of Madeley, that a certain dead body lay in the choir which seemed to have been taken down from a cross but recently. For it had five bleeding wounds after the manner of the crucified Jesus Christ. He thought that it was the sweet Jesus Christ Himself, but upon coming close to it, he saw that it was Brother Agnellus.

After many years, however, when the brothers found it necessary to move his body, when, that is, they destroyed the chapel in which he had been buried before the high altar and in the choir,[4] they found the leaden coffin in which it lay and likewise the grave filled with the purest oil; the body itself and the clothing were incorrupt and gave off the sweetest odor.

> *Incident.* It is worth remembering that a venerable man, the master Serlo, dean of Oxford,[5] advised Brother Agnellus to eat but rarely outside the convent. It happened once that a certain guardian, on the same day that he preached to the people, was joking after the meal with

---

3. In 1236 most probably.
4. The Friars built a new church in 1246.
5. Some manuscripts have Exoniae, others Oxoniae, as was the case in an earlier place. We chose Oxford here in preference to Exeter, as was also done earlier. (T.N.)

a certain monk before a secular, for they had eaten with the brothers. The secular, however, said quietly to a certain brother who was his secretary that this talk was not becoming to a prelate and a preacher. But the guardian told me that he would have preferred to have had a lance thrust between his ribs than to have given such an example. For the brothers were so concerned for the good name of the Order, above all Brother Agnellus, who would not spare even the secretary of the king,[6] but removed him from the court and did not permit him to give or receive anything.

Incident. Brother Agnellus, after he had been for a long time minister of England though only a deacon, did not wish to be promoted to the priesthood before it had been obtained from the general chapter by the provincial chapter that it be commanded him. He was, however, so devout in the Divine Office, that not only when saying it at Mass, but also in choir and while on a journey, he seemed to weep continually, but in such a way that it could not be noticed by any noise or groan or twistings of the face. Likewise, he always said his Office standing, and he bitterly rebuked a brother who said his hours while sitting down after a blood-letting. When he felt that his death was drawing near, he said to Brother Peter of Tewkesbury: "You know my whole life." And when Brother Peter said that he had never made a general confession to him, he struck his head and began to cry loudly, and immediately he made a confession of his whole life to him with wonderful contrition. Afterwards,

---

6. Who he was is not known.

when the brothers had gathered, he absolved[7] them; and when they had begun, at his command, the prayers for the dying, he closed his eyes with his own hand and placed his hands upon his breast in the form of a cross.[8]

Therefore Brother Elias, when he had received the news that Brother Agnellus had died, immediately destroyed the provincial seal, the stamp of which bore the figure of a lamb with a cross, for he took it ill that the English brothers should ask for a minister by name. Wherefore, he delayed for almost a year to send them a minister. Finally, after recalling one he had sent, he commanded Brother Albert of Pisa, who had been minister of Hungary, Germany, Bologna, and of the Marches of Ancona, Treviso, and Tuscany, to go to England to be minister of the brothers there. He came therefore to England on the feast of St. Lucy,[9] and on the feast of the Purification[10] he celebrated a provincial chapter at Oxford and preached on this theme: *Look unto the rock whence you are hewn, and to the hole of the pit from which you are dug out.* Now since he did all things in regard to the brothers according to his own will, he tried in many ways the humility and meekness, the simplicity and zeal, the charity and patience of the brothers of England. Wherefore, though he had publicly told the brothers that they would find him until the end just as he showed himself in the chapter, nevertheless, from then on he day by day seasoned every sacrifice with the salt of the Gospel with more than ordinary wisdom, and thus was changed completely. For afterwards he so greatly ap-

---

7. Not sacramentally, but as the superior does in the chapter of faults.
8. Manuscripts P and E omit both these preceding incidents.
9. December 13, 1236.
10. February 2, 1237. The text is from Isaias 51, 1.

proved of the brothers of England that he gave himself to them with the whole affection of his heart and he bound them to himself by a bond that is beyond words; he found them at one with him in every proposal for greater perfection and ready to go with him to jail or into exile to effect the reform of the Order.

He commanded, therefore, that in the guest houses silence be kept aways at table, except when preachers or brothers from other provinces were present. He wanted the brothers also to put old tunics on top of new ones, both out of love for poor things and that the new ones might last longer. He destroyed the cloister at Southampton which was made of stone, though with great difficulty because of the opposition of the people of the village; and the deed or agreement that had been made between the monks of Reading and the brothers, namely, that the monks could not put them out just any time they wished, he returned to them with great fervor and offered to remove the brothers if the monks so wished. [Concerning the chapel of the place, however, since he could not destroy it because of the lord king who had built it, he wished that it would be destroyed by heaven.][11]

He placed brothers at Chester and Winchester, but only with great difficulty.[12] He received a mandate from Pope Gregory that the Friars Preachers might obligate no one in such a way that he would not be free to enter any Order of

---

11. This passage enclosed in brackets is only in manuscript E.
12. It seems the Bishop of Lichfield was opposed to their coming to Chester; this appears from a letter of Grosseteste to him, rebuking him. They got permission, however, and the king contributed toward their house, 1240. They were established in Winchester about 1237. See Little, p. 80.

his choice, and that his own novice brothers might not be received to profession except they had completed the year of probation. For they had been accustomed to make profession the very day they entered, if they so wished, as did Brother Robert Bacon.[13] The Friars Preachers, therefore, were much upset and they asked of the lord pope Innocent IV that no Friar Minor be allowed to receive those already obligated, and that, if any one did, he should be excommunicated by that very fact; and they wanted to be bound in the same way with regard to ours.[14] They put them under obligation in so many ways, and they published their privilege so much, that they left hardly any one unbound. But this sad condition did not last long. For Brother William of Nottingham of blessed memory and Brother Peter of Tewkesbury showed the pope what his predecessor had ordained; and, declaring that he had been deceived, the pope revoked his decree, though only after a harmful delay.[15]

One time Brother Albert said that we ought to love the Friars Preachers very much, because in many things they had helped our Order and occasionally they had taught us how to avoid future dangers.

Brother Albert said that three things especially have exalted our Order, namely, the bare feet, the poor quality of our clothing, and the rejection of money.

Brother Walter of Reigate said that it had been

13. He was a friar Preacher who died in 1248, according to A.G. Little.
14. There was considerable disturbance at this time among the Orders. They were trying to get young men and boys at a very early age and make them promise to enter a particular Order.
15. By the Bull *Non Solum*, June 17, 1244, which repeated the Bull of Gregory IX. It insisted too on the year of novitiate.

revealed to a certain brother in the province of St. Francis that the devils celebrated a council every year against the Order and that they had found three ways to injure it,[16] namely, familiarity with women, the reception of unworthy persons, and the touching of money.[17]

The minister, however, Brother Albert, was accustomed to say to his companion, Omnebonum by name, when he visited spiritual friends: "Eat, eat, now we can safely do so." But he remained away from all secular people as much as he could.

In those days it happened that two very famous brothers went to a house of a certain franklin[18] who received them honorably and set before them an abundance of food. And when they were sitting at dinner, the rector of the church came and rebuked them for not coming to him; and when he had repeatedly urged them to eat the meat set before them and could not shake their restraint, he became angry and said: "Eat, eat; for cold kills your bodies and gluttony kills your souls"; and rising he left.[19]

At Divine Office Brother Albert always stood devoutly, and with his eyes closed controlled the distractions of his mind. In the company of the brothers, he was always joyful and jocund and won for himself the affection of all.

Wherefore, when once he had had a blood-letting with the rest in the convent, he proposed the following parable to

---

16. Manuscript P adds these words: "contra ordinem ipsum."
17. The preceding two paragraphs occur at the end of chapter 13 in manuscript E.
18. A middle-class land owner.
19. The preceding two paragraphs are in reverse order in manuscripts C and E.

his companions, primarily for the sake of a certain novice who was present and was much too wise in his own eyes and presumed to inject himself into things that did not pertain to him. A certain farmer, he said, hearing that there was such great quiet and so many delights in Paradise, set out to find where it was and to learn if he might somehow get himself admitted. And when at last he had come to the gate, he found St. Peter and asked admittance. But when St. Peter asked him if he could keep the laws of Paradise and if he were determined to do so, he said he could, if he would deign to tell him what they were. Peter therefore said that he need only keep silence. When he willingly agreed to this, he was admitted. Going through Paradise, he saw a certain plowman with two oxen, the one thin, the other fat, and he allowed the fat one to go as he pleased, but the thin one he kept prodding on. And going up to him, he began to argue with him. Immediately St. Peter was there and wished to expel him; but he spared him this time, and commanded him to be on his guard. But going on, he saw a man carrying a long piece of wood who wanted to enter a house and always turned the wood crosswise to the door; and going up to him, he instructed him to turn the end of the wood to the door. Immediately there was St. Peter and he wanted in every way to expel him; but he spared him again this time. A third time he went on and saw a man cutting down trees in a woods; and he passed up the old trunks and crooked trees[20] and felled and cut up those that were straight and green and most beautiful. And going up to him, he rebuked him. And immediately there was St. Peter, and he did expel him. But Brother

---

20. Manuscripts P and E have *arboribus;* the others have *roboribus.* The former seems to be the correct form.

Albert wished that subjects everywhere should hold their superiors in reverence, saying: "Far be it from us that familiarity should breed contempt."

Brother Adam Marsh related that a certain extremely delicate boy, when he became ill and his father asked him to eat out of love for him, since he was his dearest son, replied that he was not his son. In the same way he answered his mother when she begged him strongly to eat. And when she asked whose son he was if not hers, he replied indignantly and impudently: "I am my own son." Thus too are those who are slaves to their own senses and will.[21]

Incident. In the conversation mentioned before, Brother Albert spoke a parable against the presumption of young men, saying that a certain bull used to go daily through the meadows and fields wherever he wished. One day, when about the first or third hour, he turned aside toward a plow and saw older oxen going along very slowly and plowing but little, he rebuked them and said that he could do as much with one pull. So they asked him to help them. When he was put under the yoke, he ran with great energy to the middle of the row and then, tired out, he began to breathe hard; and looking about, he said: "Now how is this? Is it not yet all finished?" And the older oxen answered that it was not yet done, ridiculing him. The bull said he could not go on. But the oxen said that they therefore worked more moderately because they had to work continuously and not just for a time.

[Brother Albert was present at Oxford for the sermon of a certain young brother in the chapter; and when he boldly

---

21. This passage is in the margin in manuscripts C and P.

condemned the superfluity of houses and the abundance of food, he corrected him for being vainglorious.][22]

He compelled Brother Eustace de Merc to eat fish contrary to custom, saying that the Order lost many good persons because of their indiscretion. He said, however, that when he was staying at a certain hospital with St. Francis, the saint compelled him to eat twice as much daily as he was accustomed to eat. He[23] showed himself so generous on another occasion that he severely rebuked a certain guardian and also the procurator because they had not provided the convent more abundantly after the labor of a certain solemn occasion. He was a man of such great piety and compassion that he gave an obedience to a certain brother in weak health to go to his native region and to travel about from place to place in the whole custody, if he wished, and he himself would repay his expenses, if the brothers were thereby burdened. After he had ruled nobly over England for two and a half years, he proceeded with many others against Brother Elias, and after serving as minister general he died a happy death at Rome amongst the English brothers.

Brother Haymo succeeded him; he cared for the brothers in a kindly way, in all peace and charity, in as much as he was a most kind and gentle person. He clothed with the habit of the Order the lord bishop of Hereford, Ralph of Maidstone,[24] in accordance with a vision he had of him when he was still archdeacon of Chester;[25] namely, that a certain boy came while he was seated and arranging the clergy in a

22. This passage in brackets occurs only in manuscript E.
23. Brother Albert, that is.
24. He resigned his see in 1239 and died in 1243.
25. Perhaps as early as 1221.

synod and threw water into his face, whereat the boy was immediately changed into a miserable young man. And Ralph came to the bed where Brother Haymo lay, and he asked him to let him lie there; and this he did. And in this way he gained a happy end in the Order. Brother Haymo ruled for one year in England and afterwards was elected minister general.

When Brother Haymo was minister provincial of England, [he said that a certain wave of troubles came upon the Order when the brothers had altars and cemeteries dedicated in their places so that they could not thereafter be converted to profane uses.][26] He was so zealous for poverty that in a provincial chapter he sat with the brothers upon the ground in the refectory, clothed in a very poor and torn habit.[27]

His vicar succeeded him, namely, Brother William of Nottingham; he was elected by the community and confirmed by those to whom this was committed.[28] Therefore Brother William, though he had not gained experience in the lower offices, such as those of guardian and custos, conducted himself so zealously that his zeal and uprightness became known throughout all the provinces.[29]

Brother William used to tell how St. Stephen, the founder of the Order of Grammont,[30] put a chest in a

---

26. The part enclosed in brackets occurs only in manuscript E.
27. This paragraph occurs at different places in the various manuscripts.
28. He was elected probably in the provincial chapter at London in 1241 and confirmed by the general.
29. He died in 1254.
30. He died in 1124.

secret and safe place and forbade any one to go there as long as he himself lived. The brothers were therefore tempted to find out what was in the chest; for the saint himself wanted all to follow his example in holding it in the greatest reverence. After his death, therefore, they could not wait and they broke it open and found nothing but a piece of paper with this on it: "Brother Stephen, founder of the Order of Grammont, salutes his brothers and begs that they keep themselves away from seculars. For, just as you, while you knew not what was in the chest, held it in great honor, so will they act with regard to you."[31]

---

31. This last paragraph occurs earlier in manuscript C.

15. The Advancement of Certain Brothers

Finally, I think it should be recorded for memory how, while many brothers were still living by whom the vineyard of the Friars Minor was planted in the English province, both in this province and in others the branches grew to such an extent that brothers were raised to various dignities and offices within the Order and outside of the Order, and indeed, they above all who had humbled themselves the most. For Brother Nicholas, who, while he was a lay brother, learned his letters in England, later became the confessor of the lord pope Innocent IV and after that bishop of Assisi.[1]

Likewise, a very young man, who was received as a lay brother, and to whom afterwards the glorious Virgin appeared and put her finger into his mouth as a sign that he would be a preacher and a lector, became not only a renowned preacher and a lector, but also an outstanding superior in the Order.[2] But who is capable of relating how singularly they advanced who entered the Order with such extraordinary fervor when

---

1. Nicholas of Carbio, who also wrote a life of Innocent IV.
2. A. G. Little seems to think that this could refer to St. Bonaventure (see the *Archivum Franciscanum Historicum*, XIX, p. 289-291). There is little likelihood that this is correct, since Brother Thomas is speaking about the English province.

the first Friars Minor came to England? Though they were capable university men and men of noble birth, they wore the caperon of probation; and later they conducted themselves both zealously and laudably as preachers or as lectors and in the government of the Order.

Brother Eustace de Merc, who first was guardian at Oxford for a long time, and later custos of York, observed even unto his death his customary abstinence, vigils, and bodily penances; but toward others he always maintained the suavity of angelic affection. When he was dying he repeatedly called upon the Mother of mercy with these heartfelt words: "By thy Son, oh Virgin, and by the Father and the Paraclete be with me at my death and my last going forth."[3]

Brother Robert of Thornham, who was at first guardian of Lynn and afterwards custos of Cambridge for many years, later still, with ineffable fervor, asked permission to go with the crusaders to the Holy Land;[4] after he had gained incomparable fame[5] both among seculars and among the brothers in the discharge of an important office, he showed us such great signs of salvation at his death that no one of the faithful could doubt about his salvation.

Brother Stephen Belassise,[6] who was at first guardian of Lynn, then custos of Hereford, was a man of such great kindness and perfection, that he gave witness to the zeal of his heart even by tears, when he saw that the strictness of

---

3. There seems to be a word missing in the manuscripts before the final *exitum*. Judging from the thought expressed it should most probably be *ultimum*. See A. G. Little, p. 89.
4. It was about 1250 that he asked to go to the Holy Land.
5. A word is missing here in the manuscripts. A. G. Little supplies *famam* or perhaps *affectum*.
6. The Latin is *de Belase;* A. G. Little suggests Belassise, but hesitantly.

religion was being relaxed. Released from all offices because of his overly great desire for quiet, he had *fruit unto sancti-fication, and as [his] end, life everlasting.*[7]

Brother William Cook,[8] though he was a man of great strength, nearly exhausted himself by his early labors in the custody of London and by other cares. At length he gave up his active life and gave himself to contemplation; rich in good works, he died in peace.

Brother Augustine, the blood brother of Brother William of Nottingham of blessed memory, at first belonged to the household of the lord pope Innocent IV; later he went to Syria with a nephew of the pope, the lord patriarch of Antioch,[9] and later still was made bishop of Laodicea.[10] He related publicly in the convent at London that he had been in Assisi for the feast of St. Francis and that Pope Gregory was there; when the pope went up to preach, the brothers chanted: "This one the saint chose as his father, when he ruled over a lesser church,"[11] and the pope smiled. The holy father related in that sermon how two heresiarchs were con-verted at Venice and sent to him with letters from the cardinals who were legates there. These letters told how both these heretics had seen one night at the same hour our Lord Jesus Christ seated as a judge with His apostles and all the religious Orders of the world; but they did not see any Friars Minor, not even St. Francis, who one of the legates said in a sermon was greater than St. John the evangelist

---

7. Romans 6, 22.
8. The Latin has *William Coche;* manuscript E has *de Coche.*
9. A. G. Little gives the name as Opizo de Flisco.
10. This was about 1250.
11. The antiphon at the first Vespers: "Hunc Sanctus praeelegerat in patrem, quando praeerat ecclesiae minori." See also I Celano II, 5.

because he had been marked with the stigmata. But they saw the Lord Jesus reclining on the bosom of St. John, and St. John on His. When they therefore accepted it as certain that this vision was given them in confirmation of their opinion—for they had thought that the legate had blasphemed and they were gravely scandalized and spoke out against the sermon—behold, the sweet Jesus opened the wound in His side with His hands and St. Francis appeared most clearly within His breast; and the sweet Jesus closed the wound and enclosed him completely within it. The heretics then awakened and, when they met each other the following day, they told each other the vision they had had; they then confessed publicly to the cardinals and, as was said, were sent to the pope and were fully reconciled by him.

Oh how deeply obligated, oh how sweetly overwhelmed by divine gifts, oh how immensely honored were they who could be guided in doubts by the advice of so many and such great persons who had the first-fruits of the Holy Spirit, and could be refreshed in sorrows, and spurred on in important affairs by the examples of such persons. Oh ineffable grace, oh incomparable privilege, oh inmost depths of inexhaustible sweetness, to enjoy familiarity with such great men, to be gladdened in the present pilgrimage of life by the special affection of such remarkable men, to be commended by the favor of such renowned persons.[12]

After the sermon there came some recently enlisted soldiers to the pope, and he placed a wreath of flowers upon the head of each; and from this there grew up the custom that all who would become soldiers received their arms on this

---

12. Manuscripts C and P have this paragraph in the margin.

feast.[13] On that feast the pope celebrated Mass outside the church on a table in the open air, because it could not be held in the church on account of the multitude of people.

Brother Peter of Tewkesbury, minister of Germany,[14] defended the status of the Order, with the help of God's grace, against the king and the legate and certain false brothers,[15] and he did this so well that the fame of his deed came to many provinces and zeal for truth proved invincible.

He merited the special affection of the lord bishop of Lincoln, from whom he often heard many secret words of wisdom. Once he said to him that unless the brothers fostered studies and gave themselves to the study of the divine law, it would most certainly happen to us as it happened to other religious, whom we see, sad to say, walking in the darkness of ignorance.

Likewise he said to Brother John of Dya[16] that he should provide for himself six or seven suitable clerics from his own territory upon whom he might confer benefices in his church, such clerics, namely, as could preach by example even though they did not know English. Whence it is certain that he did not refuse those whom the pope appointed and the nephews of cardinals on the grounds that they did not know English, but because they sought nothing but temporal advantages. Wherefore, when a lawyer said to him in the curia, "The canons ordain this," he replied, "Indeed, the canines ordain

13. The feast of St. Francis, that is.
14. Of Cologne in 1250.
15. The cause of the trouble is not known.
16. Or Diva, a prominent Friar Minor who served as papal nuncio to England in 1254 and served the pope and the king in other capacities.

this."[17] He arose and confessed in English, on bended knees, before the young men presented to him by the cardinals, and he struck his breast with weeping and wailing, and thus they withdrew in confusion.

Moreover, when the chamberlain of the lord pope sought a thousand pounds for his visit to the curia, and wanted him to borrow them from the merchants, he replied that he did not want to give them an occasion of sinning grievously, but if he returned safe to England he would deposit the money with the temple at London,[18] otherwise he would never get a penny.

Likewise, he said to a Friar Preacher: "Three things are necessary for the health of the body: food, sleep, and a joke." Also, he enjoined upon a certain melancholic brother that he drink a cup of the best wine as a penance; and, when he had drunk, though he did so unwillingly, he said to him: "My dearest brother, if you would have this penance more frequently, you would also have a better conscience."

Again Brother Peter related how, when the clerics of the saintly Edmund, the archbishop,[19] asked for a post for a certain relative of theirs who was a courier, the holy man replied: "If his cart is broken, I will have it repaired out of deference for your pleas; and if it cannot be repaired, I will buy him a new one. But, know you for certain, I will never change his status." The same holy bishop said, when some precious jewels were offered to him and he was admonished by those close to him to accept them: "If I take them, I will

17. The Latin has a play on words here which we have tried to give also in the English: "Canones hoc volunt." "Immo, canes hoc volunt." (T.N.)
18. That is, a house of the Knights Templar, which was used as a bank.
19. Edmund Riche, died 1240.

hang. For between the words *prendere* and *pendere* there is the difference of but one letter."[20]

Again, the same father, Brother Peter, related that when the lord Robert, bishop of Lincoln, was very much in need of horses at his promotion, his seneschal came to him while he was sitting at his books and announced to him that two white monks had come to present to him two very beautiful palfreys; and when he pestered him to accept them and urged that the monks were exempt,[21] he did not agree, nor did he move from his place, but said: "If I accept them, they will drag me to hell at their tails."[22]

The lord Robert Grosseteste, bishop of Lincoln, was once so gravely offended because the minister would not let a certain brother stay at his guest house, though he had done so before, that he did not want to talk to any brother, not even his confessor; and then Brother Peter said to him that if he were to give all his goods to the brothers but would not give them the affection of his heart, the brothers would care nothing for these things. The bishop began to weep and said: "In truth, you are sinning because you afflict me too grievously; for I cannot *not* love you, though I show such a face to you." Even though the brothers ate at his side at his table, he still would not speak to them.

The bishop told Brother Peter that places above water are not wholesome unless they are set on a high location. He also said that it had pleased him very much to see the patched sleeves of the brothers. Again, he

---

20. *Prendere* means to grasp, take; *pendere* means to hang.
21. And therefore there could be no suspicion of a bribe in their gift.
22. The foregoing anecdotes are in the margin in manuscript C.

said that pure pepper was better than ginger in a sauce. Again, he said that he rejoiced when he saw that his scholars did not care about his lecture, so long as he had provided it with the greatest diligence; because then there would be lacking to him any occasion for vainglory and he would not lose any of his merit.[23]

Now Brother Mansuetus, the nuncio of the lord pope Alexander IV, related to that same father[24] in the same place on the same day on which there was read in an audience the Letter by which Pope Innocent IV enacted eight propositions against the Friars Preachers and Friars Minor,[25] that he lost his speech except for this that he said afterwards: *"With rebukes for guilt you chasten man."*[26] Very frequently too he invoked St. Francis; for he said that even when he was in health he had not experienced so many favors from any other saint. But the lord Alexander IV, when he was at Ostia,[27] had said that it was certain the Lord would quickly take the pope from their midst because of the favor he granted that ran counter to the interests of the Order. Indeed, at his death, all his friends deserted him, except, however, the Friars Minor; and in the same way, it happened also to Popes Gregory, Honorius, and Innocent; at the death of the latter St. Francis himself was present. The same Brother Mansuetus added that no beggar, in fact no man at all, died so miserably and wretchedly as any pope.

---

23. The two preceding paragraphs are in the margin in manuscript C.
24. Brother Peter of Tewkesbury. They both were giving their reminiscences.
25. *Etsi animarum* of November 21, 1254. It restricted the religious in their ministerial functions even in their own churches.
26. Psalm 38, 12.
27. He was at that time protector of the Order.

Brother Mansuetus said that on the very day of his election the lord pope Alexander IV[28] suspended the Letter that the lord Innocent had granted against the Friars Preachers and Friars Minor, and afterwards the first act the pope executed was to revoke it. For Innocent had decreed that all brothers would be excommunicated if they allowed any parishioner to be present on any feast day to hear Mass and other things like this.[29]

He said also that a certain brother, standing in the garden in prayer in Sicily, saw a great army of five thousand horsemen marching into the sea; and the sea made a hissing sound as though they were all made of burning brass; and one of them said to him that it was the emperor Frederick entering into Mount Etna. Indeed, Frederick died at that very time.[30]

The same Brother Mansuetus also related how, when he was a boy of about ten years of age, he was told by the Friars Minor to hold the Blessed Eucharist in the greatest reverence. Therefore, in order that he might receive Holy Communion worthily on Easter, he, when he was still a little boy, fasted almost the whole Lent. And behold, on Easter day, when all the people were receiving Holy Communion, a certain very wicked and infamous man named Execius went to receive Holy Communion; and after thus receiving Holy Communion without the proper reverence, he immediately went aside and sat upon a bench and began to gossip with those standing by, caring no more at all than if he had just a morsel of bread in his mouth. And behold, Brother

---

28. He was elected December 12, 1254. The Bull *Nec insolitum* is dated December 22, 1254, the day after his coronation.
29. This paragraph is placed a few sentences earlier in some of the manuscripts.
30. Frederick II died December 13, 1250.

Mansuetus saw the sacred host go out of the mouth of that man and fall to the ground a great distance from him. He immediately went up to the priest, a most venerable man, and told him what he had seen. The priest immediately told him to go and seek where the sacred host had fallen; and when he sought, he quickly found it in that same place, even though the people had been going back and forth over that place for a long time to receive Holy Communion. The boy therefore reverently received that host and all the consecrated hosts that remained on the altar and he was confirmed in his faith beyond saying.

Brother Peter, the minister of England, also related how, when he was on the most familiar terms in the home of Sir Geoffrey le Despenser,[31] it happened that he came once to that house, and the son of the lord, John by name, a small boy, came to him, as was always his custom, in a most friendly way. But after the boy had gone with his mother to the chapel and was present while the said Father Peter celebrated Mass, when the latter came again to that house, the boy fled from him, nor could he be compelled in any way by his mother to go up to him. When his mother asked why he fled in that way, he said that he saw him eat an infant in the chapel at the altar and he was afraid he would do the same to him.[32]

Brother Warin of Orwell[33] entered the Order when he was still very young, and later he progressed so much that he lectured solemnly in many places not without the admira-

---

31. A marginal note is added in one manuscript: *Galfridus Spencer nota.*

32. See a similiar story about Brother Peter of Brabant in the *Chronica XXIV Generalium, Analecta Franciscana*, III, p. 240.

33. Little remarks that this is probably not the Warin of Ashwell known to Brother Adam Marsh.

tion of many; and he conducted himself prudently in dealing familiarly with the great, he carried on the business of the Order in a praiseworthy manner, and he excelled incomparably in the office of preaching and in the practice of contemplation. Finally, at the same ninth hour,[34] he died before the altar at Southampton, clasping and kissing the crucifix. There appeared to Brother Simon of Wynbourne at Salisbury a certain brother by the name of John who had died long before, and he said that all was well with himself and that Brother Warin had passed through Purgatory without any delay and had gone to the Lord Jesus Christ.

The English province advanced to such great perfection that the minister general John of Parma frequently said when he was in England: "How I wish this province were placed in the middle of the world that it might be an example to all." This general celebrated a provincial chapter of England at Oxford in which he confirmed the provincial statutes concerning frugality and poverty in regard to buildings. When he gave the brothers the option of confirming or releasing the minister provincial, they asked unanimously that he be confirmed.[35]

But the aforementioned Brother William told how once, when the bishop of Lincoln of pious memory, who at that time was lecturing to the Friars Minor at Oxford,[36] preached in the chapter of the brothers on poverty, he put mendicancy on the rung of the ladder of poverty closest to the attainment of heavenly things. But he told Brother William privately that there was still a higher degree, namely, to live by one's

---

34. The same hour at which Christ died.
35. William of Nottingham, spoken of again in the next paragraph.
36. Probably from 1230 to 1235.

own labor; wherefore he said that the Beguins[37] belong to the most perfect and most holy religious state, because they live by their own labor and do not burden the world with their demands.

That same memorable father also said that there was a certain novice who wished to abstain[38] and he told his master that he was resolved to try little by little to see what he could do. His master gladly granted him permission. And after he had gone on a while and had told the master at his frequent asking that he was well, he finally began to be afraid that he was growing weak and he told his master this. The latter answered: "Hurry, then, for the love of God and eat and drink, else you will fail, for your faith is failing. Thus too when Peter began to fear, he sank beneath the waves."

Moreover, he said that it was necessary to consider the mind of St. Francis and his intention in the Rule; otherwise, as the hairs of the beard grow insensibly, so also do super-fluities grow in the Order. It is important also to struggle against the temptations of the world even more than is just necessary, otherwise it will draw us lower than we would wish, just as the water does to those who wish to cross to the other side and head directly for the opposite shore.

He also said that a man does not know if it will be hard for him to move from a place, except by experience, just as he does not advert to the fact that his hair are attached to his head unless they are pulled.

He himself studied most earnestly the Holy Scriptures

---

37. Beguins or Beghards were a semimonastic Order of laymen founded in the thirteenth century in Flanders.
38. The Latin word is *abstinentiam*, but fasting seems to be meant; the one was included in the other.

and he zealously helped those studying them. He always wanted to have a reading at the tables outside the refectory, and he venerated the name of Jesus with a special affection and he meditated most devoutly on the words of the holy Gospel; wherefore he compiled some very useful canons on the *Unum ex quatuor* of Clement[39] and he arranged that the explanation the same Clement made be written out completely for the Order.

In the meditation after Matins he sat for an especially long time, nor would he hear confessions or give advice at night as his predecessors had done. He also said that just as it is worse to give a false principle for doing something than to do something badly, so also are false opinions about the deeds of the Order worse than imperfect works. Only with the greatest difficulty would he believe what some one would tell him, unless he were willing to tell before many what he wished to denounce, and he tried to avoid above every thing else the vice of suspicion.

Familiarity with great persons and with women he avoided most studiously, and with admirable magnanimity he made light of the anger of the powerful in matters of justice. He said once that the great ensnare their friends by words of advice, and women, since they are deceitful and malicious, turn the heads of even the devout by their words of flattery. He tried with all diligence to restore the reputation of those who had lost their good name, so long as he saw that they were contrite, and he took care with the greatest wisdom to strengthen the hearts of the desolate, especially if they held offices in the Order.

---

39. Clement of Llanthony's *Concordance of the Four Gospels.*

Therefore, after he had ruled the province of England for fourteen years, he was released from office in the chapter of Metz,[40] and was sent to the pope on behalf of the general chapter. But when he had come with the minister general to Genoa, his companion Brother Richard was stricken with a pestilence that was raging; and when all others fled, Brother William remained to console his companion, and he too was struck down and died. The brothers of England, however, after they had heard that he had been released from office, and being unaware of his death, called together a provincial chapter and re-elected him. When the minister general heard that this had been done more out of an impulse of affection than out of a judgment of reason, he called together again the chapter through the vicar, namely, Brother Gregory of Bossells, and commanded that none should be re-elected who had been released by the general chapter; the confirmation of the one elected, however, he left to Brother John of Kethene, Brother Adam Marsh, and Brother John of Stamford.[41] But Brother Peter of Tewkesbury was elected and confirmed at the chapter.

When Brother Elias was released from office it was asked of Pope Gregory if he could then be re-elected, and the pope replied that he could not be.[42]

When certain brothers wished that debts should not by any means be contracted, Brother William told me that the brothers ought not oblige themselves in any way to pay a debt, nor should they fix a time for payment,

---

40 In 1254.
41. He was custos of Oxford at this time and later, 1258, minister provincial.
42. This sentence is in the margin in manuscripts C and P.

but they might licitly oblige themselves to do what they could to bring about payment.

He also said that in a hundred cases the brothers could licitly contract debts. And he said that a brother did not sin, if he dispensed with his own hands another person's money as alms.

Brother William said too that when he was staying for a long time in the convent at Rome and the brothers had no food but chestnuts, he became so fat that he was very much ashamed. Moreover, he told me that when he was growing up in his father's house and the poor boys came asking alms, he gave them some of his bread and accepted a crust from them, because it seemed to him that a piece of hard bread, begged for the love of God, was sweeter than the dainties on which he and his companions were nourished; wherefore, to make their own food sweet, the young boys went out and begged from one another for the love of God.

He said also that after a visitation he found it necessary to take some recreation to get his mind off the things he had heard. He told me that the sweet Jesus would raise up a new Order to spur us on to greater effort, and this I think was fulfilled in the Order of Penance of Jesus Christ.[43] For he had previously recommended to our brothers the brothers of the Order of St. Augustine in the chapter at Stamford.[44] Also he had

---

43. These were the Saccati or Brothers of the Sack. Salimbene speaks of them at the end of chapter 6 of his chronicle in this volume. Their founder was Raymond Atanulfi. They came to England in 1257.

44. These brothers were granted the protection of Henry III in 1249.

long before received everywhere as guests of our brothers the brothers of the Order of Carmel, whom Sir Richard de Grey[45] brought to England when the Earl Richard returned from Syria.[46] [The lord bishop Robert of Lincoln rejected the Order of the Crucifers; and in a similar way the brothers of the Order of the Cross were rightly rejected.][47] But the brothers of the Order of the Trinity had come to England long before; this Order was founded by divine guidance under Innocent III by the master of theology John, to whom Jesus Christ appeared while he was celebrating Mass in the presence of the bishop of Paris and his clergy.[48]

Brother Peter first received the brothers of Penance of Jesus Christ and recommended them in the chapter at London. This Order had its beginning in Provence at the time of the Council of Lyons and was founded by a novice who had been dismissed.[49] In the third year of the administration of Peter[50] the brothers of the Order of Martyrs came to England;[51] their founder was a certain Martin who at Paris had been somewhat the fool of the nobles of Germany.[52]

---

45. Baron of Cudnor.
46. The Earl of Cornwall; he returned from Syria in January 1242.
47. Fratres Ordinis S. Mariae de Ordine Cruciferorum came to England in 1244. The Fratres de S. Cruce came in 1249. The sentence in brackets is only in manuscript E.
48. That is, in 1224.
49. Raymond Atanulfi was rejected because of weak health.
50. Probably, therefore, in 1257.
51. Nothing more is known of these brothers, except that Alexander IV denounced them in a Bull in 1260.
52. This last sentence is not found in manuscript E. Manuscript E

adds the following paragraph and comes to a conclusion with it. Obviously it was not written by Brother Thomas:

A certain brother discreet said there are two things that the brothers love very much and a third that they are often given to: the two things they love are poverty without penury and patience without insults; the third thing that they are often given to is prayer without devotion.

Manuscript P concludes with the following paragraph, written in another hand, and evidently not pertaining to the *De Adventu*:

A certain John, who, while he was in the world, was a man of great strength, in as much as he was very tall, and a man of substance, though but poorly educated, after he had been clothed with the habit and professed, fulfilled the office of janitor even until he was an old man. A little before he died, he announced the hour of his death with the greatest certitude, saying that on a certain night it had seemed to him in a dream that he had to go up a high mountain. But when he had gotten half way up on hands and feet, behold, many boys, dancing and with very happy faces, cried to him from the top: "Brother John, why do you halt your progress there? Come on up." And immediately some took him by the arms, others by the cord, others by the sleeves, and led him joyfully to the top of the mountain. "I believe," he said, "that the young and the poor whom I refreshed at the door with what was left from the brothers' table will help me get to heaven quickly." And saying this, he soon gave forth his spirit into the hands of the Savior.

THE CHRONICLE

of

BROTHER SALIMBENE

degli ADAMI

Selections

INTRODUCTION

1. THE AUTHOR

Brother Salimbene degli Adami never received any dignity in the Franciscan Order, although, as he tells us, he would not have refused such. Yet, we are told more about him than about the most eminent personages of his Order, since he is an incorrigible busy-body, and, besides, being rather vainglorious, he delights in giving us a multitude of details about himself and about his kindred. In a familiar way, he mixes in his own history with the history of the world and the history of his Order, and the result is a chronicle that is very animated and very interesting. He is moreover our only witness about himself; since he filled no offices in the Order, since he knew how to give up his somewhat dubious ideas when they got to be dangerous, since he shunned anything that would compromise himself, he has remained in obscurity and no one has told us about him. Outside of his own chronicle we find just his name mentioned and that only once as a witness to an act of religious investiture.

Our chronicler was born at Parma on October 9, 1221 of a middle class family. He received at baptism the name of Balian of Sagitta, or of Sidon, which was the name of his godfather; but his parents called him familiarly *Omne bonum,* in Italian *Ogni bene.* He studied the seven liberal arts, and then on February 4, 1238 he left his father's house, betook himself to the convent of Friars Minor at Parma and asked to be admitted into the Franciscan Order. After some long discussions with his father, he obtained permission to stay. He was sent to Jesi, later to Lucca. After a year of novitiate, he made profession; from then on he went by the name of Brother Salimbene. Shortly after his profession, he met the last brother who had received the habit from St. Francis. When this brother heard in astonishment that he was called Ognibene, he said: "Brother, only one person is entirely good, and that is God; I say therefore that your name will be Brother Salimbene,[1] for you have leaped well in entering a good religious Order."[2] He accepted the name Salimbene, though he said he would have preferred to be called Dionysius, "not only on account of the greatness of that eminent doctor who was a disciple of St. Paul," but also because he had been born on the day of his feast.[3]

---

1. Thus his name was changed from *All-good* to *Leap-into-good.*
2. Chronicle, η. 38 in the Holder-Egger edition.
3. Chronicle, p. 39.

He lived afterwards at Lucca, at Sienna where he was ordained subdeacon, at Pisa where he was made deacon in December 1246, at Cremona, and at Parma. From this city he was sent in 1247 to Paris to study. His stay in that most famous house of studies in the Order lasted but one week; but he made two long journeys through France between which he spent the winter of 1248-1249 at Genoa where he received the priesthood. In May 1249 he returned to Italy for good and he lived at Ferrara from 1249-1256. After that he lived in the following cities: Modena, Borgo San Donnino, Bologna, Ravenna, Faenza, Parma, Forli, Imola, Bagnacavallo, Reggio, Montefalco, etc. He lived at some of these places several times and the chronology of his various residences is therefore not always easy to establish.

We do not know when he died. The last event for which the date is given in the chronicle is the siege of Monte-cavalo which took place in June 1288. It is therefore probable that he died shortly after that; but since the last pages of the chronicle are lost, in the same way as are the first, we cannot know precisely when he died.

He wrote other works too that are however lost. Also, we do not have that part of the chronicle that he wrote during his stays at the convents of Reggio and Montefalco between the years 1283 and 1288 for his niece, Sister Agnes, a Poor Clare nun. "I use a simple and understandable style so that my niece, for whom I write, can understand what I write; I do not bother myself over elegance of words, but rather to write historical truth."[4] His chronicle, however, does not seem to be something one would recommend for reading

---

4. Chronicle, p. 187.

to a young religious since there are a great number of im-
proper stories found in it.[5]

Brother Salimbene does not allow us to be ignorant about
himself; we can therefore come to know perfectly his character,
his good qualities, and his faults which he does not seek by
any means to hide. He is a boon companion, always gay;
he loves good cheer, good wines, and good stories. He is
very inquisitive and very loquacious and in this we are lucky,
for he gives us a multitude of details about the history of
his Order that other more serious authors pass over in silence.
He is often sharp-tongued, but because of him we know
also the reverse side of the tapestry. He is prudent, however,
in always trying to verify the subjects he proposes when they
are other than mere gossip.

A question that a person does not think to propose with
regard to Brother Jordan or Brother Thomas merits discussion
here. At that period, the secular clergy gave cause only too
often to remark about their deplorable morals, and one can
speak with reservations in the same way about the life of
many of the religious. But what about Salimbene, who loved
stories a bit off color and who loved the pleasures of life
so much; were his morals pure? He tells us they were. He is
our only witness to this though; but even so it seems that
one can believe him; he does not hide his faults, and, since
he is so boastful, we can suppose with a good deal of prob-
ability that if he had had some extra-curricular escapades
he could not have resisted the pleasure of telling us about
them. Moreover, he was otherwise prudent too, and he fled
carefully from the occasions of sin. He gets angry at the clerics

5. Brother Jordan and Brother Thomas, on the other hand, have
   nothing like this in their chronicles.

who wished to lead him to do wrong and he employs the most violent terms for impure priests.

His faults are otherwise redeemed by his more solid qualities. He is very much attached to his Order; he defends it with ardor and on every occasion against the calumnies of the enemies of the Friars Minor. He is deeply pious; his religious sensibility is lively and sincere, perhaps on occasion a little naive. He respects profoundly whatever pertains to religion. Like his confrere Brother Thomas of Eccleston, he has the greatest respect for the sacrament of the Eucharist. On the other hand, he seems little attached to the memory of St. Francis. This profound piety, this lively attachment to the Order are traits that are had in common by Brother Jordan, Brother Thomas, and Brother Salimbene, and, without a doubt, by many, many other Franciscans of that period.

2. THE MANUSCRIPTS AND EDITIONS

The problems of textual criticism that arise for the chronicles of Brother Jordan of Giano and of Brother Thomas of Eccleston do not arise for that of Brother Salimbene. We must be content with the single incomplete manuscript that we possess and which has been in the Vatican Archives since the seventeeth century.[6] The pages have been folioed from ancient times so that we know with certainty that the first 207 pages are missing. The part that remains begins with considerations of world history, copied faithfully from another chronicle which we possess. We have therefore lost the first part of the copy of this history which probably went back to Ptolemy, but the loss is not too important. From the allusions

---

6. Vatican 7260.

that occur in the course of the chronicle we learn that Salimbene had begun by writing a prologue in which he set down some of his personal philosophical reflections. The loss of this prologue is more regrettable.

Some pages are missing in the course of the narrative as well as the last part of it. The last page is page 492, but we have a reference to page 506; at least fourteen pages therefore are missing.

It is almost certain that the manuscript is an autograph. The handwriting is that of the end of the thirteenth century. It would be a mistake to consider it a copy made by a contemporary of the author. This is not very likely, for since that time no one seems ever to have made a copy of the manuscript. The chronicle has too much the character of an autobiography to have offered anything of interest to a fourteenth or fifteenth century copyist. Moreover, the manuscript is free from copyists' errors; words are not misread, or badly transcribed; lines are not skipped. A copy so perfect is just not conceivable.

In 1857 the chronicle of Salimbene was edited in part at Parma. Unfortunately this edition was too defective to be really useful.[7] A new edition was necessary. The direction of the German collection *Monumenta Germaniae Historica* was entrusted to the care of Dr. Holder-Egger who produced an edition that one can cite as an example. Its exactitude is surprising and the editor was careful to use different type to distinguish the text of Salimbene from the very many quotations he incorporated into his narrative. The editor tried to identify these quotations and he succeeded admirably

---

7. Salimbene d'Adam, *Chronica Fr. Salimbene Parmensis Ordinis Minorum ex codice Bibliothecae Vaticanae nunc primum edita*, Parma, P. Fioccadori, 1857.

in almost all cases; this is all the more noteworthy since Salimbene often cites texts from memory in an imperfect form and, when he indicates the references, he sometimes gives them erroneously.

In 1942 a scholarly Italian, who had published a great number of articles about Brother Salimbene, Ferdinando Bernini, prepared a new edition of the chronicle of Brother Salimbene in a more manageable format.[8] According to Bernini, the mediocre knowledge of Italian that Holder-Egger had led him to make some errors in reading Latinized Italian words. Bernini corrected these. But his edition, more simple than that of Holder-Egger, does not render the same services. If the reading is better on certain points, there is not, on the other hand, that same research with regard to the citations; there are no footnotes, unlike the Holder-Egger edition, so that one must use the latter in reading the text of Bernini.

3. The Style and Historical Value
of the Chronicle

The chronicles of Brother Jordan and Brother Thomas are relatively short. Brother Jordan recounts events in a simple manner, without adding commentaries. Brother Thomas is more prolix, and in the narrative of events he adds some narratives of apparitions, visions, and miracles which break up the unity of the narrative and make his chronicle almost twice as long as that of Brother Jordan. Brother Salimbene has written an enormous narrative and one that is occasionally without form. He had the ambition to write a universal history, but this history is lost since it occupied the first part of his

---

8. Salimbene degli Adami, *Cronica*, edited by Ferdinando Bernini, 1942, 2 vols. (Scrittori d'Italia, 187 and 188.)

chronicle. He followed that with a history of his personal adventures mixed with a history of the Order and a history of his times. In the beginning he follows a chronological order, but thereafter he roams about in interminable digressions, goes backwards, makes mention of future events, mixes into the whole thing biblical and profane texts, then takes up again the thread of his narrative after interminable pages of desultory subjects.

However, in spite of the number of digressions, the chronicle is amusing and pleasant reading. Brother Salimbene traveled about a good bit; he went over all the roads of Italy and France; he lived in a large number of convents. When he writes his chronicle, in his sixties, he tells us what he has seen. He mentions the name of a town or a person, and then recalls immediately a number of memories associated with them; he lets himself go in telling about these and, since he has an excellent talent for telling stories, his animated narratives captivate us. His portraits are very vivid and well drawn; his descriptions, precise and imaginative.

The language he uses is not worse than that of his contemporaries. His Latin is clear; he does not try too much to construe lofty phrases. He cites some proverbs, some expressions of popular wisdom. He likes figures of speech and comparisons.

The personal nature of the work is perhaps what makes the chronicle such an agreeable reading experience. Brother Salimbene keeps himself constantly in the scene; in the narrative of events he adds his own reflections. They are often very sagacious and they have this merit that they give us the intimate and spontaneous sentiments of an historian contemporary with the facts he relates.

Brother Salimbene had a part in many events and he knew some great personages. He had seen the Emperor Frederick II, had conversed familiarly with Pope Innocent IV; he met St. Louis when the latter was going on the crusade. Few of the other Franciscans had such encounters. He also knew some outstanding personages within the Order; Brother Elias, the Blessed John of Parma, Brother Hugh of Digne, and Brother John of Pian di Carpine whom he met on the latter's return from a mission to the Tartars which was one of the great adventures of the Middle Ages. The personal memories he reports about all these great people add an interesting and often very graphic point of view to things we already know.

But we regret that we do not find there are some memories about St. Francis; the person of the holy founder of the Order is almost completely absent from the chronicle, and, if we had no other testimony than the narrative of Brother Salimbene, we would be led to think that the radiance of the master had been dimmed almost to extinction.

Apart from the interesting memories presented in the chronicle, Brother Salimbene recounts some stories that are trifling and without importance so far as the events of the times are concerned. We learn that in 1282 there was such an abundance of caterpillars that the trees lost all their leaves; but the "Sicilian Vespers,"[9] which occurred the same year, is merely mentioned. One year he tells us there was an abun-

---

9. That is, the great massacre of the French in Sicily by the people there in 1282. The massacre began at Palermo on the Monday of Easter week at the hour of Vespers. See: Webster's *New Collegiate Dictionary*.

dance of early fleas and another year an abnormally high death rate amongst the chickens. He therefore scatters about an abundance of useless details.

We encounter entire pages that we might just as well pass by, some biblical quotations side by side with profane quotations, some interminable and obscure theological discussions, made up, for the most part, of citations of all kinds. Salimbene also gives us his opinion about events, great and small; but about great events he does this with extraordinary aplomb. Often he is interesting; but occasionally he is not interesting at all. It is necessary therefore to cut freely from this jumble of dull material.

What value is to be given to the testimony of Brother Salimbene? He recounts unlikely stories along with serious things, stories of visions and fantastic miracles. He has some historical errors. He puts Henry III, for instance, for Henry IV and sends to Canossa an emperor who never went there. But the errors are rare, and in general he is well informed. Wherever we can verify his testimony from other sources, we find that he is almost always exact. However, he occasionally lets himself be carried away by passion and in his treatise *De Prelato,* inserted into the chronicle and devoted to Brother Elias, there are some items of bitter gossip that are entertaining but proposed without prudence.

We learned from Brother Jordan and Brother Thomas how the Franciscans spread through Germany and England and how they lived in those countries. It is now time to learn how the Friars lived in France. Brother Salimbene made two trips into that country, he spent about a year and a half there, and these trips remained for him the most conspicuous event of his life; accordingly, he gives us a rather long account of them. His stay in France came between the years 1247 and 1249. This is a little after the events of the greater part of the narrative of Brother Jordan who wrote in 1262 but whose narrative covers for the most part the years from 1219 to 1238. But Salimbene's account of his travels in France falls within the years covered by Brother Thomas's chronicle. The latter's chronicle covers the years from 1224 to 1258 and, as was said, Brother Salimbene's stay in France occurred between 1247 and 1249. Salimbene's account of his stay in France complements, therefore, the very useful testimony of Brother Jordan about Germany and of Brother Thomas about England.

With these latter two chroniclers we have witnessed the arrival of the Friars Minor in Germany and in England and the spread of the ideal of St. Francis in those countries. With Brother Salimbene we come to France after the Friars Minor have been established there for almost twenty-five years. We do not see, therefore, the Franciscans arriving in France, and the sources for the history of their arrival are very meager. On the other hand, Brother Salimbene lets us get more intimately into the interior of the convents. We live with him the life of the Franciscans and we participate with great abandon in their conversation, for Brother Salimbene is quite loquacious. We likewise accompany him on his journeys. His testimony about the life of the simple brother, of the "average" Franciscan, completes in a useful way that of Brother Thomas who expatiates but little on this subject and that of Brother Jordan who does not give us many more details. But we regret that Brother Salimbene was not present when the Friars Minor first arrived in France for we are obliged on that account to be satisfied with what Brother

Jordan and Brother Thomas tell us and with what we can find in other rare texts.

4. FRANCE AND THE FIRST FRANCISCANS

When St. Francis sent his sons traveling through the world in the general chapter of 1217, he reserved for himself the founding of the mission of France. The saint had a special predilection for that country which is explained, perhaps, by a possible French origin of his family.[10] Francis spoke French and often expressed himself in that language; he knew the medieval epic poems, the chansons de geste, and the poems of the troubadours. At his baptism he was given the name John in the absence of his father; but when his father returned he changed it to Francis, perhaps because of his love for France. It is probable, though not certain, that in his youth Francis accompanied his father on his business trips through France. Thomas of Celano gives a moving testimony to St. Francis' love for France: "He loved France in as much as it was the friend of the Body of Christ, and he wished to die in that country out of respect for the love of the people of France for sacred things."[11] St. Francis expressed this same idea in the chapter of 1217 when he said: "In the name of our Lord Jesus Christ and of the glorious Virgin Mary, His mother, and of all the saints, I choose the country of France in which there is a truly Catholic people. What pleases me above all is the great reverence they, more than all other Catholics, show for the Body of our Lord Jesus Christ. Surely

---

10. Cf. G. Bastianini, *Lorsque Dieu passe,* Paris, Editions Franciscaines, 1957, appendix II, pp. 268-272.
11. Thomas of Celano, *Vita II,* no. 201, apud *Analecta Franciscana,* Vol. X, p. 245.

there can be nothing more agreeable on account of which I would wish to live among them."[12]

But the journey of St. Francis was interrupted at Florence; Cardinal Hugolino prevented him from going farther. "He advised him not to continue the journey he had begun, but to devote himself solicitously to the care and protection of those whom the Lord had committed to him."[13] Another witness states that Cardinal Hugolino said: "My brother, I do not want you to go beyond the mountains, because there are, in the Roman curia, a number of prelates and other people who seek to do harm to the interests of your Order."[14] So St. Francis sent in his place Brother Pacificus of the Marches[15] who became also the first minister provincial of France.

The brothers were totally unknown beyond the Alps. They presented themselves without letters of recommendation. Now the Council of Paris, about 1212, had forbidden clerics to be admitted to its celebration who could not show letters attesting to their good character and had forbidden any unknown stranger to be admitted to Holy Communion or to be given ecclesiastical burial.[16] On the other hand, the fourth Lateran Council, two years before the friars went to France, had forbidden the foundation of new religious Or-

---

12. Brother Leo, *Speculum Perfectionis,* ed. by Paul Sabatier, Vol. I, p. 180, Manchester, University Press, 1928.
13. Thomas of Celano, *Vita I,* no. 75, apud *Analecta Franciscana,* Vol. X, p. 56.
14. *Legenda Antiqua,* 74.
15. Brother Pacificus was court poet for King Henry VI before his entry into the Order and had been named "King of Verses" by that king. He died about 1230, perhaps in France.
16. Charles Joseph Hefele and H. Leclerc, *Histoire des Conciles,* Paris, Letouzey et Ané, 1907-1921, Vol. V, p. 1309.

ders. The brothers therefore were immediately seized as Albigenses. Brother Jordan tells us of their misadventures.[17]

It seems that Brother Pacificus led his brothers to Paris, but before he arrived there, according to one tradition, he left some of them at Vézelay with Brother Louis.[18] They built a small convent there next to the church of the Holy Cross; the convent was called the "Cordelle." The rest went on to Paris. Their first establishment there was on the outskirts of the city, near the Benedictine Abbey of St. Denis. Brother Gregory of Naples wrote somewhat later to the abbot of St. Denis, as is recorded in a letter of October 26, 1231:[19] "Not long ago we came as Pilgrims to St. Denis; we had not whereon to rest our heads; you installed us in a house that belonged to you. . . . We recognize without evasions that in that house behind the church of St. Peter we were received to live there as guests and we claim nothing as our own; besides, we will leave that house, with no complaint, on the day you should choose to order us to do so. . . ." The brothers were still living at St. Denis in 1231 and it was at this house that Haymo of Faversham received the Franciscan habit on April 12, 1224, a fact that Brother Thomas of Eccleston records in his chronicle.[20]

Two authors of the sixteenth century, Gilles Corrozet[21]

17. See number 4 of Brother Jordan's chronicle.
18. Cf. Abbé M.A. Despiney, *La Cordelle de Vézelay, premier couvent franciscain de la province de France,* Le Pélerin de Vézelay, No. 15, April 1926, pp. 180-198.
19. Archives nationales, L.854.
20. Chapter VI.
21. Gilles Corrozet, *Les Antiquitez, croniques et singularitez de Paris,* Paris, Nicolas Bonfons, 1586-1588.

and Francois de Belleforest,[22] assure us that they saw the remains of the convent of the Friars Minor on the Montagne Ste.-Geneviève, in the place where a little later the Collège de Navarre stood. Corrozet is quite certain of this: "Next to the convent of the Friars Preachers, the good St. Louis founded that of St. Francis and of the Friars Minor who are called cordeliers. The holy group of Friars lived of old on the spot where at present stands the Collège de Navarre; one can still see traces of the dormitory and of the cells of the Friars. But the saintly king, seeing that the place was ill suited for the solitude of these angelic men, moved them near the gate of St. Germain and on the Rue Haute-fueille. . . ."[23]

But how can we reconcile this text with that of Brother Thomas who tells us: "When Brother Henry of Burford was clothed at Paris, there were only thirty brothers in that convent. They were building at that time in a place which was called Valvert, in which they built a long and high house, which seemed to many brothers to be contrary to the state of poverty of the Order. Wherefore, some of the brothers, and in particular Brother Angeler,[24] begged St. Francis to destroy it. And behold, when the brothers were about to go into it, by divine disposition no one took up his abode there, for the roof and the walls collapsed to the very basement. . . . And so they gave up the place."[25]

We know, however, that the house of Valvert collapsed in 1229, for a contempory, Jean de Garlande, tells us: "In the year of our Lord 1229 . . . the high house of the Minors,

---

22. Francois de Belleforest, La Cosmographie universelle de tout le monde, Paris, M. Sonnius, 1575.
23. Corrozet, op.cit., Vol. I, p. 82.
24. All the manuscripts give Angeler. Perhaps Agnellus is meant.
25. See chapter 10 of the chronicle of Thomas of Eccleston.

which was built for them at Valvert, collapsed."[26]

Did the Friars ever live at Valvert or on the Montagne Ste.-Geneviève? A text of Bartholomew of Pisa may help us to understand a little what happened: "The latter [Brother Agnellus] was the first to build a convent in Paris; he was the custos of Paris."[27] Now Brother Agnellus went to England in September 1224. There cannot be question here therefore of the house that collapsed in 1229, for it is hardly likely that the brothers would spend five years building a house that would collapse at the moment they were ready to take possession of it. It is therefore probable that Brother Agnellus built before 1224 the convent of the Montagne Ste.-Geneviève, traces of which Corrozet and Belleforest saw in the sixteenth century, so that the brothers at St. Denis could follow the courses of theology at Paris. This is confirmed by a legacy of ten pounds in January 1223 by "Master Barthèlemy de Bruyères ... to the Friars Minor of Paris,"[28] which seems to indicate that at that time the Franciscans were already established elsewhere than at St. Denis.

It seems, therefore, that the brothers had settled at St. Denis in 1217 and that, keeping that house, they went before September of 1224 and very probably before January of 1223 to the Montagne Ste.-Genevieve. A little before 1229, they made an effort to build a house at Valvert, which, however, collapsed.

---

26. Jean de Garlande, *De Triumphis Ecclesiae*, ed, by Thomas Wright, London, J. B. Nichols, p. 99.
27. Bartholomew of Pisa, *De Conformitate vitae Beati Francisci ad vitam Domini Jesu, Analecta Franciscana*, Vol. IV and V.
28. Leon Briele, *Archives de l'Hotel-Dieu de Paris*, Paris, Ernest Coyecque, 1894.

We find them afterwards, according to Corrozet, "near the gate of St. Germain and on the Rue de Haute-fueille." We possess, in fact, an act of May 1230 in which William of Auverne, bishop of Paris, gave notice to the abbot and the abbey of St. Germain des Près, that they should cede, on certain conditions, a site, with some houses, to the Friars Minor where they could live as guests. ". . . They can have neither bells, nor a cemetery, nor a consecrated altar, nor a portable altar, nor a consecrated chapel, and they must safe-guard the rights of the parish church of SS. Cosmas and Damian. . . ."[29]

The Friars Minor were now solidly established there. Little by little, in the course of the thirteenth century, a series of donations and acquisitions put the "great convent of the cordeliers" on a firm basis and it lasted up to the Revolution, even though the church, built through the gen-erosity of St. Louis, burned down in 1580.

Brother Pacificus did not contribute to these transfor-mations; he returned to Assisi, probably in 1223. Brother Gregory of Naples was sent to succeed him as minister pro-vincial and he held this office from 1223 to 1233; under his direction the Order developed rapidly and many convents were established in France. In less than twenty-five years they occupied more than thirty convents; for some of these we are certain about the date of their foundation.[30] A ne-crology of 1233, that of William of Barres, names twenty-one

---

29. Archives nationales, L. 767, published by P. Heinrich Denifle and Emile Chatelain, *Chartularium Universitatis Parisiensis*, Paris, Delalain, 1889-1897, 4 vols., I, pp. 134-135.
30. P. Antoine de Sérent, *Géographie de la province de France*, 1217-1792, La France Franciscaine, t.I, 1912, pp. 91-135.

Franciscan convents:[31] Meaux, Paris, Etampes, Sens, Compiègne, Amiens, Beauvais, Pontoise, Vernon, Rouen, Evreux, Chartres, Senlis, Noyon, Soissons, Provins, Troyes, Vendome, Blois, Orlèans, and Chatillon-sur-Seine. But this list is only a list of convents praying for the dead. In reality, there were more Franciscan convents than these. We know that there was one at Vèzelay, Sèzanne from 1224 on, Auxerre in 1225, Dijon before 1243, Tours in 1224, Sèez, Bayeux, Quimper, Rennes, and other places.

When he sent his brothers out, St. Francis sent another group to southern France. They were under John Bonelli of Florence, and they founded the province of Provence. The Blessed Christopher of Cahors was in this group and, a little later, St. Anthony of Padua contributed to the development of this province.[32] From 1220 on we find the Friars established at Arles, Aix-en-Provence, Montpellier, and Périguex. In 1222, at Draguignan, Nimes, and Toulouse; about 1223, at Limoges and at Brives; about 1225, at Nice, Bordeaux, La Réole, St. Jean d'Angely and Le Puy. The foundations at Avignon, Bourges, Carcassone, Narbonne, Beaucaire, Hyères, Marseilles, and at a number of other places followed in quick succession.

By the time Brother Salimbene went to France, there were already a number of provinces in France. St. Francis had at first reserved for himself the office of minister provincial of France, though he was persuaded not to go to France, as was said before. The province of Provence was also established by St. Francis. From the province of France,

---

31. Léopold Delisle, *Les Rouleaux des morts du IX au XV siecles*, Paris, 1896, pp. 407-420.
32. Cf. *Chronica XXIV Generalium, Analecta Franciscana*, Vol. III, pp. 23 and 161 ssq.

properly so called, there were detached the province of Aquitaine, perhaps as early as 1219, and the provinces of Burgundy and Tours, which seem to have been erected in the general chapter of Rome in November 1239. These provinces each developed, in the course of time, a number of custodies. Thus, by the first part of the fourteenth century, the province of France had 9 custodies; that of Tours, 5; that of Burgundy, 6; that of Aquitaine, 10; that of Provence, 8. In all, at this time, there were some two hundred and forty-seven houses in France.[33]

But of all these convents, the most important and the most renowned establishment was that at Paris which became in a few years the greatest house of studies in the Order. Brother Gregory of Naples played a decisive role and it seems he was one of the most influential defenders of the scientific tendencies within the Order.[34] Brother Thomas of Eccleston tells us that he was one of the great preachers of the times. Through his influence many scholars entered the Order. Somewhere around 1236 the celebrated master of the University of Paris, the Englishman Alexander of Hales, received the habit. He did not interrupt his teaching, but he simply transferred it to the convent of the Franciscans where he gave his courses for the brothers at the same time that he gave them for other students. Thus the Franciscans had a public school incorporated into the university. Several years later they obtained a second chair at the university. These things, however, did not go by without stirring up a

33. *Archivum Franciscanum Historicum*, Vol. I, pp. 1-22. (T.N.)
34. Fr. Hilarin Felder O.F.M., *Geschichte des wissenschaftlichen Studien im Franziskanerorden bis um die Mitte des 13 Jahrhunderts*, Freiburg, 1904.

violent reaction among the masters of the University of Paris.

Every Franciscan province had the right to send two of its religious to the convent at Paris; these religious had to have begun their studies within their own provinces. The minister provincial designated the brothers to be sent to Paris. From this time on the greater number of the lectors were trained at Paris in the great convent of the cordeliers. Brother Thomas of Eccleston gives us some of the names of English brothers who went there for their training. Salimbene was sent there in 1247 with another brother by the minister provincial of Bologna, Brother Rufinus. But Salimbene did not remain even a week at Paris; he preferred to move about from convent to convent.

Such was the province of France when Brother Salimbene was sent there. No chronicle gives us any detailed information about the great development of the Franciscan Order in France. We have only fragmentary and scattered records like the following to give us the history of the beginnings in Paris: charters of the foundation of convents; records of donations made from time to time or of the founding of a convent in some village. In the absence of such a narrative of the beginnings of the Order, the chronicle of Brother Salimbene shows us the brothers already established in the province of France and that of Provence; how they were living there; how the brothers flocked to Paris and to Toulouse for studies; or how the pontifical court attracted them to Lyons. It completes our knowledge of important personages of the Order: for instance, we assist at the return of Brother John of Pian di Carpine from his mission among the Tartars; we assist also at the departure of Brother Jordan; we are made acquainted with the minister general John of Parma in a much more complete way than we come to know him from the chronicles of Brother Jordan or Brother Thomas. The chronicle of Brother Salimbene, therefore, is a very useful complement to the chronicles of these other two Franciscan brothers.

BROTHER SALIMBENE'S FIRST JOURNEY THROUGH FRANCE

1. *LYONS, VILLEFRANCHE*

BROTHER JOHN OF PIAN DI CARPINE[1]

In the year of our Lord 1247, while my native city, Parma, was besieged by the emperor Frederick,[2] I left it and betook myself to Lyons. There I spoke familiarly with the lord Pope Innocent IV in his chamber. After the feast of All Saints I continued on my way through France.

When I arrived at the first convent of the Friars Minor beyond Lyons,[3] Brother John of Pian di Carpine arrived there that same day. He was returning from among the Tartars where he had been sent by Pope Innocent IV. He was a friendly person, spiritual, learned, a great teacher, and skilled in many things. In the past he had been minister provincial in the Order.[4]

Brother John showed me and the other brothers a wooden cup which he was bearing as a gift to the lord Pope.

---

1. The divisions of the selections presented here and the headings were supplied by the author of the French volume.
2. Frederick II, 1194-1250.
3. Most probably, Villefranche.
4. Minister provincial of Germany, Spain, and Saxony.

In the bottom of that cup was the image of a very beautiful queen, which I saw with my own eyes. The image had not been painted there by the artistry of a painter, but it was engraved there by the action of the stars. And if it had been broken into a hundred pieces, the impress of that image would have always remained. If any one finds this impossible to believe, we can demonstrate the fact by another example and support this affirmation. The emperor Frederick gave the Friars Minor in Apulia a very old church in ruins and completely abandoned. A walnut tree of exceptional size had grown on the spot where the altar had been. When it was cut up, it showed in every section an image of our Lord Jesus Christ crucified. If one had cut it a hundred times, all the sections would have shown the image of the crucified. Although God demonstrated this fact by a miracle, in as much as that walnut tree had grown on the spot where the Passion of the Immaculate Lamb is represented in the Host of salvation and by the adorable Sacrifice, some persons say that such impressions are made by the action of the stars.

Brother John told us that he had with him a beautiful set of vestments to give to the lord Pope. He sent for them and showed us all the pontifical vestments necessary for the celebration of Mass on solemn feast days. The wise man has a saying in the Book of Proverbs (18, 16) : *A man's gift clears the way for him, and gains him access to great men.* And another (19, 6) : *Many curry favor with a noble; all are friends of the man who has something to give.*

Brother John told us, moreover, that he had come to the great leader of the Tartars after great fatigue caused by the journey and suffering, and the great inconveniences of hunger, cold, and heat. He said that the people are called Tatars and not Tartars,[5] and that they eat the meat of horses and drink the milk of the mares. He saw with them people from every nation under the sun, with the exception of two. He could not get near to the emperor of the Tatars unless he were clothed in purple. He was received and treated with honor, courtesy, and kindness by him. The great emperor asked him how many there were who ruled in the West. And he replied that there were only two, the Pope and the Emperor, and that all the others held their power dependently upon these two. He also asked which of the two was the greater. Brother John said that the Pope was, and he took out the letter he had from him and gave it to the emperor. He read the letter of the Pope and said that he would write a reply and give it to Brother John. And he did this.

Brother John also wrote a large book about the deeds of the Tatars and other memorable things of the world which he had seen with his own eyes. He had the book read, as I have often seen and heard, when he grew tired from relating the deeds of the Tatars. When those who read it wondered or could not understand it, Brother John explained the strange facts and commented on them.

I do not wish to write down anything from that book, unless perhaps the letter mentioned above, for I do not have the time to do so. That letter is written in this way:

---

5. He writes thereafter Tatars in place of Tartars.

LETTER
OF THE EMPEROR OF THE TATARS
TO POPE INNOCENT IV[6]

He who is the Strength of God and is Emperor of All People
sends to the Great Pope this authentic and sincere letter.

Having taken counsel concerning the making of peace with
us, you, Pope, and all Christians have sent us an envoy as
we have heard from him and as your letter declares. Therefore, if you, Pope, and all the kings and powerful ones,
desire to have peace with us, do not in any way delay to
come to us to make terms and you shall hear our answer at
the same time you will hear our will.

Your letter stated that we ought to be baptized and
become Christians. We answer briefly that we do not understand in what way we ought to do this. For the rest, you say
in your letter that you are astonished at the slaughter of so
many men and especially of so many Christians, and, in
particular, of the Poles, Moravians, and Hungarians. We
answer likewise that we do not understand. However, not
wishing to seem to pass over the question in silence, we
give you this answer: Because they did not obey the commandments of God and the orders of Chinges Chan and of
the Chan. But they took counsel to kill our envoys, for
which God ordered us to destroy them and gave them into
our hands. For otherwise, if God had not ordained this,
what could one man do in the face of other men?

You, men of the West, you believe that you alone are
Christians and you despise others. But how can you know

---

6. The orginal letter is preserved in the Vatican Archives and published
   by Paul Pelliot, *Les Mongols et La Papauté* in *Revue de l'Orient
   chretien*, Vol. 23, pp. 1-30.

to whom God deigns to give His grace? We adore God and we have destroyed, in the name of the Almighty God, the whole earth from the East to the West. If the power of God were not there, what could men have done?

If you accept peace with us and if you wish to surrender your forces, you, Pope, and with you the strong leaders of the Christians, do not delay to come to us to make peace. Then we will know that you wish to live in peace with us. If you do not believe the truth of God and if you do not listen to the counsel that comes from us, then we will know for certain that you wish to have war with us. After that we do not know what will happen; only God knows.

Chengis Chan, first Emperor

Ochoday Chan, second Emperor

Cuiuch Chan, third Emperor

Nothing more is contained in the letter of the Emperor of the Tatars to the Pope.[7]

Note that the first rumors about the Tatars were heard in the time of Pope Gregory IX. Secondly, Pope Innocent IV sent Brother John of Pian di Carpine to them. Thirdly, Pope John XXI again sent six Friars Minor of whom two were from the province of Bologna.[8] One of these was a lector, Brother Anthony of Parma; the other, a discreet man, Brother John of St. Agatha. He likewise sent the same number of brothers from the province of the Marches of Ancona and the same number from the province of Tuscany, three lec-

---

7. The chronicle here inserts several pages about the invasions of Italy in the course of the centuries.
8. See Girolamo Golubovich, *Biblioteca bio-bibliografica della Terra sancta e dell' Oriente francescano*, Vol. I, pp. 426-427.

tors and three discreets.[9] The lector of Tuscany who went among the Tatars was Brother Gerard of Prato with whom I lived in the convent at Pisa when I was young. He was the blood brother of Brother Arlotto who belonged to the convent of Paris and who held the master's chair. The Friars Minor returned healthy and unharmed from among the Tatars, and they told many things about them, as I heard from them with my own ears.

Moreover, when Brother John of Pian di Carpine, on his return from among the Tatars, had come to Lyons to see Pope Innocent IV and had told him news about the Tatars and had given him the letter and the gifts, the pope did five things.

The first was that the pope, because he received him as one of his official family, treated him kindly and familiarly.

The second was that the pope kept him with him for three months, until the city of Victoria was captured and destroyed by the Parmesans and the emperor was expelled by them and put to flight;[10] for he always kept six Friars Minor with him as long as he lived, as I saw with my own eyes.

The third was that the pope commended him for his work and for his fidelity, as it is written in the Book of Proverbs (28, 20) : *The trustworthy man will be richly blessed.* The pope said to him: "May you be blessed, son, by the Lord Jesus Christ and by me His vicar, because in you I see fulfilled the word of Solomon recorded in the Book of Proverbs (25, 13) : *Like the coolness of snow in the heat of*

9. Discreets, technically at that time, were representatives of the friars to present their complaints and grievances at the chapters.
10. February 18, 1248.

the harvest is a messenger for the one who sends him. He re-freshes the soul of his master. And a little later in the same chapter (25): *Like cool water to one faint from thirst is good news from a far country."*

The fourth was that the pope gave him the archiepis-copal see of Antivari, saying, as it is found in Matthew (25, 23): *Well done, good and faithful servant; because thou hast been faithful over a few things, I will set thee over many.*

The fifth was that he made him legate again and sent him to Louis, King of France.[11] But when Brother John asked him the reason why he was being sent to the King of France, the pope did not want to tell him and said: "It is written in the Book of Proverbs (25, 9): *Discuss your case with your neighbor, but another man's secret do not disclose.* And in Isaias (24, 16): *My secret to myself, my secret to myself.* And another text of Holy Scripture (Psalms, 119, 11): *Thy words I have hidden in my heart, that I may not sin against thee."*

The reason for this mission is thought to have been this. Pope Innocent had deposed Frederick from his em-pire,[12] and the Parmesans had rebelled against the emperor and, in addition, had expelled him from his village and put him to ignominious flight; and they destroyed so completely his city Victoria, which he had built near Parma, that no trace of it was left. All these injuries made the emperor very angry, and *as a bear raging in the wood when her whelps are taken away,*[13] the emperor was thoroughly enraged and

---

11. Louis IX, St. 1226-1270.
12. By the Council of Lyons, July 17, 1245.
13. II Kings, 17, 8.

filled with fury. After his flight Frederick II went to Cremona, and afterwards he went to Torricella; then he returned to the neighborhood of Parma and inflicted what injuries he could upon the Parmesans, and what he could not, he threatened. And he did many evil things before he returned to his kingdom, as we will tell later and as we have said in another chronicle.[14] The pope knew that Frederick was a very great persecutor of the Church and that he would pour out his spite if he could. Fearing for his own person, the pope sent Brother John to ask the King of France to put off his trip across the sea[15] until he could know what God would ultimately do with regard to Frederick. He alleged, moreover, that in Italy there dwelt many infidels, and many evil, perverse, and pernicious men, *needy men and robbers*,[16] and oppressors in the hire of a stranger, who, united by Frederick, *followed him as their prince*[17] and destroyed the goods of the Church. What more shall I say? The pope labored incessantly, but in vain, for he could not turn the king from his desire to cross the sea, in as much as the crusaders were prepared and insisted on sailing.

The king of France sent Brother John back saying that the pope should confide the affair of Frederick to the justice of God, because God it is who will abase those who walk in pride, as the prophet Daniel said.[18] For, *God is the judge; one he brings low; another he lifts up. For a cup is in the Lord's hand, full of spiced and foaming wine.*[19] Consequent-

---

14. This chronicle has not survived.
15. On a crusade, the seventh.
16. Judges 11, 3.
17. *Ibid.*
18. Daniel 4, 34.
19. Psalm 74, 8-9.

ly, *various is the event of war: and sometimes one, sometimes another is consumed by the sword.*[20]

Therefore, Louis, King of France, obstinate in mind and irrevocably determined, his whole being consecrated to his task, set about immediately to cross the sea.

---

20. II Kings 11, 25.

2. *TROYES, PARIS, SENS, AUXERRE*

The Wine in France

The day after I saw Brother John of Pian di Carpine on his return from among the Tatars he went on to Lyons to Pope Innocent who had sent him to the Tatars. And for my part, I continued on my journey in France. I stayed fifteen days at Troyes, in Brie, which is in Champagne.[1] There were many Lombard and Tuscan merchants there; as in Provins, there is a fair there which lasts two months. The village of Troyes is the birth place of Pope Urban IV[2] and of the priest, Master Peter, who wrote some histories.[3] Then I went on to Provins and I lived there from the feast of St. Lucy until the Purification.[4]

On the feast of the Purification of the Blessed Virgin, I went to Paris and stayed there eight days. There I saw many things that pleased me.

After that stay I took the road back and dwelt in the convent at Sens; the brothers of France liked to have me with them because I was a peaceful and jolly young man and because I praised their doings. But as I lay on my bed in the

---

1. Salimbene's geography was not too good. Brie is not in Champagne, a region in northeastern France.
2. Pope from 1261-1264.
3. Author of *Historia scolastica.*
4. From December 13 to February 2 (1247-1248).

infirmary, sick because of the cold, certain brothers of the convent came to me full of joy, holding a letter and saying: "We have very good news from Parma; the Parmesans have driven Frederick from the village of Victoria which he had built; they have put him to flight in shame and they have destroyed from top to bottom his village in such a way as is described in the Apocalypse (17, 11) : the village *that was, and is not.* They have taken the entire imperial treasure and also the chariot of Cremona which they brought back to Parma. Here is a copy of the letter the Parmesans sent to the lord Pope at Lyons." They asked me for what purpose that chariot could be used. I told them that the Lombards call a chariot like that their coach, and that if the coach of one village is taken in war that village thinks they have received a great injury. In the same way that if the oriflamme[5] were taken in war, the French, and their king, would consider it a great disgrace. When they heard this, they marvelled and said: "My God! We have heard an astonishing thing."

After that, I recovered. At that time Brother John of Pian di Carpine was returning from the king to whom he had been sent by the pope. He had the book which he had written about the Tatars. The brothers read it in his presence, and he explained and interpreted whatever seemed to them to be obscure and hard to believe. I ate with Brother John in the convent of the Friars Minor and abroad in some abbeys and illustrious houses more than once or twice. People invited him gladly and often to lunch and dine,

---

5. The oriflamme was the ancient banner of St. Denis, a red silk banderole on a lance, carried into battle by early French kings. Cf. Webster's *New Collegiate Dictionary.*

because he was the legate of the pope, sent to the king of France; because he had come from the Tatars; and because he belonged to the Order of Friars Minor and the people therefore thought he lived a holy life. For they said: *One that is a priest of the seed of Aaron is come, he will not deceive us.*[6] When I was at Cluny, the monks of the abbey said to me: "Would to God that the pope would always send legates like Brother John. The other legates despoil the Church whenever they can and carry off whatever they can. When Brother John was amongst us, he did not wish to accept anything except a bit of cloth to make a tunic for his companion."

Understand, reader, that the monastery of Cluny is the most eminent of the monasteries of the black monks of the Order of St. Benedict in Burgundy. There are several priors in the convent. It is made up of such a large number of buildings that they can give hospitality to the pope, to the cardinals, and their entire court, and at the same time to the emperor, without inconvenience to the monks, and it would not be necessary for any monk to quit his cell or suffer any kind of discomfort.[7]

Note also, reader, that among the black monks of the Order of St. Benedict, the Rule is kept much better in the lands beyond the mountains than in Italy.[8]

Note likewise that in the Order of St. Benedict there are four important monasteries of black monks: Cluny in Burgundy; St. Gall in Germany; in Lombardy, in the dio-

---

6. I Mach. 7, 14.
7. The abbatial church of Cluny was demolished between 1800 and 1811. It had been the grandest church of Christendom next to St. Peter's at Rome.
   8. Salimbene was writing, of course, in Italy.

cese of Mantua, between the Po and the Lario, there is a monastery of St. Benedict where the countess Mathilda is buried in a stone tomb; the fourth monastery, the head monastery of the Order, is situated on Monte Cassino.

After my stay at the convent at Sens, where I found myself when the village of Victoria was captured and destroyed and the emperor expelled and put to ignominious flight, I betook myself to Auxerre. I lived there because I had been assigned specifically to that convent by the minister provincial of France. It was said of Auxerre that the city was like a place sacred to the gods or like a lofty star because it held many bodies of saints who had been martyred. There was there a monastery of St. Germain with the saint's body; he had been bishop of that city. He was like a brilliant star and like a *rainbow appearing in the cloudy sky,*[9] or so it seemed to those who had read his life.

Likewise, Auxerre was the birth place of Master William, who wrote a *Summa Theologica* and another *Summa* about the offices of the Church. I frequently entered his house.[10] The priests of the diocese of Auxerre told me that Master William had been a master of controversy. When he took part in scholastic discussions at Paris, no one could do better than he. He was a great logician and a great theologian; but, when he undertook to preach, he did not know what to say, although he had some good rules in his *Summa*. . . .[11]

We return to Auxerre. When I lived in the convent at Cremona, the year my village, Parma, rose up in revolt

---

9. Ecclesiasticus 50, 7.
10. William of Auxerre died some time after 1231.
11. Salimbene puts in here some pages of examples.

against the deposed emperor, Frederick, I remember that Brother Gabriel of Cremona, of the Order of Friars Minor, a most learned man and a man of saintly life, told me that there were more vineyards in Auxerre than in Cremona, Parma, Reggio, and Modena together. I was shocked at this and thought that it was beyond belief.

When I lived in Auxerre, I found out for myself that he had spoken the truth. Now there was a large district or diocese, a vast territory, that I saw with my own eyes, where the mountains, the hillsides, and the plains were covered with vineyards. The people of the region *do not sow, or reap, or gather into barns,*[12] but they send their wine to Paris, because next to the village, there is a river that flows to Paris. They sell it at a good price and from this they get all their food and clothing.

I went over the diocese of Auxerre three times on foot. The first time I went with a brother who preached and gave the cross for the crusade of the king of France.[13]

Another time I tramped around the country with another brother who, on Holy Thursday,[14] preached to the Cistercians in a very beautiful monastery.[15] We celebrated Easter[16] with a countess,[17] who at dinner served us and her whole court twelve kinds of dishes, that is to say, twelve servings of different dishes. The count, her husband, was not at home; had he been present, there would have been

---

12. Math. 6, 26.
13. The seventh crusade.
14. April 16, 1248.
15. Probably at Nevers.
16. April 19, 1248.
17. Countess Mathilda I. Her husband was Guy II who died in 1241. Either she remarried or Salimbene is in error.

served an even greater number of dishes. The brother showed me the monastery of Potigny where the Blessed Thomas, archbishop of Canterbury, after he had been expelled from England by the king, was welcomed kindly by Pope Alexander III, who was then at Sens.[18]

The third time I traveled with Brother Stephen, I saw and heard many things worth telling, but I will omit them for the sake of brevity and hasten on to tell of other things.

Note, reader, that in the province of France,—I speak from the point of view of the Order of Friars Minor,— there are eight custodies: four drink beer and four drink wine. Note also that there are three regions in France that give a great quantity of wine: La Rochelle, Beaune, and Auxerre. Note also that red wines are looked down upon in Auxerre, because they are not as good as the red wines of Italy. Again, note that the wines of Auxerre are white, sometimes golden; they give off a delicate aroma; they are very comforting and very delicious; they give to all who drink them *peacefulness and cheerfulness,*[19] and they transform them entirely; thus the passage of the Book of Proverbs (31, 6-7) can be applied to the wines of Auxerre: *Give strong drink to one who is perishing, and wine to the sorely depressed; when they drink they will forget their misery, and think no more of their burdens.* And note that the wines of Auxerre are so strong that, when they have been for a time in jugs, tears gather on the outside.

We note also that the French are accustomed to say jokingly that good wine should have three B's and seven F's,

---

18. Thomas à Becket, exiled in France from 1164-1170 by Henry II. He returned to England and was murdered in his cathedral on December 29, 1170.

19. From the apocryphal III Esdras 3, 20.

for such wine is the best and deserving of praise. They say it in fun:

> *El vin bon e bels e blance,*
> *Forte e fer e fin e franble,*
> *Freit e fras e formijant.*
> Good wine is lovely and white,
> Strong and proud and fine and real,
> Cold and fresh and sparkling bright.

Master Morandus, who taught grammar at Padua, commended wine in his own way in song:

> Honey sweet and blessed wine
> Gives us strength and courage fine.
> Ripened long, with flavor full,
> Whets our wits and cheers our soul.
> Strong and pure wine makes us bold,
> Drives away the piercing cold.
> But the wine that tastes so sour,
> Stings the tongue with piercing power,
> Turns the stomach deeply sour,
> Breaks the body's healthy power.
> Muddy wine with hoarseness coats
> Heavy drinker's tender throats.
> Wine fermented reddens man's face,
> Gives his body supple grace.
> Even weak wine has its worth,
> On your cheeks gives redness birth.
> Golden wine of citron hue
> Warms your body through and through,

Keeps anemia far from you.
But the cursed water clear,
Never let it come too near.
If you do you'll lose your cheer.
Blessed wine to me so dear!

The French, therefore, enjoy drinking good wine; and this is not astonishing, for good wine *cheereth God and men,* as is said in the Book of Judges (9, 13). For good wine rejoices the heart of man and gives peace and joy to his spirit.

It knows no sadness, no obligations, and it makes the whole heart virtuous. It knows neither king nor magistrate, and it reveals all secrets. When one drinks, one knows no friendship or brotherliness, and, after having drunk even a little, one has recourse to the sword. When one has drunk wine and when one gets up, one does not know how to go to work.[20]

Literally, the French and English are persistent in their draining full cups. As a result, the French have purulent eyes, because they drink so much wine. Their eyes are red, bleary, and rimmed around. Early in the morning, after they have slept off their wine, they go, with eyes like that, to the priest who has celebrated Mass and ask him to put into their eyes the water he has washed his hands in. Brother Bartholomew Guiscolo of Parma, used to say at Provins, as I have heard with my own ears: "Alé! Ke malonta ve don Dé! Metti del aighe in le vins, non in lis ocli." That is to say: "Go! and God give you an evil lot! Put the water into your wine when you drink it, and not into your eyes." Again,

---

20. Salimbene is quoting loosely various passages of Scripture. We omit many of the quotations.

in the book of Proverbs (20, 1), it is said: *Wine is arrogant, strong drink is riotous; none who goes astray for it is wise.*

The English, too, delight in such things and like to drain full cups. For, when an Englishman takes a large glass of wine, he will drain it and say: "Ge bi, a vu," that is, "You must drink as much as I." He believes he is saying and doing a great act of courtesy and he will take offense if someone does otherwise than he has said and shown by example. And yet he acts against Holy Scripture which says in the Book of Esther (1, 7-8): *Wine also in abundance and of the best was presented, as was worthy of a king's magnificence. Neither was there any one to compel them to drink. . . .* Another passage in Holy Scripture (Ecclesiasticus 31, 30): *More and more wine is a snare for the fool; it lessens his strength and multiplies his wounds.* And it continues to talk about sobriety to the end of the chapter.

Still, one must forgive the English if they drink good wine with such great pleasure whenever they can, for they have but little wine in their country. The French are less excusable, for they have much more wine; but of course some will want to plead that it is hard to give up a habit. Note what is said in these verses:

> Normandy gives you the fish of the sea;
> England, abundance of corn;
> Scotland gives plenty of milk;
> France, an abundance of sparkling wine.

But enough of this. One notes, as I saw with my own eyes, that in France the days are longer than in Italy during the same periods. Thus in May and in winter the days are shorter in the latter country.

3. SENS AND VEZELAY

JOHN OF PARMA AND ST. LOUIS

Let us return now to our own affairs and talk about the King of France.

In the year of our Lord 1248, around the feast of Pentecost, or a little later,[1] I went down from the convent at Auxerre to that at Sens. The provincial chapter of France was to be held there; and the lord Louis, King of France, was to come there. When the chapter had been convened, the minister provincial of France,[2] with his definitors,[3] approached the minister general, John of Parma, who was in the convent, and said to him: "Father, we have examined and approved forty brothers who had come to the chapter to obtain the office of preaching; we have given them that office and have dismissed them to return to their convents, so that the place where we are holding the chapter may not be burdened with such a great multitude of brothers."

The minister general replied that they had acted with little wisdom, and that they had acted incorrectly, in as

1. Pentecost fell on June 7. It was probably a little after this, for Louis left Paris on June 12 and stopped at Corbeil and Melun on the way to Sens.
2. Brother Geoffrey of Brie.
3. Definitors are the counselors of the minister provincial (provincial definitors) or of the minister general (general definitors).

much as the giving of that approbation was not permitted to the ministers provincial and the definitors except in the absence of the minister general. He added: "I consider it a valid examination that you have given the brothers, but I wish that they be recalled and that they receive the office of preaching from me alone as is prescribed in the Rule."[4] And this was done. The brothers returned to the place of the chapter and they stayed there until it was over.

When the King of France was on his way to the chapter and approached the convent, all the brothers went out to meet him that they might receive him with great honor. Brother Rigaud, of the Order of Friars Minor, master of the University of Paris and archbishop of Rouen,[5] clad in his pontifical robes, hastened out of the convent, calling as he went, asking for the king: "Where is the king? Where is the king?" I went after him, because he went alone and was very distraught, and had his mitre on his head and his crozier in his hand. He had been slow in vesting, so that the other brothers had gone on ahead and were standing on one side of the street or the other, their faces turned in the direction from which the king would come, for they

---

4. "Let none of the brothers dare to preach to the people, unless he has been examined and approved by the minister general of this fraternity and the office of preaching committed to him by the same." *Regula Bullata,* Chapter 9.

5. Eudes Rigaud was one of the very remarkable men of that period. He entered the Order in 1236; in 1247 he was made archbishop of Rouen. He was active in visiting and correcting his clergy, and did much to improve the education of his candidates for the priesthood. We possess a day-by-day account of his episcopate from 1248 to 1269. He traveled to Rome and to London, took part in the crusade of 1270 and the Council of Lyons in 1274. He died July 2, 1275.

were anxious to see him. Astonished beyond expression, I said to myself: "I am certain that once or twice I read that the Senonians were so powerful a people that, under the direction of Brennus, they took possession of Rome. But now their women have, for the most part, the air of servants." If the king of France had passed through Pisa or Bologna, the flower of the ladies of these villages would have gone out to meet him. I remembered that this is indeed the custom of the French: in France, only the middle class people live in the cities; the knights and noble ladies live in their country homes and on their estates.

The king was slender and elegant, a bit thin and tall; he had the face of an angel and a gracious mien. He came to the church of the Friars Minor, not with royal pomp, but in the costume of a pilgrim, bearing a pilgrim's staff and a cloak that adorned his shoulders beautifully. He did not come on horseback, but by foot. His brothers, three counts, followed him with the same humility and the same garments. The eldest was Robert,[6] and the youngest Charles[7] who accomplished great deeds worthy of praise.[8] One might have said in the words of the prophet: *Some are strong in chariots; some, in horses; but we are strong in the name of the Lord, our God.*[9]

The king did not care to have a train of nobles, but he preferred the prayers and suffrages of the poor. Thus he accomplished what was said in Ecclesiasticus (4, 7): *Make thyself affable to the congregation of the poor.* Truth to say,

---

6. Robert, count of Artois.
7. Charles of Anjou, count of Anjou and Provence, pretender to the throne of Jerusalem.
8. The third brother, not named here, was Alphonse, count of Poitiers.
9. Psalms 19, 8.

one might rather take the king for a monk, considering his piety, than for a knight trained in the profession of arms. He entered the church of the brothers, genuflected piously before the altar and prayed. When he left the church and paused at the threshold, I was at his side.

Someone offered the king, on behalf of the treasurer of the church at Sens, a large pike that was alive, in a basin made of fir-wood and filled with water; such a basin as the Tuscans call a *bigonza* and in which they wash and bathe tiny infants. In truth, the pike has a reputation in France of being a precious fish of great value. The king thanked the donor and the one who had brought it. Then, in a loud and clear voice, he said that no one should enter the house of the chapter except the knights and the brothers with whom he wished to speak.

When we were gathered together in chapter, the king spoke first of his own affairs. He recommended himself and his brothers, the queen, the queen mother, and his whole retinue to them. He knelt piously and ask the prayers and suffrages of the brothers. Certain brothers of France, who were at my side, wept so out of devotion and piety that they were inconsolable. After the king, a cardinal of the Roman curia, the lord Oddo, who was chancellor of the church at Paris,[10] and who was about to go across the sea with the king, made a speech and concluded in a few words what he had to say, according to the teaching of Ecclesiasticus (7, 5): *Before the king flaunt not your wisdom.* And even more, Job (29, 9): *They dared not add anything to my words.*"

---

10. He became a master of theology about 1230, a chancellor of the church in Paris in 1238 to 1244, cardinal archbishop of Tusculum in 1244. He died January 26, 1273.

Again, in the Book of Proverbs (30, 6) : *Add nothing to his words, lest he reprove thee, and you be exposed as a deceiver.*[11]

After these, Brother John of Parma, the minister general, upon whom the duty of replying fell because of his office, made a speech and said: "Ecclesiasticus, in chapter 32, teaches: *Speak, thou that are elder, for it becometh thee, to speak the first word with careful knowledge.*[12] Our king and lord, father and benefactor, who makes himself *affable to the congregation of the poor,*[13] came to us in humility, desiring to be useful, courteous, and kind. He spoke to us first, as was right. He does not ask for gold or silver: by the grace of God his treasury is sufficiently full; he asks the prayers and suffrages of the brother for a project that seems to us highly laudable. The lord king has in truth undertaken this voyage and this crusade for the glory of the Lord Jesus Christ, to bring help to the Holy Land, to fight the adversaries and the enemies of the faith and of the cross of Christ, for the honor of the universal Church and for the Christian religion and for the salvation of his own soul and the souls of all who are to go across the sea with him. Wherefore, seeing that he has been a special benefactor and defender of our Order, not only at Paris, but throughout his realm, and that he has come humbly to us with so worthy a company to ask the prayers of the Order for this enterprise, it is fitting and just that we respond to his kindnesses. And since the brothers of France are all disposed to undertake this, and intend to do more than I know how to impose upon them,

---

11. This passage is not found in the place cited. The passage is probably the one found in Deuteronomy 4, 2.
12. Ecclesiasticus 32, 4-5.
13. Ecclesiasticus 4, 7.

I do not therefore put any precept upon them. But, since I have begun the visitation of the Order, I have decided for myself to enjoin upon each priest the obligation to say four Masses for the king and for his companions. The first will be the Mass of the Holy Spirit; the second, that of the Cross; the third, that of the Blessed Virgin; the fourth, that of the Holy Trinity. If it should happen that the Son of God should call the king from this world to His Father, the brothers will add even more Masses. If I have not responded sufficiently in accordance with the wishes of the king, he himself is our lord to command; for on our part there is none wanting who will obey, but only such as will command."

At these words, the king thanked the minister general, and he so appreciated the response that he wished to have it confirmed in a letter and by the seal of the minister general. And this was done.

Moreover, the king paid the expenses that day and dined with the brothers. We ate in the refectory. There were present the three brothers of the king, the cardinal of the Roman curia, the minister general, the archbishop of Rouen, Brother Rigaud, the minister provincial of France, the custodes, definitors, and discreets, and the guest brothers whom we call strangers.

Since the minister general knew, therefore, that there was a noble and worthy company with the king, namely, the legate and cardinal of the Roman church, the archbishop of Rouen, he did not wish to push himself forward, according to the word of Ecclesiasticus (11, 4) : *Be not exalted in the day of thy honor.* Though he had been invited to sit by the side of the king, he preferred to practice the courtesy and humility our Lord taught by the example He gave us. The

Lord said in the Gospel according to St. Luke (14, 8-11) : *When thou art invited to a wedding feast, do not recline in the first place, lest perhaps one more distinguished than thou have been invited by him, and he who invited thee and him come and say to thee, "Make room for this man"; and then thou begin with shame to take the last place. But when thou art invited, go and recline in the last place; that when he who invited thee comes in, he may say to thee: "Friend, go up higher!" Then thou wilt be honored in the presence of all who art at table with thee. For everyone who exalts himself shall be humbled, and he who humbles himself shall be exalted.* Another text says (Ecclesiasticus 13, 9-10) : *When invited by a man of influence, keep your distance; then he will urge you all the more.* Another text, one from the Book of Proverbs (25, 6) : *Claim no honor in the king's presence, nor occupy the place of great men.*

Brother John preferred, therefore, to sit at the table of the humble who were ennobled by his presence. Many of those at the banquet were edified by this good example. And, just as a generous countenance ennobles a mean repast,[14] so also the presence of a humble man who seats himself humbly at table lends dignity so much to a place that the table is enriched with magnificence. Consider, moreover, that God did not create the light of heaven for one place alone, but He placed it in diverse places for greater beauty and to be useful to diverse places. That day the king accomplished what is written in Scripture (Ecclesiasticus 4, 7) : *Endear yourself to the assembly.* In another place it is said in Ecclesiasticus (9, 16) : *Have just men for your table com-*

---

14. L. Hervieux, *Les Fabulistes Latins*, Paris, Firmin-Didot, 1884, vol. 2, p. 289.

panions; in the fear of God be your glory.

At dinner we had first cherries, then bread that was very white, *wine in abundance and of the best, ... worthy of a king's magnificence.*[15] And, according to the custom of the French, there were many guests who were eager to invite and *compel them to drink that were not willing.*[16] We then had fresh beans boiled in milk, fishes and crabs, eel-pasties, rice cooked with the milk of almonds and cinnamon, eels baked with excellent sauces, tarts, new cheese, and fruits. We had everything necessary in abundance and fittingly arranged. All was brought in with much ceremony and served with care.

The next day the king continued on his way. When the chapter ended, I followed the king. I had a letter of obedience from the minister general to go to live in the province of Provence. It was easy for me to catch up with the king, for he often turned aside from his main route to visit at the right or at the left a hermitage of the Friars Minor or of other religious to recommend himself to their prayers. He did this every day until he came to the sea and embarked for the Holy Land.[17]

After I had visited with the brothers at Auxerre, the convent to which I had belonged, I went on in one day to Vézelay, which is a celebrated village in Burgundy where it is believed the body of Mary Magdalen is to be found.[18] The next day was Sunday.[19] Early in the morning the king betook

---

15. Esther 1, 7.
16. Esther 1, 8.
17. August 25, 1248.
18. This was a popular shrine for pilgrimages.
19. June 12, 1248.

himself to the brothers[20] to ask their prayers, according to the word of the Book of Proverbs (11, 27) : *Well doth he rise early who seeketh good things.* The king left his whole escort in camp; therefore the brothers were very little disturbed. He took with him only his three brothers and some servants to watch the horses. After they had made a genuflection and reverence before the altar, the brothers brought them seats and benches on which to sit. The king sat on the ground, in the dust; this I saw with my own eyes, for the church was not paved. The king called us to him, saying: "Come to me, my very dear brothers, and hear my words." We formed a circle around him, sitting with him on the ground; his brothers did the same. He recommended himself to us and asked the prayers and suffrages of the brothers in the same manner I described earlier.

After we had made answer, he left the church to continue on his way. It was told him that Charles was still praying with fervor. The king was happy and waited with patience, without mounting his horse, for his brother to finish his prayers. The two other counts, his brothers, waited in the same way with the king. Charles, the count of Provence, was the youngest of the brothers. He had taken as his wife the sister of the queen.[21] He made numerous genuflections before

---

20. In the convent of Cordelle, founded by Brother Pacificus. It had many vicissitudes during the centuries. It burned in 1390. In 1596 the Calvinists massacred the religious of the convent. In 1790 it was taken over by the government, sold, and dismantled. In 1949 the Friars took possession again and built a small hermitage there.
21. She was Beatrice, the sister of Marguerite of Provence, queen of France. The two were daughters of Raymond Bérenger, count of Provence.

the altar which was in the wing of the church near the entrance there. I saw for myself with what fervor Charles prayed and how the king waited patiently outside. I recognized how true is the saying of Holy Scripture (Proverbs 18, 19) : *A brother is a better defense than a strong city.*

Then the king, continued on his way; his affairs having been taken care of, he hastened to get ready to embark.

4. *LYONS, ARLES, MARSEILLES*

BROTHER HUGH OF DIGNE

As for myself, I went to Lyons and found there the lord pope Innocent IV and his cardinals. Then I went down the Rhone as far as Arles, which is about five miles from the sea. I arrived there on the feast of St. Peter.[1] Brother Raymond, the minister provincial of Provence, who later became bishop, arrived there about the same time, and he received me with honor. The lector of the convent of Montpellier accompanied him.

Then I went by sea to Marseilles, and from there to Hyères to see Brother Hugh of Bareola, who is called Brother Hugh of Digne also, and whom the Lombards call Brother Hugh of Montpellier.[2] He was one of the great clerics of the world,[3] an eminent preacher, beloved of the clergy and the people, excellent in controversy and competent in everything. He entangled all and confounded all; he was a facile speaker, and had a voice that resounded like a trumpet, or like the crash of thunder, or like the falling of water in torrents. He

---

1. June 29, 1248.
2. Salimbene gives considerable information about him and is our main source of information. He died in the year 1256, according to Salimbene. His sister Douceline was a tertiary and died in the odor of sanctity in 1274.
3. Salimbene uses this formula frequently.

never imposed his ideas on any one; he never made terms with any one; he was always ready with an answer. He spoke wonderful thoughts about the heavenly court, that is to say, about the glory of Paradise, and terrible things about the pains of hell. A native of the province of Provence, he was small of stature and not unsuitably swarthy of complexion. He was a man of more than average spirituality of the kind that would make one think he was looking upon another Paul or another Elias.

He spoke in consistory to the pope and the cardinals as he might have done to children gathered together at play; this he did at Lyons as he had done earlier at Rome. And listening to him speak, they all trembled like reeds in the water. And why? Because he fulfilled the words of Isaias (51, 7-8): *Fear ye not the reproach of men, and be not afraid of their blasphemies. For the worm shall eat them up as a garment; and the moth shall consume them as wool.* And again in the same chapter (12-13): *Who art thou that thou shouldst be afraid of a mortal man, and of the son of man, who shall wither away as grass? And thou hast forgotten the Lord thy maker.*

Asked by the cardinals about what news he had brought, he reprimanded them as asses, saying: "I have no news, but I have complete peace within my conscience and with my God, peace *which surpasses all understanding*[4] and that guards my heart and my mind in Christ Jesus, my Lord.[5] I know though that you seek after news and that you are busy about such things all day. You are Athenians and not disciples of Christ, Athenians of whom Luke wrote in the Acts of the

---

4. Philippians 4, 7.
5. *Ibid.*

Apostles (17, 21) : *Now all the Athenians and the visitors there from abroad used to spend all their leisure telling or listening to something new.* The disciples of Christ were fishermen and weak men according to the judgment of the world; yet, they converted the whole world, for the Lord was with them, according to the word of Mark in his last chapter (16, 20) : *But they went forth and preached everywhere, while the Lord worked with them and confirmed the preaching by the signs that followed.* They accomplished the mission described in these words: *Through all the earth their voice resounds, and to the ends of the world, their message.*⁶ For you, however, has not been accomplished what was written: *The place of your fathers your sons shall have; you shall make them princes through all the land.*⁷ In reality, you are they *who build up Sion with blood, and Jerusalem with inquity.*⁸

"You have called your grandnephews and relatives to benefices and ecclesiastical dignities to elevate and enrich your families, and you have excluded able men who might have been useful to the Church of God. You have given prebendaries to infants in the cradle. . . . ⁹

". . . How you have done this, reflect and judge for yourselves. For, you have not sought men in all classes of society when you wished to create cardinals, but you have chosen from amongst your relatives and your grandnephews those who were to be cardinals, archbishops, bishops, and primates. These latter times you have enlarged the dignity

---

6. Psalm 19, 5.
7. Psalm 45, 17.
8. Micheas 3, 10.
9. Salimbene loves phrases like this. Parts of the talk are omitted here.

of these ceremonies greatly. Pope Innocent IV has given you a red hat,[10] so that, when you travel on horseback, people can distinguish you from other chaplains. But, in ancient times, your equals and your predecessors were not called cardinals, but priests and deacons of the Roman curia. . . ."[11]

At these words, the cardinals were cut to the heart and gnashed their teeth at him.[12] Yet they did not have the audacity to reply, for fear of the Lord had pierced them and *the hand of the Lord was with* him.[13] They were astounded that he had dared to speak to them so boldly; it seemed long to them till he would depart from them and leave the chamber, nor did they say to him: *We will hear thee again on the matter,* as the Athenians said to St. Paul.[14]

Before Brother Hugh left, the pope said courteously to him the words of the Book of Job (32, 8) : *"It is a spirit in man, the breath of the Almighty, that gives him understanding.* For, *the wind blows where it will*[15] and *there is no man who is master of the breath of life so as to retain it.*[16] May you be blessed, my son, by God the most high because you have spoken many good things to us. *Blessed are they that saw thee, and were honored with thy friendship.*[17] Go in

---

10. At the Council of Lyons in 1245.
11. Brother Hugh continued to berate the cardinals: for assuming honors, living too comfortably, neglecting the ministry, neglecting their own spiritual welfare. We omit the rest of this here and return to what happened at the end of his talk.
12. Acts 7, 54.
13. Ezechial 3, 14.
14. Acts 17, 32.
15. John 3, 8.
16. Ecclesiastes 48, 11.
17. Ecclesiasticus 48, 11.

peace, and *the blessing of him that appeared in the bush*[18] be upon your head."

These things took place at Lyons, at the consistory of Pope Innocent IV, in presence of the cardinals of the Roman curia who wished to hear the news from him and to get knowledge of future events. I heard this narrative from the mouth of Brother Hugh himself just as I have transcribed it here.

When I spoke to Brother Hugh, two things astonished me: first, that the cardinals had borne his speaking to them so many words; and secondly, that they could have confounded him by the authority of the Bible and the fullness of their power, if they had known how. He told me that they could not for two reasons: "First, because of the guarantee of the sovereign pontiff who had supported me with his help and had given his assurance. For the sovereign pontiff had sent for me, and the cardinals being gathered in consistory, he had placed me in their midst and said to me: 'We have heard that you are a great cleric, a good man, and a highly spiritual man. But we have also heard that you are the successor of the abbot Joachim[19] by your prophecies and that you are a great

---

18. Deuteronomy 33, 16.
19. Joachim of Fiore in Calabria was a Cistercian abbot who died in 1202. He had made a number of prophecies which were suspect from a theological point of view. The Lateran Council condemned in 1215 his teaching about the Trinity which in effect posited three Gods. He divided history into three periods: that of the Father, the Old Testament; that of the Son, the New Testament; and that of the Holy Spirit, which was about to begin at that time, namely 1260, according to his prophecy. The "eternal gospel" would replace the sacraments and every outward sign. The Franciscan "spirituals" became involved in these teachings.

Joachimite. *Now, therefore, we are all present in thy sight to hear whatever has been commanded thee by the Lord.*[20] That is why, if you propose to speak *any word of exhortation, speak!*[21] For, as regards this sect, *we want to hear from thee what thy views are'.*"[22]

Moreover, Brother Hugh told me that it was impossible for them to do him any harm, for the pope had promised that he could speak whatsoever he wished and he gave him his guarantee that he would defend him, and also because God was with him.

Brother Hugh used to say that he had four friends that he liked in a special way.

The first was the minister general John of Parma. This was proper for the two were great clerics, both were spiritual men,[23] and both great Joachimites. Brother Hugh was my intimate friend too, because I seemed to believe in the writings of the abbot Joachim of Fiore.

The second was the archbishop of Vienne,[24] a saintly, learned, and distinguished man, who loved the Order of St. Francis very much. Through his friendship for the Friars Minor he had a bridge of stone built across the Rhone because he had given them a place to live within his territory.

---

20. Acts 10, 33.
21. Acts 13, 15.
22. Acts 28, 22.
23. Salimbene uses this term in several senses: one meaning simply a man of spirit (as he used it of John of Pian di Carpine); another meaning a highly spiritual man; and a third meaning more precisely the "spirituals" in the Franciscan Order, who were men devoted to an exaggerated observance especially of poverty. It is in this last sense that he uses it of Hugh of Digne.
24. Vienne in France. The archbishop was John I.

When I was at Vienne, Brother William of the Order of Preachers,[25] who had written a *Summa of the Vices and Virtues,* came there. He had come from Lyons to Vienne to preach and to hear confessions. And because the Friars Preachers did not have a convent in that city, he turned aside from his route to be the guest of the Friars Minor. It pleased the guardian that I associated with him; and I treated him familiarly and he me, for he was a humble and courteous man, though he was small of stature. When I asked him why the Friars Preachers did not have a convent in Vienne, he told me that they preferred to have one large convent in Lyons rather than have many smaller ones. I asked him to preach to the brothers on the feast of the Annunciation of the Blessed Virgin,[26] which was approaching, because I wanted to hear him. For, besides the *Summa* he also had written a treatise on preaching. He told me that if the guardian would tell him to he would obey gladly. This was done. He gave a beautiful sermon on the annunciation of the Blessed Virgin. He announced his subject with the text: *The Angel Gabriel was sent.*[27]

Another day, finding myself in the same city, I happened upon Brother William the Breton, of the Order of Friars Minor, whose book is worthy of memory. Because of the smallness of his size, he resembled the first William I spoke about a little earlier; not, however, in character, for he seemed hot-headed and impatient, as is often the case of people of small size. Also it is said: "A small man is rarely humble; a great man is rarely endowed with reflection; a red-haired

25. Archbishop of Lyons.
26. March 25.
27. Luke 1, 26.

man is seldom without perfidy."[28]

At the convent at Lyons, I heard him give a reprimand at table in the presence of the minister general, Brother John of Parma, and of Pope Innocent IV, then at Lyons. But Brother William had not yet written the book that bears his name.

The third friend of Brother Hugh was Robert Grosseteste, bishop of Lincoln;[29] he was one of the great clerics of the world. He was the second one after Burgundio, judge of Pisa,[30] to translate St. John Damascene, the Testaments of the twelve patriarchs, and many other books.

The fourth friend of Brother Hugh was Brother Adam Marsh, of the Order of Friars Minor, one of the great clerics of the world.[31] He was a brilliant light in England and, like the bishop of Lincoln, composed a number of writings. Both these men were English, they were good friends, and they are buried together in the cathedral.[32] A third friend of these two was Alexander, of the Order of Friars Minor, an Englishman, a master of the University of Paris;[33] he wrote a number of works and, as all said who knew him well at that time, there was no person in the world who equalled him. . . .

Another time I heard Brother Hugh preach in the province of Provence at Tarascon on the Rhone. Many men and women of Tarascon and Beaucaire were present at his sermon. These were two celebrated cities, one facing the

---

28. Salimbene does not cite any reference for this quotation.
29. See the chronicle of Thomas of Eccleston, especially chapter 15.
30. A celebrated jurist and translator of the 12th century.
31. See Eccleston, chapter 11.
32. The catherdral of Lincoln.
33. Alexander of Hales who became a Franciscan and an eminent teacher in the Order.

other, separated only by the Rhone. In each there was a large convent of the Friars Minor. Men and women from Avignon and Arles also came there. He spoke to them, as I heard with my own ears, words of edification, very useful words, and words filled with unction, words of salvation. They listened gladly, as they would have listened to John the Baptist or Jesus Christ made man, for they considered him a prophet; and they said: *"This is indeed the prophet who is to come into the world."*[34] Those who are deprived of grace do not believe these things. It is not without reason that Ecclesiasticus says (44, 19-20) : He *kept his glory without stain, he observed the precepts of the Most High.*

It would be most ridiculous if I would not want to believe that someone is a bishop or the pope simply because I am not a bishop or the pope.

At the court of the count of Provence,[35] there was a certain Raynier, a native of Pisa, who called himself a universal philosopher. He so confounded the judges, notaries, and physicians of the court that no one could live there with honor. They therefore explained their vexation to Brother Hugh and asked him to help them and to protect them from this evil adversary. Brother Hugh said to them: "Arrange with the count a day for discussion in the palace and let the knights, nobles, judges, notaries, and natural philosophers be present. Engage him in discussion and then let the count send for sky is a frying pan." This was done. Brother Hugh entangled and so confounded him that he was ashamed to remain at the court of the count. He left without taking leave of his host me. I will demonstrate and prove that he is an ass and that the

34. John 6, 14.
35. Raymond Bérenger.

he thought to entangle the whole world in his sophistries. But, as is said in Ecclesiasticus (37, 20-21) : *Though a man is wise, if his words are rejected he will be deprived of all enjoyment.* Brother Hugh delivered therefore *the poor man when he cries out, and the afflicted when he has no one to help him.*[36] They sought to kiss the hands and feet of Brother Hugh, for he had freed them from the hands of a powerful person.

The count of whom I spoke above is called Raymond Bérenger. He was a comely person, a friend of the brothers. He was the father of the queen of France and of the queen of England.[37] His third daughter married the brother of the king of England,[38] and the fourth daughter married Charles, the brother of the king of France.[39] She bore him the count of Provence.[40]

In that province of Provence there is a very populous city between Marseilles and Vintimille, or Nice, close to the sea, and located on the road to Genoa. There are salt works and thereafter he never again dared to live there or even to show his face there. He was, in fact, a great sophist and there, because there salt is extracted from the sea; from this fact the city takes it name, Hyères. There is a great number of men and women there who, wearing their regular wordly clothing, do penance in their homes.[41] They are very much

---

36. Psalm 71, 12.
37. Marguerite of Provence, spouse of St. Louis IX of France. And Eleanor, spouse of Henry III of England.
38. Sancia, spouse of the Duke of Cornwall.
39. Beatrice, spouse of Charles of Anjou.
40. Dante puts it: "Four daughters were there born to Raymond Bérenger; and every one became a queen." Paradiso, VI 134.
41. They were Third Order members.

attached to the Friars Minor and they listen gladly to the word of God whenever the brothers preach there. For the Brothers Preachers do not have a convent there, because large convents please them more and they prefer to live in these rather than in small ones.

Brother Hugh liked very much to live at Hyères. There were many notaries, judges, natural philosophers and other learned people there who, on feast days, would gather in the room of Brother Hugh to hear him talk about the doctrine of the abbot Joachim and teach and explain the mysteries of Holy Scripture and predict future events. For he was a great Joachimite and he had all the works of the abbot Joachim in a flowing handwriting.

Before I had been instructed in this doctrine, I had heard of it, when I lived at Pisa, from an abbot of the Order from Fiore, an elderly and very saintly man, who had placed in the convent for safekeeping his books of the abbot Joachim, for fear that the emperor Frederick would destroy his monastery which was situated between Lucca and Pisa on the road to Luni. He believed that, with Frederick, the period had come in which would be fulfilled all the mysteries because the Church was greatly disturbed. Brother Rudolph of Saxony, lector of the convent at Pisa, a great logician, a great theologian, and a great contraversialist, abandoned the study of theology and became a great Joachimite because of these books that had been placed in our convent.

5. PROVINS AND AUXERRE

JOACHIMISM

A little later, at the time when the king of France was preparing to go to the help of the Holy Land and I was living at Provins, two brothers, fervent Joachimites, did all they could to persuade me to study the teaching of the abbot Joachim. One of them was from Parma and he was called Brother Bartholomew Guiscolo. He was born in the same city I was born in. He was a courteous and spiritual man, but a great talker and a great Joachimite. He belonged to the party of the emperor. At one time he had been guardian of the convent of Capua. He was very brisk in everything he did. He died at Rome the last day of a certain general chapter. In the world, he taught grammar; in the Order, he could copy, illuminate, dictate, and do other things as well. *In life he performed wonders, and after death, marvelous deeds.*[1] When he was dying he saw such visions that all the brothers present were filled with admiration.

The other brother was Gerard of Borgo San Donnino,[2]

---

1. Ecclesiasticus 48, 14.
2. In reality he was born in Lombardy, spent some time in Sicily, then in Provins, and later in the convent of studies in Paris. He pubished *The Introduction to the Eternal Gospel,* which was replete with Joachimism. The masters of the University of Paris pointed out many errors in the book. In July, 1255 the book was condemned by Alexander IV.

a native of Sicily and a teacher of grammar. He was a man well-mannered for his youth, honest and good, except for this one thing that he was too obstinate in believing in Joachim and in holding his doctrine tenaciously.

These two tried hard to persuade me to believe what Joachim wrote and to study it. For they had the *Exposition of Jeremias* of Joachim and many other books. And since, at that time, the king of France was preparing to go across the sea with the other crusaders, they sneered at the project and turned it to derision, saying that if the king went, he would fare ill, as the event afterward showed. They showed me that this was written in the *Exposition of Jeremias* of Joachim and told me that we would have to expect the events to unravel just as he had written. Since, in all of France, there was said daily in the conventual Mass the psalm: *O God, the nations have come into your inheritance,* etc.,[3] they mocked them saying: "It is necessary that Scripture be fulfilled which says in the Lamentations of Jeremias (3, 44): *Thou hast set a cloud before thee that our prayers may not pass through.* For the king of France will be taken, the French will be conquered, and a pestilence will carry many off." For this reason these two were disgraced before the brothers of France who said that these events had been fulfilled on the preceding crusade.

There was at that time in the convent of Provins a lector, Brother Maurice, who was a comely person, noble, and very learned. In the world he had made his studies at Paris and continued them for eight years in the Order. He was a native of the region of Provins, for, in France, the

---

3. Psalm 79, 1.

nobles live in the country, on their estates, and the middle class people live in the cities. Provins is a celebrated city in Champagne, about twenty-five leagues from Paris. Brother Maurice became my friend and he said to me: "Brother Salimbene, have no faith in these Joachimites; they cause trouble to their brothers with their teaching; but help me rather with my writing, for I wish to compose a treatise on *Distinctions* which will be very useful for preachers." The Joachimites withdrew themselves at this time of their own free will.

As for me, I went to Auxerre to live there. Brother Bartholomew went back to the convent at Sens. Brother Gerard was sent to Paris to make his studies for the province of Sicily, for which province he had been received into the Order. He spent four years studying there and he expressed his folly in a treatise he composed.[4] He made his foolishness public by publishing it amongst the brothers who knew no better. I will speak again of the treatise when I talk about Pope Alexander IV who condemned it.[5] This work was the occasion, at Paris and elsewhere, of much reproach being heaped upon the Order; its author, Gerard, was deprived of the office of lector, of preaching, of hearing confessions, and of all other privileges of the Order. He did not wish to repent and humbly acknowledge his fault, but on the contrary, like a headstrong person, he persevered with insolence and arrogance. The Friars Minor cast him into prison, in chains, and *fed him with bread of affliction and water of distress,*[6] saying with Josue (7, 25) : *Because thou hast troubled us, the Lord trouble thee this day.* That evildoer would not even

---

4. The *Introduction to the Eternal Gospel.*
5. In July, 1255.
6. III Kings 22, 27.

then withdraw from his obstinacy and listen to what is said, *vexation alone shall make you understand what you hear,*[7] to the point that there was fulfilled the word of the Book of Proverbs (27, 22) : *Though you should pound the fool to bits, his folly would not go out of him.* Wherefore he permitted himself to die in prison; he was deprived of ecclesiastical burial and buried in a corner of the garden. Let all know, therefore, that the Order of Friars Minor acts with rigor and justice against those who transgress the Rule of the Order. No one, therefore, should impute the fault of one man to the whole Order, for just as *the number of fools is infinite,*[8] so *a great number of wise men is the safety of the world.*[9]

---

7. Isaias 28, 19.
8. Ecclesiasticus 1, 15.
9. Wisdom 6, 24.

6. *HYERES*

Two Dominicans, Converts to Joachimism

Therefore in the year of our Lord 1248, when I was at Hyères with Brother Hugh, the latter, seeing that I was curious about the teaching of the abbot Joachim and that I listened gladly, with applauding and rejoicing, said to me: "Are you carried away like the others who follow this doctrine?" In fact, most of the people consider the Joachimites to be infatuated. . . .[1]

. . . When I saw that judges, notaries, and learned men and other scholars congregated in the room of Brother Hugh to hear him teach the doctrine of the abbot Joachim, I remembered Eliseus of whom it is said in the Book of Kings that *Eliseus sat in his house, and the ancients sat with him.*[2] In those days two other Joachimites arrived who had been in the convent of Naples. One of them was called Brother John the Frenchman, and the other Brother John Pigolino the Little of Parma, chanter of the convent of Naples. They had come to Hyères to see Brother Hugh and to hear him talk about Joachimism.

Then two Friars Preachers arrived; they were returning from their general chapter which had been celebrated at

---

1. Here are inserted some thoughts on Joachimism which are, however, of little interest.
2. IV Kings 6, 32.

Paris. One was called Brother Peter of Apulia, a lector of the convent of his Order at Naples; he was a learned man and a good speaker. They were waiting for a suitable time to sail. For the Friars Preachers do not have a convent in this country.

One day after dinner, Brother John the Little, the chanter of the convent of Naples, who knew Brother Peter very well, said to him: "Brother Peter, what do you think of the teaching of the abbot Joachim?" Brother Peter replied: "I care as much about Joachim as I do for a fifth wheel on a wagon; in his homily on the Gospel, *There will be signs in the sun and moon and stars,*[3] St. Gregory expressed the belief that the end of the world would come in his own day because the Lombards had come at that time and were destroying everything."

Brother John the Little went with haste to find Brother Hugh in his room, and, asking assistance, said: "There is a Friar Preacher here who will not believe this doctrine." Brother Hugh said to him: "It is not my business if he does not believe. He will have to bear the consequences. Let him look to it when *vexation alone will make him understand.*[4] Yet, invite him to join us and I will hear what he doubts about it."

Brother Peter, thus invited, came, though unwillingly; on the one hand, because he despised Joachim, and on the other, because he did not think there was any one in the house who could compare with himself in culture and in knowledge of the Scriptures. When Brother Hugh saw him,

---

3. Luke 21, 25.
4. An adaption of Isaias 28, 19.

he said to him: "You are the one who doubts the teaching of the abbot Joachim?" Brother Peter answered: "Yes, I am he." Brother Hugh said: "Have you ever read Joachim?" Brother Peter answered: "I have read him and I have read him with care." "I believe," said Brother Hugh, "that you have read him as a woman reads the psalter. When she comes to the end, she does not know what she read at the beginning and she remembers nothing. Many read and do not understand, either because they despise what they read, or because *their senseless minds have been darkened.*[5] Now tell me what you would wish to hear about Joachim so that we will know what you doubt about so much."

Brother Peter said: "I would have you prove to me by Isaias, as the abbot Joachim teaches, that the life of the emperor Frederick must be ended in seventy years, for he is still living; and that he cannot die except by the hand of God, that is to say, that his death cannot be brought about by violence but only by natural causes." Brother Hugh said: "Gladly; but listen with patience, without crying out, without sneering; with that teaching, one must come to believe gradually. The abbot Joachim was a holy man; he says that the events which are predicted by him are revealed by God for the good of men, according to the word that is written: *You have raised for those who fear you a banner to which they may flee out of bowshot.*[6] In consequence, I am not incredulous of the divine revelation, for, if I believe that at a future time there will be tribulations caused by the sins of man, no punishment will have been promised to me by

5. Romans 1, 21.
6. Psalm 59, 6.

this revelation, but a great advantage can result, as St. Gregory said: 'The arrows hurt less if they are not expected; we show ourselves more tolerant to the wicked of the world if Providence has not provided us with a shield.' The Wise Man says in the Book of Proverbs (28, 14) : *Blessed is the man that is always fearful: but he that is hardened in mind, shall fall into evil.* Again in Ecclesiasticus (18, 27) , it is said: *A wise man will fear in every thing.* And St. Jerome: 'One must fear with prudence whatever could come upon one.' And Ecclesiasticus (1, 27) : *The fear of the Lord driveth out sin. For he that is without fear cannot be justified.* And a little after that (36): *Be not incredulous to the fear of the Lord.* And again in Ecclesiasticus (33, 1) : *No evils shall happen to him that feareth the Lord, but in temptation God will keep him, and deliver him from evils.*

"Behold the example of a young man who was urged on to sin by another young man; he prayed and he found himself transported to the other bank of the river, because the Lord has said in the Apocalypse (3, 10) : *Because thou hast kept the word of my patience, I too will keep thee from the hour of trial, which is about to come upon the whole world. . . .*

"With regard to the life of the emperor Frederick which must come to an end, take note of the passage in Isaias (23, 13) , where this is said about the evildoers of Tyre: *Behold the land of the Chaldeans, there was not such a people, the Assyrian founded it.*' And a little after that (15) : *It shall come to pass in that day that thou, O Tyre, shalt be forgotten, seventy years, according to the days of one king.* Notice that, in these words, for the land of the Chaldeans the abbot Joachim wished to say Romans and the Empire;[7] for Assyrian, the emperor Frederick himself; for Tyre, Sicily; for the days of the one king, the entire life of Frederick; for the seventy years, the end of his life fixed by Merlin.[8]

"Frederick must not die at the hand of man, but rather by that of God, as is said in Isaias (31, 8-9) : *And the Assyrian shall fall by the sword not of a man, and the sword not of a man shall devour him, and he shall flee not at the face of the sword: and his young men shall be tributaries. And his strength shall pass away with dread, and his princes fleeing shall be afraid: the Lord hath said it, whose fire is in Sion, and his furnace in Jerusalem.*" Brother Hugh went on: "These prophecies apply above all to Frederick at Parma when he was put to flight by the Parmesans and his village of Victoria destroyed. The princes and the barons of his kingdom,[9] in great number, wished to kill him, but could not."[10]

. . . When these words had been spoken, a messenger came from the ship to the Preachers to tell them to hurry to go to the boat.

---

7. The Holy Roman Empire, whose subjects could therefore be called Romans.
8. The English prophet and magician.
9. Sicily.
10. The discussion continues on at some length between Brother Hugh and Brother Peter. Brother Hugh appeals to the English Merlin, quotes certain prophecies of his, and explains their application to the emperor Frederick. Brother Hugh succeeded in entangling his opponent. The latter's companion tried to come to his assistance, but he would have none of it. In the end, Brother Peter commended Brother Hugh's wisdom. The whole discussion is of little interest to us and hence we take the liberty to omit the rest of it here. (T.N.)

After their departure, Brother Hugh said to the learned men who had remained and had heard the discussion: "Do not be scandalized if we have said some things it would have been better not to say. In the heat of the discussion, it is easy to let oneself be carried away to such exaggerations." And Brother Hugh added: "These good people always brag about their knowledge and say that in their Order is the fountain of wisdom, according to what Ecclesiasticus says: *All wisdom comes from the Lord.*[11] They say also that they have passed among imbeciles when they have passed through a convent of the Friars Minor, where they are received with charity and eagerness. But, by the grace of God, they will not now be able to say that they have passed among men weak in mind. For I have done as the Wise Man teaches in the Book of Proverbs (26, 5): *Answer the fool according to his folly, lest he become wise in his own eyes.*" After these words his hearers withdrew much edified and consoled, saying: "Today we have heard admirable words. We would like to hear some words about the doctrine of Our Lord Jesus Christ on the next feast day."

Brother Hugh said to them: "If God lets me live, I will do so gladly; therefore come."

But the same day, the Brothers Preachers returned to us for the time was not suitable for sailing. After dinner Brother Hugh came to them in a friendly way. Brother Peter arose and went to seat himself at the feet of Brother Hugh. No one could make him get up to sit on the same bench with him. Brother Hugh himself could not, though he in-

---

11. Ecclesiasticus 1, 1. There was a great friendship between the Friars Minor and Friars Preachers, but there was evidently some jealousy too.

sisted that he should. Brother Peter said: "In the Book of Proverbs it is written: *It is better to be humble with the meek than to share plunder with the proud.*[12] *He who humbles himself shall be exalted,*[13] *the man of humble mien he saves,*[14] *and, they that approach to his feet, shall receive his doctrine.*[15]

Brother Peter, without disputing or contradicting, but in a humble attitude, listened to the gentle words of Brother Hugh. All of them would be worthy of being recorded, but I will omit them for the sake of brevity, for I hasten to tell of other things.

Then the companion of Brother Peter took me apart and said to me: "For the love of God, Brother Salimbene, tell me who this brother is? Is he a prelate, a guardian, a custos, or a minister?" I replied to him: "He has no prelacy because he does not want one. He was once minister provincial, but now he is a simple brother. He is one of the greatest clerics in the world, and those who know him esteem him as such." Then he said to me: "In truth, I believe I have never seen a man who speaks so well and is so ready to answer to all things. But I am astonished that he does not live in some great convent." I said to him: "It is because of his humility and holiness and because he finds greater consolation living in a small convent." Then he said: "May he be blessed, for he seems to be a heavenly man."

The Friars Preachers stayed at Hyères until they found a suitable time to sail. At their departure, Brother Peter

---

12. Proverbs 16, 19.
13. Luke 14, 11.
14. Job 22, 29.
15. Deuteronomy 33, 3.

said to Brother Hugh: "In truth, now that I have heard you speak, I would like to remain with you always to hear you discuss the Holy Scriptures." After many mutual commendations, the Brothers Preachers left consoled and greatly edified.

After their departure, on the feast that followed, all the learned men of Hyères came together in the room of Brother Hugh to hear his teaching. He preached an admirable sermon to them, full of usefulness, very beautiful, and one that filled them with delight. I will omit it to be brief, for I hasten on to speak of other things.

When the sermon was finished, a man from the city, whom I saw and knew and who was a layman, asked Brother Hugh if he were worthy to be received as a Friar Minor, for the love of God. For the minister provincial had given Brother Hugh permission to receive brothers into the Order, because he was a very respectable person, a great cleric, a man of high spirituality, and because he had once been minister provincial.

That man who asked to enter the Order of Friars Minor was the founder of the Order of Saccati. He had a companion who also wished to enter. They were urged on by a sign from God which they found in the sermon of Brother Hugh. The latter said to them: "Go into the forest, learn to eat roots, for the day of tribulations is approaching." They went into the forest and made for themselves robes that were gray like those that the converts to the Order of Saint Clare once had the custom of wearing. They begged their bread in the same city where the Friars Minor dwelt. The people gave them an abundance, for the Friars Preachers and we ourselves had taught all men to beg; and the whole world wished to wear a capuch and to follow the Rule of the Order of beggars. This group multiplied rapidly; the Friars Minor of Provence called them ironically "the men of the forest."[16]

---

16. Or "Wild Men."

7. AIX, TARASCON, BEAUCAIRE, ARLES

BROTHER JOHN OF PARMA

Let us come back now to Brother Hugh, the minister provincial in the Order of Friars Minor,[1] who was one of the great clerics of the world, a man of high spirituality, and let us continue what we have to say.

In the year of our Lord 1248, at the time that I found myself with Brother Hugh in the province of Provence, in the convent at Hyères, where the Saccati had their origin, I received from him what he had in his possession of the *Exposition* of the abbot Joachim on the four Gospels, and I betook myself to Aix. I lived in the convent of the Friars Minor there, and, with the help of my companion, I transcribed the *Exposition* of the abbot Joachim for the minister general who was also a great Joachimite. . . .[2]

. . . Therefore, when I had written what I had undertaken, the seventh month, that is to say, September,[3] around the feast of the Exaltation of the Cross,[4] Brother Raymond, the minister provincial of Provence, wrote me to go to meet the minister general who was coming from France. He had

---

1. More exactly, "who had been minister provincial in the Order."
2. Brother John of Parma.
3. The year was sometimes reckoned from March 25, the feast of the Annunciation.
4. September 14.

visited England, France, and Burgundy, and he wanted to visit Provence and Spain. He had also written to Brother Hugh to meet him.

We met him at Tarascon where the body of St. Martha is to be found and where the countess of Provence, the mother of the queen of France and of the queen of England, resides habitually. The canons showed us the arm of St. Martha to kiss. When, in ancient times, miracles were being performed at her tomb, the king of the Franks, Clovis, who had become a Christian through baptism at the hands of St. Remy, recovered his health completely there after he had come to the tomb suffering great pains in his kidneys. That is why he endowed the place of pilgrimage with grants extending for three miles round about, from each side of the Rhone, and decreed that the lands, towns, and villages would be exempt from all taxes.

In that same convent at Tarascon we said Compline one evening with the minister general. The latter was living in the building where beds were assigned to the guest brothers to sleep. He went to the cloister to pray. The brothers who were strangers in the convent feared to go to their beds before the minister general first went to his. They murmured because they would have liked to go to sleep, but could not, since tapers of wax were lighting up the whole room where their beds were.

Seeing their weariness, I went to find the minister general, with whom I was intimate, and he with me, since we were from the same country and he was a neighbor of my relatives. I found him praying in the cloister and said to him: "Father, the brothers who are strangers are fatigued from their journey and would like to go to sleep, but they fear to go to their beds before you have given them the example." He then said to me: "Go find them and tell them for me that they should go to bed with the blessing of God." This was done. But for myself, I preferred to wait for the minister that I might show him his bed.

When Brother John of Parma had finished his prayers, he came out, and, I said to him: "Father, you must go to rest in this bed prepared for you." He said to me: "My son, in the bed you are showing me the pope himself might sleep; Brother John of Parma will never sleep in it." He then threw himself upon the bed which I had thought to occupy and which was therefore empty. I said to him: "Father, may God forgive you. You have deprived me of the bed I thought to sleep in, for it was assigned to me." He said to me: "My son, you sleep in the papal bed." When I would have refused, following his example, he said to me: "I desire absolutely that you sleep there and I command you to." I had therefore to do as he commanded.

The next day the guardian of the convent of Beaucaire, a well-known town on the other bank of the Rhone, came. He asked the minister general to come, with his retinue, to visit his sons at Beaucaire when he finished at Tarascon. This was done.

When we were at Beaucaire, two brothers arrived, coming from England. One was Brother Stephen, a lector who had entered the Order of St. Francis in early youth. He was a comely person, full of spirit, well instructed, of good counsel and always ready to preach to the clergy. He had with him the very best writings, that is to say, those of Brother Adam of Marsh, whose lecture on Genesis I heard from him. At the time of his visit to England, Brother John of Parma, the minister general, gave a promise to him for his consolation that he could go to Rome to teach there. His companion was another Englishman, Brother Jocelyn, a man of good looks, learned, and full of spirit.

At the same time there arrived two other brothers who asked the minister general to provide a good lector for the convent at Genoa. These brothers were Henry of Bobbio, a chanter at the convent of Genoa and the uncle of Brother William who later became a lector and minister provincial. I have forgotten the name of his companion. They insisted to Brother John of Parma that he should accede, for the love of God, to the wishes of the brothers of the convent at Genoa and of the minister provincial, Brother Nantelmo.

The minister general knew how to expedite affairs in a short time. He was a man of good counsel and he quickly found a good solution. He said to Brother Stephen: "Here are the letters in which the brothers of the convent of Genoa ask us to send them a good lector. If it pleases you to go there to teach, this will be very good, and when I come to Genoa, I will send you to Rome." Brother Stephen answered: "Father, I am ready to obey you willingly and gladly." The minister said: "Bless you, my son, you have answered well. Go therefore to Genoa with the brothers and your companion. I will write to the minister provincial and to the brothers, that they will give you a good welcome." This was done.

After these events, we left the brothers of Beaucaire and went down the Rhone in a boat to Arles, a town a little distance from Tarascon. The brothers of Arles rejoiced at the arrival of the minister general, for he was a man of good example and great edification.

One day when the minister general was alone, I went to find him. My companion who was from Parma and was called Brother John the Little of Olle happened along unexpectedly. He said to the minister: "Father, grant that Brother Salimbene and I may obtain the aureole."[5] The minister smiled and said to my companion: "How can I arrange that you may have the aureole?" Brother John the Little answered: "By giving us the office of preacher." Brother John, the minister general, then said: "In truth, if you were both my blood brothers, you should not have that office otherwise than by the sword of examination."[6] After hearing the minister I replied and said to my companion: "Away then with your aureole! Last year I received the office of preacher from Pope Innocent IV at Lyons, and now I should receive it from Brother John the Little of San Lazarro? It is enough that this office has been conferred upon me by him who has the power to give it." Brother John was called Master John the Little when he taught in the world. He had been given the surname *di San Lazarro,* because, as an infant, he had been brought up in the house of San Lazarro at Parma, by his paternal uncle who was a priest and had that house in his charge. He had educated his nephew at his own expense. . . .[7]

. . . Therefore, as I have said above, I was boasting before Brother John at Arles that I had received the office of

---

5. This refers to the special glory in heaven that was to be the reward of virgins, doctors, and martyrs. Preachers were thought to rank with the doctors in the expectation of that reward.
6. According to the Rule the office of preaching is to be awarded only after an examination. Chapter IX.
7. Several pages about John of Parma are omitted here.

preacher from Pope Innocent IV at Lyons. My companion, Brother John the Little of Olle, replied: "I prefer to have the office from the minister general rather than from a pope. If it is necessary for us to pass by the sword of examination, I ask that Brother Hugh examine us." He was speaking of the renowned provincial Hugh who was then in the convent of Arles on the occasion of the journey of the minister general, and whose great friend he was. Brother John answered: "I do not want Brother Hugh to put you through the examination; he is your friend and will go easy on you. Summon for me the lector of the convent and his assistant." When they were summoned, they came. The minister said to them: "Take these two brothers separately and examine them on their ability to preach. If they are capable of receiving that office, let me know." This was done. He gave me permission to preach, but he did not want to give permission to my companion for he was found wanting. The minister general said to him: "What is deferred, is not refused. *Study wisdom, my son, and make my heart joyful, that thou mayest give an answer to him that reproacheth.*[8] For Ecclesiasticus has said: *Learn before thou speak.*"[9]

At that time two brothers came from Tuscany who were going to Toulouse to study: Brother Gerard of Prato, a blood brother of Brother Arlotto, and Brother Benedict of Colle. They were deacons at that time. They were young men and good students. They had studied with me in the convent of Pisa for a number of years. They wished to leave Arles the next day, so they sent Brother Mark, the companion of the minister general, to ask him to grant them

---

8. Proverbs 27, 11.
9. Ecclesiasticus 18, 19.

the office of preaching and the authorization to be promoted to the priesthood.

Just then the minister general was saying his Compline
and I was alone with him. Brother Mark came and interrupted our office to tell us what he had to say. The minister
replied with great ardor of spirit what he thought, as was
his custom when he was filled with zeal for God. He said
to his companion, Brother Mark: "These brothers are acting
badly in asking shamelessly for such things, for the Apostle
has said, *And no man takes the honor to himself.*[10] They
have come away from their own minister provincial who
knew them and who could have given them what they are
seeking from me. Let them go therefore to Toulouse where
they have been sent to study and continue their instructions
there. It is not necessary for them to preach here; at the
opportune time they can have what they are asking for."
Then Brother Mark, seeing that he was angry, withdrew,
saying: "Father, you must believe that it is not they who
make this request, but Brother Salimbene who told me that
I should present the request on their behalf." The minister
answered: "Brother Salimbene has been all this time saying
his Compline beside me; it seems evident to me that he did
not speak to you about these things." Brother Mark then
went out, saying: "Father, I will do as you wish."

I noticed that Brother Mark welcomed with little favor
the answer of Brother John of Parma; when Compline was
over, I went to console him. He said to me "Brother Salimbene, Brother John has done wrong, for he has made me

---

10. Hebrews 5, 4.

lose face in not wishing to accede to my request that was of little importance. I suffer for the Order in accompanying him and in writing his letters at a time when I am advanced in age. He is correct that they have been sent by their minister provincial who knew them and that the latter knows whether or not they are good brothers; he sent them to study at Toulouse; they will go afterwards to study at Paris. But these brothers would have had greater joy in receiving the office of preaching from Brother John because of his dignity and his reputation for sanctity than in receiving it from their minister provincial, Peter of Cora. They wished to have authorization to be promoted to the priesthood because the village of Pisa where they lived has remained, as you know, without religious offices for thirty years because the Pisans had made prisoners of the cardinals and other prelates on the sea, because they had taken possession by violence of ten cities situated in the mountains and belonging to the bishop of Lucca and, finally, because they invaded the province of Garfagnana against the will of the Church."[11] Garfagnana is the region surrounded by mountains between Lucca and Lombardy. "These two brothers, because they are from Pisa, are not troubled so much about the promotion to the priesthood, but they wished rather to become priests so that they could celebrate Mass for the living and for the dead; I think that this is by no means a sin; they could be more useful to the brothers to whom they go. These young people were considered good all their lives and now they recognize the grace that is given them. God knows that I am ashamed to return to them without my prayer having been satisfied."

---

11. In May, 1241.

I replied briefly to him, saying: "Your words please me more than those of the minister general, but *let patience have its perfect work.*"[12]

That evening the minister general sent for me, and also my companion, and he said to us: "My sons, I hope soon to leave you, for I want to go to Spain; consequently, choose for yourselves any convent in the whole Order where you wish to go and I will send you there, with the exception of the convent at Paris; you have the whole night to consider, choose, make your decision, and tell me tomorrow."

The next day he said to us: "Have you decided, and what do you choose?"

I answered him: "We do not want to choose a convent that we will later regret having chosen; but we leave it to your will to send us to a convent which you will choose; we will obey you." He was edified at the good answer and said to us: "Go then to the convent at Genoa; you will dwell there with Brother Stephen the Englishman whom I have sent there. Moreover, I will write to the minister provincial and the brothers that they may welcome you with the same favor they would show to me, and that you, Brother Salimbene, may be promoted to the priesthood and your companion, Brother John the Little, to the diaconate. When I come there, if I find you are satisfied, I will be happy; if not, I will console you anew." These things were accomplished in their entirety.

---

12. James 1, 4.

8. *MARSEILLES, HYERES, NICE, GENOA*

That same day Brother John of Parma said to Brother Hugh, his friend: "What do you think, Brother Hugh? Should we go to Spain and fulfill the desire that St. Paul had of going there?"[1] Brother Hugh replied: "Go you there, Father; as for me, I want to die in the country of my fathers." Forthwith, we conducted Brother John to his ship, which was ready on the Rhone to sail. It was the feast of St. Michael,[2] about None. After we had said our farewells, he left us to go on to St.-Gilles that same day.

As for us, we went by sea to Marseilles and we found Brother Stephen the Englishman there. He asked me to tell the guardian that he would gladly preach to the clergy and to the brothers for the feast of St. Francis.[3] The guardian replied that it would give him pleasure to hear him, but he feared to give offense to the bishop who was coming to the feast.

After the feast of St. Francis we took to the sea and went to Hyères to the convent of Brother Hugh. Brother Stephen, not being able to find a boat, made the trip by land with his companion to go back to his convent at Genoa.

---

1. Romans 15, 24-28.
2. September 29, 1248.
3. October 4.

My companion and I remained at Hyères with Brother Hugh from the feast of St. Francis to All Saints Day.[4] I was happy to have the chance to remain with Brother Hugh and we conversed all day long about the teaching of the abbot Joachim. In fact, he had all the latter's books and he was a great Joachimite and one of the great clerics of the world; he was incomparable for his sanctity and his knowledge.

On the other hand, I was grieved to see that my companion grew very ill, that he would not take care of himself, and that the time for sailing was becoming less and less favorable because of the winter.

That year, this region was extremely unwholesome because of the wind off the sea; all night I could hardly breathe, even when I lay in the open air. I heard wolves howling and moaning in great numbers *more than once or twice.*[5] I said to my companion, a rather irresponsible young man: "You will not keep yourself from doing things harmful to your health and every day you are relapsing into your illness. But I have found that this country is very unwholesome and I do not wish to die yet, since I would like to see the things that Brother Hugh predicts. Know therefore, that, if a propitious occasion comes to leave here in the company of our brothers, I am going." He said to me: "What you say pleases me; I will go too." He hoped, however, that none of the brothers would come.

And behold, by the grace of God, a certain Brother Pontius arrived. He was a holy man who had been with us at Aix. He was going to Nice, of which place he had

4. November 1.
5. IV Kings 6, 10.

been named guardian. He was happy to see us. I said to him: "We will go with you for we must go to Genoa to live there." He answered: "That will please me greatly; I will go and make inquiries about a ship."

The next day, after dinner, we went to the boat about a mile from the convent. My companion did not wish to go, but, seeing that I was really going, he took leave of the guardian of the convent and followed us. When I gave him my hand to climb aboard, he pushed back violently and said: "God forbid that you should touch me. You have not kept faith with me and you have not shown yourself a good companion." I said to him: "Wretched man, understand God's goodness in your regard, for the Lord has revealed to me that if you had stayed at Hyères, without doubt you would have died. The Wise Man said in Ecclesiastes (7, 18) : *Be not foolish, lest thou die before thy time.* And in the same way it is said in the Book of Job (22, 16) : *They were taken away before their time, and a flood hath overthrown their foundation,* that is to say, the stream of human mortality."

What more is there to say? He would not believe until *vexation would make him understand.*[6] All that winter, in the convent at Genoa, he could not shake off the illness he had contracted in Provence. On the feast of St. Mathias,[7] I again took to the sea and went in four days from Genoa to the convent of Brother Hugh; I found that six brothers of the convent had died and been buried, of whom the first was the guardian who had accompanied my companion to the boat. Another who died was Brother William of Pertuso,

6. An adaption of Isaias 28, 19.
7. February 24, 1249.

a good preacher with whom I had lived in the convent at Parma. Four other brothers, whose names it is not necessary to mention, also died.

At my return to the convent at Genoa, I reported to my companion the news of the death of these brothers; he thanked me for having snatched him away from the portals of death. He recovered his health at last, and, some years later, the year when the king of France took to the sea for the second time to go to Tunis,[8] he went to the province beyond the sea. He was made custos and went in that capacity to the general chapter celebrated at Assisi in which Brother Bonagrazia was elected minister general and in which an explanation of the Rule was given to the brothers. . . .[9]

. . . Therefore, Brother John the Little, Brother Pontius, the new guardian at Nice, and I arrived at Nice the same day that we left Hyères and Brother Hugh. Nice is a city on the shore of the sea; we met there Brother Simon of Montesarculo in Apulia, who was procurator of the Order at the curia of the pope, who was living at that time at Lyons. He wished to go to Genoa and, with the brother in charge of the refectory of the convent at Lyons, he was waiting on the shore to find a boat. I said to them: "We have a ship ready to sail and tomorrow we will continue on our way." And they were glad to hear this.

The next day we traveled all day, as well as the next night; at daybreak we entered the port of Genoa, which is near the city. It was Sunday. The brothers were happy to

---

8. 1270.
9. 1279.

see us, and we all rejoiced, especially the lector Brother Stephen the Englishman. The minister general later sent him to Rome, as he had promised. He became lector at Rome and died there, as did his companion Brother Jocelyn, after they had realized their desire to see Rome and the holy places, according to the word of the Book of Proverbs (10, 24) : *The desire of the just will be granted.*

The guardian gave me two new tunics, an outer tunic and an under tunic. He did the same for my companion.

Brother Nantelmo, the minister provincial, who had been a lector and was from Milan, was a pious and saintly man. He told me that he would accord me all the favors and all the gratifications that I would be pleased to ask of him. He designated his own companion, Brother William of Piedmont, a man of great worth, learning, and goodness, to teach me to say Mass and to sing.[10] These have all passed from this world to the Father; *their names are written in the book of life,*[11] for they have ended their lives well and they have been made worthy of praise.

---

10. Salimbene tells us elsewhere that he was ordained in December of 1248.
11. Philippians 4, 3.

BROTHER SALIMBENE'S SECOND JOURNEY THROUGH FRANCE

In the year of our Lord 1249,[1] at the time that I was staying at the convent at Genoa, it pleased my minister provincial, Brother Nantelmo, to send me to the minister general to talk with him about the affairs of the province of Genoa. On the feast of St. Mathias,[2] I put out to sea and, on the fourth day, came to Hyères to the convent of Brother Hugh, who was very glad to see me. Since he was vicar of the guardian, he ate with my companion and me in great familiarity. No brother, apart from the one who served us, was with us. He gave us a grand meal of sea fish and all kinds of other things. We were at the beginning of Lent. My companion, who was from Genoa, and the brothers of the convent of Hyères were astonished that Brother Hugh showed such great friendship for me and was so intimate with me, for he was not in the habit at that time of taking meals with other brothers, perhaps because Lent was approaching.[3] During that dinner we spoke of God, of the teaching of the abbot Joachim, and of future events.

As I said above, I found out that six brothers of the convent had died and had been buried. I had left them alive

---

1. Before this paragraph there are a number of pages about Salimbene's stay at Genoa during the winter 1248-1249.
2. February 24, 1249.
3. Actually Lent began that year on February 17; Salimbene is a little off the mark.

around the feast of All Saints.[4]

At my departure from Genoa, there was an almond tree in bloom near the sacristy; in Provence I found fruit already formed with the green shells. I saw also some new beans.

After the meal, I went on my way to the minister general. After some days, I found him at Avignon. He was returning from Spain, having been recalled by Pope Innocent IV, who was residing at Lyons and who wished him to go among the Greeks. The pope was at that time full of hope that they would be reconciled with the Church of Rome through the mediation of the emperor John Vatatzes.[5] Avignon is a city in Provence, on the Rhone, where, a little later, the minister general Brother Bonagrazia died.[6] I was there many times on various occasions.

Later I left for Lyons with the minister general. When we were in Vienne, we found the ambassador whom Vatatzes had sent to the pope asking him to send the minister general to him. He was a Friar Minor and, like me, he was called Brother Salimbene. He was a Greek by one parent and a Latin by the other. He spoke Latin excellently, though he was not a cleric. He knew also the popular Greek and Latin tongues. Brother John of Parma took him and went on to Lyons.

When the minister general arrived before the pope, the latter received him with a kiss on the mouth and said to him: "God forgive you, my son, for being so tardy. Why did you not come on horseback to get here sooner? Do you there-

---

4. November 1.
5. There were many attempts at negotiations by this emperor. Haymo of Faversham was also involved in one of these attempts, as we saw in Brother Thomas' chronicle. But the efforts came to naught when both the pope and the emperor died.
6. A native of Bologna, he was minister general from 1279-1283.

fore think that I cannot afford the expense?" Brother John replied: "Father, I came swiftly enough after I had received your letters. But the brothers with whom I stopped on the way held me up." The pope continued: "We have heard some good news, namely, that the Greeks want to be reconciled with the Church of Rome. That is why I want you to go among them with a retinue of brothers of your Order, and it may be, that with your help, God may deign to work some good. From me you will receive all the help you may wish."

Brother John replied: "Father, there is no lack of one who will carry out what you wish, but of one who will command, for I am ready and not fearful to carry out your commands."[7]

The pope said: "Bless you, my son, this is an excellent answer."

There was at that time at Lyons the lector of the convent of Constantinople, a Greek, the Friar Minor Thomas, who was a holy man and who spoke Greek and Latin excellently. Brother John of Parma took him with him to go among the Greeks. For he had been sent by Vatatzes for this purpose. Brother John took with him Brother Drudon, the minister provincial of Burgundy, a distinguished person, of commanding appearance, a learned and saintly man. He was a very good professor of theology and he would have liked to preach to the brothers every day. He took with him also Brother Bonaventure of Jesi, a well-known brother who had been minister provincial of various provinces,[8] and also some

---

7. A reference to Psalm 118, 63.
8. He was minister provincial of Genoa, Bologna, and the Marches of Treviso.

other worthy brothers whose names there is no need to transcribe here. He left Lyons finally after Easter week.[9]

At that time, Brother Rufinus, the minister provincial of Bologna, was at Lyons, together with his companion Brother Bonaventure of Forli and Brother Bassetto. Brother Rufinus said to me: "I sent you to France to make your studies for my province, and you went to the convent at Genoa where you are now dwelling? Know that I do not like this at all, all the more so, since, for the honor of my province, I had students from other provinces come to Bologna." I answered: "Pardon me, Father; I did not think these things would displease you." He replied and said to me: "I pardon you, but, on this condition, that you write out a letter of obedience with which you will return to the province of Bologna, from which you came, and also your companion who is at Genoa." This was done. The minister general did not know of this obedience when he was at Lyons.

At that time, there was at Lyons Brother Raynald of Arezzo, from the province of Tuscany. He had come to find the pope to release him from being bishop.[10] When he was lector at Rieti, the bishop of that place died. There was so much good in him that the canons elected him unanimously. Pope Innocent, hearing of his wisdom and holiness, did not wish to release him, and, moreover, on the advice of his brothers, that is to say, the cardinals, he ordered him to accept the bishopric and honored him by personally consecrating him. I was at Lyons at this time.

After these events, I took to the road and went to Vienne, which is fifteen miles from Lyons going down the

9. In 1249 Easter fell on April 4.
10. The Order did not favor the acceptance of such honors.

Rhone. Afterwards I passed through Grenoble, then through the valley of Savoy, where I could judge the fall and the ruin of the mountain.[11] I went into a church called St. Gerard, which was full of dresses of children.[12]

I went next to Embrun where there was an archbishop born in Piacenza.[13] He wanted to give dinner daily to two Friars Minor. He always had places set for them at table and he set out dishes of all things for them. If any Friars Minor came there, the dinner was for them; if not, he had it given to other poor.

Thirteen brothers lived in that village. The guardian of the convent came to find me and said: "Brother, may it please you to eat with the archbishop; he will be glad to have you, for, for a long time, the brothers have not shared in his repast. They are always bothered when they go to dinner with him." I said to him: "Excuse us, Father, and do not take our refusal ill. We wish to leave without delay after we eat. The archbishop will hold us back and hinder us from going on our way by asking us for news, if he hears that we have come from the curia." Hearing what I said, the guardian was silent. In a low voice I said to my companion: "I think that it will be better for us to continue on our journey while we have propitious weather and valid letters so that we may quickly give answer to those who sent us and that the minister general may not come to Genoa ahead of us, for Brother Nantelmo, our minister provincial, is displeased with our journey." My companion approved of what I said and decided. . . .

---

11. There had been a great landslide in the valley.
12. Probably as thanksgiving offerings, perhaps for cures.
13. Henry, archbishop from 1250-1261, later cardinal bishop of Ostia.

After we left Embrun, we passed through the lands of the Dauphin and came to Susa, which belongs to the province of Genoa. When we had come to Alexandria, in Lombardy, we met two brothers from the convent of Genoa: Brother Martin, the chanter, and Brother Rufinus of Alexandria. My companion, Brother William Blanchard, said to them: "Know that you are going to lose Brother Salimbene and his companion who is at Genoa,[14] for Brother Rufinus, the minister provincial of Bologna is recalling them to his province. I myself, however, though I belong at Genoa, do not wish to return there, but I wish to return to my convent at Novara, from where the minister provincial called me when he sent me to the minister general. We have worked faithfully and have accomplished what we were supposed to do. We have left Brother Peter Lanerius, the guardian of Genoa, at Lyons where he is to see the minister general and Brother Bujolus who lives with the pope and to whom he is attached. If anything has not been yet done fully or well by us, we hope it will be done well by others. Shortly, the minister general will pass through Genoa, for he is going among the Greeks, asked for by them and sent by the pope. Meanwhile, take these letters and give them to the minister provincial, Brother Nantelmo, on the part of Brother John of Parma." After this discourse, he brought out the letters which he had and gave them to my companions.

The next day, however, we went from Alexandria to Tortona, which is a journey of about ten miles, and the day after that, we went from Tortona to Genoa, which is a long journey.[15]

When the brothers of Genoa saw me, they were very

---

14. Brother John the Little of Olle.
15. Perhaps about 35 miles.

happy, for I was coming from a long journey and carrying good news. The minister provincial and Brother Stephen the Englishman asked me if the minister general had visited Spain. I answered: "No, for the pope summoned him because of the Greeks. For he sent him amongst them, because, according to what Vatatzes wrote, they wish to be reconciled with the Church of Rome. I expect Brother John of Parma, to pass through Genoa shortly. You will see him and your hearts will rejoice. . . ."[16]

The same year, after the feast of St. Anthony of Padua, or of Spain, of the Order of Friars Minor,[17] I left Genoa with my companion and went to Bobbio, where we saw one of the jars in which the Lord changed water into wine at the marriage at Cana. It is said, at least, that this is one of those jars. . . . After this we came to Parma, from where we had departed and there we carried out what we had to do.

After our departure from Genoa, the minister general, Brother John of Parma, came there. The brothers of the convent of Genoa said to him: "Father, why have you taken away the brothers whom you sent to us? Through love for you we rejoiced to have them with us, and also because they were good brothers, who gave satisfaction and comported themselves well." The minister general answered: "And where are they? Are they then not in this convent?" The brothers said: "No, Father, for Brother Rufinus, the minister provincial of Bologna, has called them to his province." Then the minister general said: "God knows that I knew nothing of this obedience; I thought they were in this house and I was astonished that they had not come to see me."

---

16. Here Salimbene speaks for several pages about Genoa.
17. June 13, 1249.

A little later Brother John found us at Parma and, smiling, said to us: "You have traveled much, my children, in France, in Burgundy, in Provence, to the convent of Genoa, and now you are living at Parma. If I could rest myself now, like you, I would not travel so much." I said to him: "Father, it falls upon you to travel, by reason of your office of minister general, for the Lord said to the apostle John (15, 16): *I have appointed you that you should go and bear fruit and that your fruit should remain.* It has also been said of Elias that he went *whithersoever he had a mind.*[18] As for us, know that our obedience is always true and sincere." These words gave him satisfaction, for he loved us much.

When we were at Bologna, one day, in his room, he said to the minister provincial, Brother Rufinus: "Father, I had placed these brothers in the convent at Genoa to study there, and you have brought them here." Brother Rufinus replied: "Father, I did this for their consolation. I had sent them to France at the time when the emperor Frederick was besieging Parma; therefore I recalled them because I believed it would please them." I then said to the minister general: "Father, these things are as he has said." Then Brother John of Parma, the minister general, said: "Place them as well as possible then, that they may be content, apply themselves to their studies, and not wander about so much." Brother Rufinus answered: "Gladly, Father, will I do them this favor and give them this satisfaction for love for you and for them." He then kept my companion at Bologna to correct his Bible and he sent me to Ferrara where I lived for seven years in a row without changing my dwelling.

---

18. III Kings 19, 3.

BIBLIOGRAPHY

A list of books that were particularly helpful in making this translation. Others that were only of incidental help are not listed here. See also the *Translator's Foreword* at the beginning of this volume.

Chronica Fratris Jordani a Iano O.F.M., Analecta Fransiscana, Ex typographia Collegii S. Bonaventurae, Ad Claras Aquas (Quaracchi), 1885, Vol. I.

Chronica Fratris Nicolai Glassberger O.F.M., Analecta Franciscana, 1887, Vol. II.

Chronica Anonyma Fratrum Minorum Germaniae, Analecta Franciscana, Vol. I.

Chronica XXIV Generalium, Analecta Franciscana, 1897, Vol. III.

Thomas of Celano O.F.M., *Vita I* and *Vita II Sancti Patris Francisci, Analecta Franciscana,* 1941, Vol. X.

Girolamo Golubovich O.F.M., *Biblioteca Bio-Bibliografica Della Terra Santa e Dell' Oriente Francescano,* ex typographia Collegii S. Bonaventurae, Ad Claras Aquas (Quaracchi), 1906, Vol. I.

Archivum Franciscanum Historicum, edited by the Fathers of the College of St. Bonaventure, Ad Claras Aquas (Quaracchi), Volumes I, II, and III particularly.

291

Thomas of Eccleston, *Liber De Adventu Minorum in Angliam, Analecta Franciscana*, Vol. I.

A. G. Little, *Fratis Thomae vulgo dicti de Eccleston Tractatus De Adventu Fratrum Minorum in Angliam*, Manchester, University Press, 1951.

J. S. Brewer, M.A., *Thomas De Eccleston De Adventu Fratrum Minorum in Angliam*, Longman, Brown, Green, Longmans and Roberts, 1858, apud *Monumenta Franciscana*, Vol. I.

Richard Howlett, *Fragmentum Libri Thomae de Eccleston "De Adventu Minorum in Anliam,"* London, Longman and Company, 1882, apud *Monumenta Franciscana*, Vol. II.

Father Cuthbert O.S.F.C., *The Chronicle of Thomas of Eccleston*, Sands and Company, London and Edinburgh, 1909.

E. Gurney Salter, Litt.D., *The Coming of the Friars Minor to England and Germany* (translation of Brothers Thomas and Jordan), J.M. Dent & Sons Ltd., London and Toronto, 1926.

Edward Hutton, *The Franciscans in England* 1224-1538, Constable and Company Ltd., London, 1926.

Chronica Salimbene de Adam, Scrittori D'Itlalia, no. 187 and 188, a cura di Ferdinando Bernini, Guiseppe Laterza e Figli, Bari, 1942.

G. G. Coulton, M.A., *From Saint Francis to Dante*, (a Translation of all that is of primary interest in the chronicle of the Franciscan Salimbene), David Nutt, London, 1906.

INDEX

293